LOST IN THE CROWD

La collection Louis J. Robichaud/The Louis J. Robichaud Series
Directeurs de la collection/series editors: Donald J. Savoie
and Gabriel Arsenault

Collaboration entre l'Institut Donald J. Savoie et McGill-Queen's University Press, la collection « Louis J. Robichaud » regroupe des publications en français et en anglais, évaluées par des pairs et qui portent sur les politiques publiques canadiennes, le régionalisme et des sujets connexes. La collection est ouverte aux chercheuses et chercheurs de toutes les universités du Canada atlantique et offre une plus grande visibilité aux travaux universitaires qui s'intéressent aux enjeux fondamentaux de politique et comprennent des analyses rigoureuses, pertinentes et non partisanes à forte valeur sociale et contribuant à des débats publics éclairés. La collection rend hommage à l'ancien premier ministre néo-brunswickois Louis J. Robichaud, reconnu comme l'un des grands leaders politiques du XXe siècle au Canada et l'un des fondateurs de l'Université de Moncton.

A collaboration between the Donald J. Savoie Institute and McGill-Queen's University Press, the Louis J. Robichaud Series publishes peer-reviewed scholarship on Canadian public policy, regionalism, and related subjects in both English and French. The series welcomes books by researchers at all Atlantic Canadian universities and offers widespread visibility to Atlantic university research that focuses on the stakes of public policy, informed by rigorous, relevant, and non-partisan analysis that is socially engaged and aims to contribute to transparent and informed public debate. The series honours Louis J. Robichaud, a New Brunswick premier widely recognized as a leading light of twentieth-century Canadian politics and a founder of the University of Moncton.

1 The Summer Trade
  A History of Tourism on Prince Edward Island
  Alan MacEachern and Edward MacDonald

2 Eating the Ocean
  Seafood and Consumer Culture in Canada
  Brian Payne

3 Lost in the Crowd
  Acadian Soldiers of Canada's First World War
  Gregory M.W. Kennedy

Lost in the Crowd

Acadian Soldiers of Canada's First World War

GREGORY M.W. KENNEDY

McGill-Queen's University Press
Montreal & Kingston · London · Chicago

© McGill-Queen's University Press 2024

ISBN 978-0-2280-2012-7 (cloth)
ISBN 978-0-2280-2013-4 (paper)
ISBN 978-0-2280-2014-1 (ePDF)
ISBN 978-0-2280-2015-8 (ePUB)

Legal deposit first quarter 2024
Bibliothèque nationale du Québec

Printed in Canada on acid-free paper that is 100% ancient forest free (100% post-consumer recycled), processed chlorine free

This book has been published with the help of a grant from the Canadian Federation for the Humanities and Social Sciences, through the Awards to Scholarly Publications Program, using funds provided by the Social Sciences and Humanities Research Council of Canada. Additional funding provided by the Faculté d'études supérieures et de la recherché at the University of Moncton.

We acknowledge the support of the Canada Council for the Arts.

Nous remercions le Conseil des arts du Canada de son soutien.

McGill-Queen's University Press in Montreal is on land which long served as a site of meeting and exchange amongst Indigenous Peoples, including the Haudenosaunee and Anishinabeg nations. In Kingston it is situated on the territory of the Haudenosaunee and Anishinaabek. We acknowledge and thank the diverse Indigenous Peoples whose footsteps have marked these territories on which peoples of the world now gather.

Library and Archives Canada Cataloguing in Publication

Title: Lost in the crowd: Acadian soldiers of Canada's First World War / Gregory M.W. Kennedy.
Names: Kennedy, Gregory M. W. (Gregory Michael William), 1978- author.
Description: Series statement: La collection Louis J. Robichaud = The Louis J. Robichaud series; 3 | Includes bibliographical references and index.
Identifiers: Canadiana (print) 20230524990 | Canadiana (ebook) 20230525059 | ISBN 9780228020127 (cloth) | ISBN 9780228020134 (paper) | ISBN 9780228020141 (ePDF) | ISBN 9780228020158 (ePUB)
Subjects: LCSH: World War, 1914-1918—Maritime Provinces. | LCSH: Acadians—History—20th century. | LCSH: Soldiers—Maritime Provinces—History—20th century. | LCSH: Maritime Provinces—History, Military—20th century.
Classification: LCC D547.C2 K46 2024 | DDC 940.4/1271—dc23

This book was typeset by Marquis Interscript in 10.5/13 Sabon.

Contents

Tables and Figures vii

Gratitude xi

Introduction 3

1 Creating an Acadian Battalion, November 1915–June 1916 31

2 Training, Preparations, and Completing the Battalion, July 1916–March 1917 67

3 Heading Overseas, March–June 1917 111

4 Life in the Canadian Forestry Corps, May 1917–November 1918 145

5 Demobilization and Post-War Transition 203

Conclusion 236

Notes 245

Bibliography 275

Index 289

Tables and Figures

TABLES

1.1	Declared age at enrolment. 54
1.2	Declared occupation at enrolment in the 165th Battalion and the CEF. 54
1.3	Declared counties of residence of 165th Battalion originals. 58
3.1	Comparative analysis of age, height, and girth of Acadian volunteers. 132
3.2	Comparative analysis of previous military service of Acadian volunteers (%). 132
3.3	Comparison of key characteristics of CEF volunteers. 134
4.1	Acadians appointed to the position of acting CSM in 5th District, CFC. 185
4.2	Declared occupation at enrolment (%) 165th Battalion volunteers. 187
4.3	Mortality rates of Acadian volunteers overseas and CEF (%). 195
5.1	Household comparison 1911 and 1921 (%). 220
5.2	Average declared annual salaries ($) in 1911 and 1921. 224
5.3	Declared occupation of 165th Battalion volunteers at enlistment and in 1921. 225
5.4	Average weight (in lbs) of CEF soldiers and 165th Battalion volunteers. 231
5.5	1921 trends among selected subgroups of 165th Battalion volunteers. 232

FIGURES

0.1 Page from the 165th Battalion photograph album, CEAAC. 17
1.1 Key locations of the 165th Battalion. Map created by Stephanie Pettigrew using ARCGIS. 42
1.2 Enlistments by month in the 165th Battalion (January–June 1916). 58
2.1 Photo of 165th lines at Valcartier, CEAAC. 69
2.2 165th Battalion postcard from Valcartier. Courtesy of Jonathan Vance. 70
2.3 Officers of the 165th Battalion at Saint John, CEAAC. 81
2.4 Desertions from the 165th Battalion. 90
2.5 Corrected age at enrolment (%) of soldiers and deserters (n=705 and 160). 97
2.6 Declared occupation (%) at enrolment of soldiers and deserters (n=843 and 189). 99
2.7 Declared occupation (%) 1911 census of soldiers and deserters (n=262 and 59). 100
2.8 Desertion rate (%) by residence and birthplace for select regions. 104
2.9 The 165th battalion on parade in Valcartier, 1916, CEAAC. 110
3.1 Wartime portraits of Joseph Ulric LeBlanc, CEAAC. 123–4
3.2 Postcard sent from Ferdinand Malenfant to his sister Anna, CEAAC. 128
3.3 Alban Bourgeois and Marguerite LeBlanc of College Bridge, NB, CEAAC. 144
4.1 Map of the Jura region and key locations for 5th District. 153
4.2 FBM produced by 39th Company, 5th District (Jura), CFC (DROS). 155
4.3 39th Company sawmill at La Joux, CEAAC. 157
4.4 Foresters of 39th Company in 1917, CEAAC. 159
4.5 39th Company foresters with local civilians, CEAAC. 162
4.6 Nature of charges (%) in Acadian CFC Coys, 22nd Bn, 26th Bn CEF. 171
4.7 Summary charges among the 165th volunteers who went overseas. 173

4.8   A group of sergeants from 39th Company in the Jura, CEAAC. 188
4.9   Hospital admissions recorded in 5th District DROs, November 1917–October 1918. 190
4.10 Photograph of funeral parade for Pte Félicien Roy, CEAAC. 193
4.11 Author's photograph of CEF gravesite at Supt Parish Church, 2019. 194
5.1   Honeymoon photograph of J. Ulric LeBlanc and Marcelline Blanchard, CEAAC. 219

Gratitude

I am full of gratitude for all of the assistance and support I received during this project. I am profoundly thankful for the entire community of people who helped make this book possible. Any errors or omissions that remain are entirely my responsibility.

First, the heart of this project was the construction of the database of the nearly 1,200 volunteers of the 165th Battalion. This monumental task went far beyond simply transcribing information from attestation papers. An amazing team of students and researchers were up to the task of finding and accurately linking soldiers to multiple kinds of records; they then assisted me in organizing, sorting, and analyzing the results. The team included Kayleigh Blacklock, Mélanie Morin, Christine Dupuis, Rémi Frenette, Mélanie Desjardins, Danick Poirier, Josée Thériault, Julie Rennison, Emily Muckler, Samuelle Saindon, and Tanya Daigle. Julie-Michèle Lee and Samuelle Saindon added transcriptions of soldiers' letters and other family archives. Lauraly Deschambault assisted me with the references and crafted the bibliography. Mélanie Desjardins and Samuelle Saindon completed MA theses under my supervision on other aspects of Acadian military service during the First World War. Stephanie Pettigrew created the maps. Several colleagues generously shared personal research with me. Thanks to Curtis Mainville, we were able to add dozens of names to our database as well as extensive references to anglophone New Brunswick newspapers. Ronald Cormier contributed ongoing work identifying Acadian soldiers interred overseas with the Commonwealth Graves Commission. William Wicken shared findings about British women prosecuted for supposedly spreading venereal disease in CEF camps. Robert Richard identified songs and other resources from the folklore archives at the Centre d'études acadiennes Anselme-Chiasson (CEAAC).

One of the great aspects of academic life is the opportunity to learn and get feedback from colleagues. The participants in the Social Sciences and Humanities Research Council (SSHRC)–funded Partnership Development Project *Military Service, Citizenship, and Political Culture in Atlantic Canada* (2019–23) contributed much to my reflection on the meaning and importance of military service in our region. Similarly, the innovative research and engaging discussion among colleagues in the collective *Repenser l'Acadie dans le monde* (2019–23) helped me better understand the complexities of Acadian nationalism and the ongoing search for recognition and distinctiveness. These two projects formed an essential background to the evolution of this book. Other historians including Claude Léger, Jonathan Vance, Maurice Basque, Martin Hubley, Kris Inwood, and Mark Minenko shared insights from their own projects and publications that helped shape my findings.

I am especially grateful for those who read the full manuscript and offered such meaningful feedback. In addition to the anonymous peer reviewers, Cindy Brown, Lee Windsor, and Meredith Daun provided constructive criticism. In addition to guiding this manuscript to publication, the editorial team at MQUP, and especially Kyla Madden and Lesley Trites, made helpful suggestions that improved the readability, coherence, and presentation of this work. I would be remiss if I did not also mention the editors and reviewers of *Port Acadie*, *Histoire sociale – Social History* and *Canadian Military Journal*, who were involved in publishing preliminary results from this project in article form. The feedback from these endeavours contributed to the book's evolution. In addition, Corina Crainic, Philippe Volpé, and Julien Desrochers read early drafts of particular chapters and provided helpful suggestions.

The Université de Moncton and particularly the Faculté des études supérieures et de la recherche offered crucial financial support to this project. Programs including *Jeunesse Canada au travail* and *Emplois-été Canada* assisted with student hires. A Connection grant from SSHRC, *Minority Cultural Communities, Memory, and the First World War*, provided key momentum for the community-based event aspects of the research. Throughout the last ten years, my colleagues at the Institut d'études acadiennes, the CEAAC, and the Musée acadien de l'Université de Moncton have helped create a dynamic interdisciplinary space for research and knowledge mobilization. To give just one example, a team led by Jeanne-Mance Cormier and including Christine Dupuis, Madeleine Arseneau, and Mélanie Desjardins curated a temporary museum exhibit in 2016 about the 165th Battalion called *Debout peuple acadien, en avant pour l'honneur!*

Finally, I would like to thank my family for their unwavering support, starting with my partner, Meredith Daun. Your love, patient listening, and active engagement as a sounding board and as a travel partner to the Jura region are greatly appreciated. My children Avery and Aerin Kennedy, and my stepdaughter Mira Daun-Toews, as well as my parents Michael and Evelyn Kennedy, helped sustain a productive and encouraging space for me to complete this research and write the book. Friends and family from across this country have offered support over the years. While academic work can sometimes feel lonely and isolating, you also come to realize that you have a whole community of caring people around you. Thank you.

LOST IN THE CROWD

Introduction

The First World War occupies a complicated space in our national memory. In a seminal work on the commemoration of the First World War during the 1920s and 1930s, Jonathan Vance describes the development of the post-war consensus about how the conflict should be remembered as just and necessary.[1] The construction of white marble monuments emphasized the brave sacrifice and essential purity of those who had given their lives for their country, providing a sense of meaning and a place of remembering for those who remained. However, this consensus masked many internal divisions based on ethnicity, social class, and language. Andrew Theobald describes the "paradox" of a "great Canadian triumph and a costly victory in a brutal war that fractured the basic fabric of the country."[2] Mark Humphries, in his introduction to the revised edition of G.W.L. Nicholson's official history of the Canadian Expeditionary Force (CEF), emphasizes that by the time the war ended, "Canada was a far more violent, radicalized, and internally divided country than it had been in 1914."[3] Amy Shaw reminds us "we still forget that, for many Canadians, the patriotism surrounding the war emphasized duty to Britain more than an explicitly Canadian loyalty."[4] For example, before Robert Borden imposed conscription in 1917, more than half of CEF members were recent British immigrants. Meanwhile, the virulent debates around conscription reflected the limits of voluntarism and called into question national unity. French-speaking minority groups like the Acadians were at times subjected to harsh polemical discourses questioning their loyalty.[5] Terry Copp shows that the linguistic divide extended far beyond the war: education and language rights, politics, and even hockey were covered very differently in anglophone and francophone Montreal.[6]

For readers who may be unfamiliar, Acadie was a French colony from 1604 until 1763 in what are now Canada's Maritime provinces of Nova Scotia, New Brunswick, and Prince Edward Island. The colony was a contested imperial borderland between New France and New England as well as home to Indigenous peoples such as the Mi'kmaq and the Wolastoqiyik. Over time, the colonists who settled around the Bay of Fundy and in various coastal regions developed their own distinct identity within the larger Atlantic World.[7] To summarize a complex history, Acadie was destroyed during the 1750s, a time of renewed conflict that also saw the Battle of the Plains of Abraham and the Conquest of New France. British military leaders operating from Halifax led a series of campaigns to deport the Acadians and displace Indigenous peoples from the territory they referred to as Nova Scotia. Several thousand Acadians were forcibly transported in ships to the Thirteen Colonies; thousands more fled overland into the North American interior. Acadians refer to this period, somewhat ironically, as *le Grand Dérangement*.

Under the Treaty of Paris (1763), France surrendered to the British all of its North American territories except the islands of Saint-Pierre and Miquelon. British authorities then allowed some Acadians to return to the region, although their former lands had been taken over by British colonists called Planters. The Acadians founded new settlements on the periphery of Nova Scotia and New Brunswick (the latter hived off as a distinct colony in 1784). Others chose to stay in Quebec or France, while still others migrated to Louisiana, Saint-Domingue (now Haiti), and other French-speaking colonies. Today, around 300,000 French-speaking people reside in Atlantic Canada: about 32 per cent of the population of New Brunswick and between 3 and 4 per cent of the populations of Nova Scotia and Prince Edward Island.[8] Most, although certainly not all, of these francophones are descendants of the original Acadians. As we will see, the First World War coincided with an intense period of collective action by which this growing minority community sought greater rights and recognition within the Canadian state. Just as in Quebec, questions of military service and conscription divided communities in Atlantic Canada. However, the context and nature of those debates could be quite different for the Acadians.

The recent centenary of the First World War has inspired many innovative research projects aimed at advancing our knowledge of Canada's contribution to that conflict and also called into question the consensus about what it means for us today. Ian McKay and Jamie Swift have sounded the alarm over what they call "Vimyism": a deliberate policy by Stephen Harper's federal government to invent a glorious Canadian martial past anchored in victories like Vimy Ridge.[9] That policy has generated a predictable reaction from many scholars in the field, who maintain that Canada's wartime accomplishments are indeed worthy of praise. Tim Cook argues that all nations create histories in line with popular ambitions and ideals – in this case, that Canada was a force for good in the world and could rely on a patriotic population.[10] Indeed, Canada's ability to assemble a large expeditionary force essentially from volunteers contributed to a perennial "militia myth" – that ordinary citizens fighting for their country made the best soldiers and that large (and expensive) professional military forces were not required.[11] The deployment of militia during the War of 1812 and the Northwest Campaign of 1885, and even Canada's successful deployment of volunteers to the Boer War in service of the British Empire, seemed to confirm that ordinary citizens could do the job.[12]

There is no dispute that Canada made a major contribution to the war effort, especially relative to its population. The dominant national narrative of the First World War continues to emphasize nation-building through shared sacrifice. Tim Cook explains that the Battle of Vimy Ridge, during which all four divisions of the Canadian Corps fought together for the first time and achieved an important objective at great cost, emerged as the primary symbol of this narrative. At the same time, though, Cook highlights the powerful counter-narrative in French Canada of conscription forced on an unwilling population by an imperialist, anglophone majority, symbolized by the deadly Easter Riots of 1918 in Quebec City. The First World War as nation-building event simply has not resonated for most Quebecers.[13]

Where then do Acadians fit in the traditional English narrative and French counter-narrative of the war? Broadly speaking, they shared a willingness to support voluntary military service with their anglophone neighbours in Atlantic Canada but also an abhorrence of conscription with their French-Canadian counterparts in Quebec. The focus of this book on the members of an Acadian national unit offers a unique opportunity to study their perspectives and experiences of the First World War, both in their own right and also as part of a broader reflection on the legacy of that conflict for Canada and Canadians today.

WHY THIS BOOK?

This book was inspired, simply enough, by a student who asked whether Acadians had participated in the CEF. I had no idea. After some cursory research, I concluded that there had been little scholarly treatment of this question or, indeed, of Acadian military service more generally.[14] According to Anselme Chiasson, "the majority of Acadians, like other French-Canadians, saw no reason to participate in the war."[15] Michel Roy thought that the Acadian politicians who publicly supported the war did so as "the only possible defence" against the "radical" imperial emotions expressed by English-speakers in Atlantic Canada.[16] Moreover, popular histories tended to diminish the impact of the First World War and in some cases completely omit Acadian military service, which may explain why a recent paper struggled to fathom why 23,000 Acadians signed up during the Second World War.[17]

These absences in the literature are hard to understand given the clear evidence that Acadians did participate in the CEF. Cook notes that the Moncton-based French-language newspaper *L'Acadien* was one of the first to celebrate the victory at Vimy Ridge, and we know that hundreds of Acadians fought there, notably with the 26th (New Brunswick) Battalion.[18] Claude Léger's 2001 study of the 165th (Acadian) Battalion details how Acadian elites had successfully lobbied the federal government for the creation of an Acadian national unit. The effort to create this French-speaking, Catholic battalion was part of a larger renaissance movement aimed at gaining greater recognition of Acadian rights. Indeed, the president of the Société nationale de l'Acadie, Pascal Poirier, who was also the first Acadian nominated to the Canadian Senate, was among the champions of this initiative. The battalion was intended to embody all of Acadie; while most units drew from a particular city or county, the 165th established recruiting and training depots throughout the Maritime provinces.[19]

I wanted to know more about the volunteers of the 165th Battalion. Thanks to Léger's work I had a starting point – a list of more than

500 soldiers who had been sent overseas in March 1917. I also wanted to learn more about how military service and minority experience intersected in the CEF. At least some observers at the time were well aware of the irony of Acadians fighting for the British Empire. How did Acadian and anglophone observers interpret the presence of the 165th recruiting and training across Atlantic Canada?

In an important study centred on the conscription crisis in New Brunswick, Andrew Theobald affirms that "during the debate over conscription, virtually all of New Brunswick's anglophone politicians, military officers and newspapers espoused anti-French views openly."[20] As the war continued, casualties mounted, and volunteers dried up, it was easy to cast blame on those who had supposedly not sacrificed as much and to play on old linguistic and religious prejudices. Conspiracy theories abounded "about francophone and popish plots to destroy the province."[21] Far from assuaging this anti-French discourse, the creation of the 165th Battalion simply provided a new target. For example, when a group of volunteers went door to door in Moncton to raise money for the unit, one man declared that "he would like to see everyone of the 165th shot down one by one."[22] National studies have focused on the terribly divisive political debates about the war that raged in Quebec; yet a similar discourse was playing out in the Maritime provinces.

Theobald, like most researchers, assumes that Acadians did in fact contribute less to the war effort than their anglophone counterparts. He notes that in New Brunswick this was less about loyalty and more about opportunity; army recruiters had made little effort to visit French communities. Despite these obstacles, there are many indications that a considerable number of Acadians enlisted voluntarily even before the 165th Battalion was established. The same Moncton assembly of notables in December 1915 that called for an Acadian unit deplored the lack of Catholic chaplains to provide religious services to the many Acadians already serving overseas with the 26th (New Brunswick) and 55th (New Brunswick and Prince Edward Island) Battalions. In a speech given to that assembly, Poirier stressed that Acadian participation in the war had become an issue of primary importance. Accusations that they were not doing their part were due to the fact that *"nos soldats sont perdus dans la foule."* They were literally "lost in the crowd" of those who had already gone overseas.[23] Writing two years later from France, Major Arthur Legere affirmed that to his knowledge, more than 6,000 Acadians had signed up among various English-speaking units.[24] As we will see, one of the challenges for the 165th Battalion recruiters was that most of those interested in military service had already enlisted.

It is impossible to know exactly how many Acadians served in the CEF and, of these, how many spoke French as their primary language, because neither the military attestation papers nor the service files recorded such information. However, even if a total figure eludes us, we can find thousands of Acadians serving across several battalions in the Maritime provinces and we can calculate estimates of their participation rate. The Acadian contribution to the war was significant not only to the CEF in Atlantic Canada but also as part of their own national movement. Why, then, have Acadian leaders and historians paid so little attention to the creation of this national battalion? Claude Léger details the inability of the 165th Battalion to recruit up to strength, falling far short of the 1,000 fit soldiers needed. In the end, only 532 Acadians boarded the ss *Metagama* for England in March 1917.[25] With the unit disbanded soon after, the majority of the soldiers were transferred to the Canadian Forestry Corps (CFC). They would serve in France, but not in the trenches. Instead, many cut wood for the Allies in the Jura region close to Switzerland or near Bordeaux. Put simply, the battalion "brought no memorable glory to Acadie."[26] There was no Vimy moment for the Acadians. Scholars chose to highlight other, more visible, successes of the Acadian national movement at that time, such as the appointment of the first Acadian bishop in 1912.

The first objective of this book is to integrate the history of the 165th Battalion as part of a larger Acadian and Atlantic Canadian contribution to Canada's First World War. The 532 soldiers who left Canada with the 165th tell only part of the story. In fact, more than 1,000 Acadians volunteered for that unit, and thousands more served elsewhere, often at the front. In other words, I want to be able to answer the student's question about Acadian participation in the CEF, in both quantitative and qualitative terms. It should not matter whether the 165th Battalion fought in key battles like Vimy Ridge. This is a historical study and not a commemoration, so victories and sacrifices are not the only criteria for who gets to be talked about. The volunteers proudly believed they were serving Canada as well as their home communities.

Beyond making a significant contribution to Acadian and regional history, this book connects the 165th Battalion and its volunteers to national trends. Many aspects of recruitment, training, and service overseas were similar across the CEF, but the Acadian national unit was one of thirty-nine "special identity" battalions created during this time. The recruitment of minority groups like the Acadians and their diverse experiences of military service, from trenches to lumber camps, deserve our attention because they challenge broader historiographical narratives about the conduct of the war, the lower enlistment rates for French-Canadians, and what military service meant for the volunteers.

The second objective of this book is to offer a new approach to Canada's First World War using the methods of social history. The historiography is already well endowed with regimental histories, which tend to follow a standard formula that emphasizes military concerns such as training, battles, casualty rates, and officer biographies. Claude Léger integrates many aspects of this formula in his study of the 165th Battalion, but the approach has limited value for a reserve battalion that was disbanded soon after arriving overseas. It also leaves out rejected volunteers and those who abandoned the unit before it left Canada. This book proposes instead a broader examination of the soldiers themselves, who they were, their motivations in signing up, their experiences of the war, and the important consequences of their military service for themselves and their families. Such an approach is not unique; there have been several compelling local and regional studies of the First World War that apply social history methods.[27] What is exceptional about this study is that it applies a longitudinal analysis that links soldiers to a multitude of sources in order to reveal even more of the human dimensions of people living at that time. These dimensions include economic conditions, mobility, and family dynamics. While official military archives remain key sources, a rich historical record is available from other sources as well, such as personnel files, censuses, parish registers, newspapers, and personal correspondence. The reconstitution of individual and family histories from 1911 through 1921 and beyond enables new insights into the backgrounds, movements, and motivations of these adolescents and men who would pass from recruits to soldiers to veterans in the span of just a few years. The methodology used here could be applied to other groups of Canadian soldiers and units.

Finally, this study broaches topics often ignored or passed over by traditional regimental histories. We will tackle difficult questions including underage and unfit recruits, desertion, discipline, and disease. These were fundamental aspects of life in the CEF, yet for a variety of ideological and practical reasons, historians are often reluctant to treat them in detail. Nobody wishes to impugn the honour of those who died for their country or create embarrassment for veterans' families. Official sources broach these issues in complex and often contradictory ways, seeking to minimize problems and defend authorities. We might expect more frank discussions in the letters home that soldiers wrote, but these passed through censorship, and even more compelling was the desire to avoid worrying family members at home. The book will also include a discussion of the relationship between soldiers and nearby civilian communities, including financial claims and documented cases of violence. Considering these aspects of military service is a necessary step towards a more comprehensive history of the war and its impact. In some cases, there are obvious links between problems during military service and adverse outcomes upon soldiers' return to Canada.

There remains an important place for commemorative regimental histories.[28] My background in social history – in particular the family reconstitution methods of the *Annales* school – coupled with the rich and varied documentation now available and often accessible online, makes a different kind of history possible, one that is more centred on the soldiers themselves and able to integrate pre-war and post-war perspectives. While this book is certainly a regional history focused on Acadians, many of the findings and methods presented here will be applicable to other francophone and anglophone units and suggest new ways of thinking about Canada's First World War. The English-Canadian "birth of a nation" narrative does not fit comfortably with Acadian perspectives, but neither does the French-Canadian "opposition to conscription" narrative. Like other minority groups, the 165th Battalion volunteers had their own paths to and reasons for enrolment and service overseas. Some of the recruits suffered greatly, from debilitating diseases and injuries to unemployment and displacement after demobilization. At the same time, others benefited from their time in uniform, finding themselves in improved social and economic circumstances afterward. Indeed, the diversity of their views and experiences defies simple conclusions. Unpacking the host of trajectories contained within a single unit is not just possible, but necessary if more inclusive regional and national histories are to be written.

THE DATABASE AND PRIMARY SOURCES

The 532 Acadian volunteers approved for overseas service with the 165th Battalion left Saint John, New Brunswick, by train for Halifax and subsequently embarked for England on 25 March 1917. A last round of medical examinations had reduced the unit's effective strength from 784, meaning that authorities discharged approximately one-third of the recruits during these final stages.[29] This study includes all of the Acadians who volunteered for the 165th, whether they ultimately deployed overseas or not. This has required detailed work with earlier unit nominal roles, newspaper articles, and other archival sources. For example, the papers of the Commanding Officer, Lieutenant-Colonel Louis-Cyriaque Daigle, include a register of 198 deserters, that is, those who quit the unit without authorization while it was still training in Canada.[30] In the end, we identified 1,184 enlistments, although this includes some Acadians who had already been serving with other units and later transferred to the 165th. Even this does not represent the total number of volunteers. Files were lost; for example, several of the deserters listed by Daigle and some of the new enlistments mentioned in newspaper articles do not have any surviving military service record. We also have no way of knowing how many men (and boys) the recruiters turned away.

With such a large pool of volunteers, we might wonder why the unit did not get closer to the goal of reaching its full strength of 1,000. First, not everyone who deployed overseas was included in the official list. In fact, that document neglected to include several soldiers who boarded the ss *Metagama* with everyone else, a further reminder that military record keeping was far from perfect. Others did not make the list because they departed later or transferred to different units. In total, at least 598 of the 165th Battalion volunteers, not 532, ultimately served overseas with the CEF. Second, not all of the 1,184 recruits were actually Acadian or even francophone. In the desperate push to find new soldiers, and given the geographic focus of most military recruiting, it is not surprising that a few of the volunteers did not fit the profile and were simply lumped in with the unit because they were also from the area. A significant portion of these men eventually deserted, and others transferred to anglophone battalions.

Given the importance of finding Acadians for this study, this point deserves further attention. Other military historians interested in identifying French-Canadians have commented on the difficulties inherent in using attestation papers and personnel files. How, that is, can we know who actually was Acadian? Family names are an obvious starting place but are not necessarily sufficient to make the case. Jean Martin affirms that soldiers with French names, and who listed parents with French names, were probably francophone.[31] Fortunately, longitudinal analysis helps address this concern. By linking soldiers to their records in the 1911 and 1921 Canadian Census, which did ask questions related to language and ethnicity, we can much more conclusively identify Acadians and other francophones.

After completing this work, it seems that the concerns about surname identification can be overblown, particularly when one is dealing with a minority community concentrated in certain parishes. Nearly everyone with an Acadian family name turned out to be of French ancestry and to speak French. There were also a handful of men with family names like Sweeny, Ferguson, and McDonald who identified as French-speakers. This was undoubtedly the result of intermarriage, particularly among Roman Catholics. In other words, using family names as a basis for identifying francophone soldiers actually underestimates, not overestimates, their contribution. In the end, we identified 146 volunteers who had no apparent links to the Acadian community and who did not speak French. This included several anglophone residents of Saint John, where the unit trained for several months, as well as recent immigrants from a variety of countries including England, Belgium, Denmark, Italy, and Russia, who no doubt had arrived at that port. As mentioned, most of these non-Acadians did not stay long in the 165th Battalion.

Regarding the 1,038 Acadian volunteers remaining in the database, research into their complete service files (helpfully digitized by Library and Archives Canada) allowed us to determine that 237 were discharged as medically unfit, 114 deserted, and 40 more were released specifically for being under 18 (31 cases) or over 45 years old (9 cases). When compared with other battalions raised in 1916, the 165th Battalion lost a bit less to desertion and a bit more to medical exams. Of the 647 soldiers remaining, 598 served overseas at some point, and the remainder never left Canada.

An important part of this project was our endeavour to link all of these soldiers to their 1911 and 1921 Canadian Census records. The detailed information available in the attestation papers and personnel files, particularly with regard to birthplace, age, residence, and next of kin, made it more likely that we would be able to find them before and after the war. Unfortunately, not everyone could be found. Acadians often possessed multiple first names and nicknames. In addition, recruiters and census-takers often misspelled or anglicized French names. Using "*Ancestry*" to access images of the original censuses introduced another level of error, because the people employed by that organization committed frequent transcription mistakes. To complicate matters further, military authorities identified a few soldiers using false names, such as "Amable Beauséjour." Several others, including "François Bacon" seem highly suspicious. The censuses themselves were far from perfect; people not at home or travelling when the enumerator came by might be left out entirely.[32]

Regarding the 1911 Canadian Census (or 1910 American Census), we had enough information to attempt to match 1,030 of the 1,038 Acadian volunteers. Of these, we successfully linked 718 (70 per cent). For 1921 (or 1920), the pool is reduced by 28 for those who died during the war and by another 10 for those who died between the end of the war and the time of the census. Of the 992 remaining, we found 621 in the censuses and another 116 in travel documents, especially those for people crossing the border. These latter records do not provide as much information, but they do usually indicate their destination and sometimes include other details such as their trade and next of kin. In total, after the war we accounted for 737 volunteers (72 per cent). While there is much overlap, in some cases we did not find the same soldiers in both censuses. A total of 521 (almost exactly half the group) were found in both 1911 and 1921. At first glance, this may seem disappointing, but it is actually pretty remarkable. In their study of a sample of 974 French-Canadian (Quebec) soldiers, Carl Bouchard and Michael Huberman could find only 22 per cent in the 1911 census, 18 per cent in the 1921 census, and just 15 per cent in both.[33] The detailed work of my research assistants using multiple sources proved highly effective, netting more than three times the successful matches as this other similar sample. Angela Cunningham notes that previous attempts in several countries to link First World War personnel records to just a single census have had varying results, ranging from 28 to 85 per cent.[34]

Although the focus of this book is on the 165th Battalion, some space is devoted to Acadian volunteers who served elsewhere. To this end, we constituted two samples of additional recruits, one composed of men who signed up earlier, up to the end of 1915, and the other drawn from the complete nominal role of the 26th (New Brunswick)

Battalion. Each sample includes 100 volunteers linked to their 1911 and 1921 Census records. Since nearly all of these men ended up at the front, their experiences of the war would have been quite different – most obviously they would have suffered higher casualty rates. The rare and valuable source constituted by the detailed personal correspondence of J. Ulric LeBlanc, one of the first Acadian volunteers for the CEF, allows us to travel to the great battlefields of the war. He mostly wrote in English because, as he explained, his censors could not read French.[35] Together, these additional sources add crucial details to our analysis of the Acadian experience of the war and serve as a point of comparison with the trends identified with the 165th Battalion.

Newspapers provided additional information, especially for the time that the 165th Battalion was recruiting and training in Canada. French-language newspapers in the Maritime provinces such as *L'Évangéline* and *Le Moniteur acadien* dedicated particular attention to the unit and published letters from Acadian soldiers throughout the war. English-language newspapers including *The Daily Times* (Moncton) and the *Saint John Standard* also published many articles, editorials, and other texts concerning the 165th alongside information for other anglophone battalions in the region. In total, we compiled more than 1,200 documents from these newspapers, and while many were simple stubs of information about recruiting assemblies or officers travelling in the area, these sources sometimes provide information on unique details about army life, particular unit challenges such as desertion, and public support for the war. Readers were clearly interested in following the Acadian national unit, and at least some of the editors strongly believed in the cause. These texts also frequently emphasize Catholicism – an important reminder for readers today of the importance of faith and religious obligation for historical actors. This was particularly the case for many Acadians, because the Church played a strong role in education and provided a key focal point for the larger national movement. In his pastoral letter for Lent in 1915, Bishop Édouard A. LeBlanc commented on the many empty places in the pews across his diocese of Saint John, yet another indication that some Acadians had already enlisted and died in considerable numbers.[36]

These local sources are much less helpful when it comes to knowing what happened to the Acadian volunteers overseas, particularly after they were transferred to the Canadian Forestry Corps (CFC). The CFC has recently received a little more attention from scholars interested in its ethnically diverse units such as No. 2 Construction Battalion.[37] In many ways, the CFC provides a compelling microcosm of the war as global phenomenon. Acadians from the 165th Battalion ended up logging alongside Chinese labourers, Russian conscripts suspected of Bolshevik sympathies, and other individuals deemed unsuitable for trench duty. The stigma must have been obvious to the men involved, but, as Fred Frigot prosaically wrote to his sister, service in the CFC greatly increased their chances of survival.[38] Acadian officers such as Major Arthur Legere lobbied hard to preserve the cohesion of the 165th in the CFC. For example, both the 39th and 40th Companies of the 5th District, located in the Jura region of France, near the Swiss border, were composed almost entirely of former members of the Acadian national unit, and the men were authorized to continue wearing the 165th Battalion cap badge. The complete routine orders from 27 November 1917 through 12 December 1918 conserved at Library and Archives Canada (LAC) provide many details about life in the camps.[39] For example, there is information about discipline, promotions, pay, hospital admissions, lumber production, and general orders. This includes instructions related to the influenza pandemic and the demobilization process. A recent study by David Devigne using similar sources provides valuable insights into the experiences of Acadian foresters in the Bordeaux region. Devigne notes that being francophone was an advantage for the Acadians in the CFC, who forged strong bonds with many of the local residents that led to several marriages.[40]

Naturally, official records are incomplete and often limited in scope. Fortunately, private archives such as those located at the Centre d'études acadiennes Anselme-Chiasson (CEAAC) at the Université de Moncton add unique documents to the record. The Commanding Officer of the 165th Battalion left several documents, including reports and the aforementioned register of deserters. He also organized the publication of a unit photo album, which included pictures of the volunteers. Family archives yield additional unpublished letters, photographs, and postcards. We even stumbled upon an extraordinary notebook kept by one of the volunteers. While censors always screened the letters sent home, this notebook appears to have been kept by the soldier for his own thoughts. It contains many tantalizing details about life in the camps that do not appear in the official record, such as a brawl that broke out at the showers and the misfortunes of an accident-prone soldier nicknamed "Fricot."[41] We also learn of the soldier's profound loneliness and sense of isolation from home. Unfortunately, few records like this have survived, although others may eventually be discovered in basements, flea markets, and uncatalogued boxes stored at local archives. Indeed, some of the knowledge mobilization activities accompanying this research project included organizing pop-up museums in communities like Pubnico and Chéticamp, Nova Scotia, and Bathurst, New Brunswick. We were grateful for those who shared letters and photos from their family collections.[42]

A note on references. First, primary (and secondary) sources in English and French were consulted for this book. I have translated from French to English unless otherwise indicated. Second, this book regularly uses individual examples to highlight trends and exceptions among the 165th Battalion volunteers. As discussed earlier, we reconstituted soldier biographies and created a database from a variety of sources that included military personnel files, official unit archives and census records (LAC), newspapers, correspondence, and family archives (CEAAC), as well as civil registration, parish registers, and border control records (*Ancestry*). To avoid encumbering the book with long footnotes, I decided not to provide detailed references to every case. A simplified version of the soldier database is available on the website of the Institut d'études acadiennes (https://www.umoncton.ca/iea).

It remains to better situate this research in the broader historiography of the First World War, a significant undertaking. While making no claims to be exhaustive, the following sections outline some of the key contributions of this study and how they intersect with recent trends and ongoing debates in the field.

FRENCH-CANADIAN ENLISTMENT IN THE CEF

It is easy to forget that in the early twentieth century, Canada was still very much a country divided between two nations, French and English. The hanging of Louis Riel in 1885, coupled with the introduction of anti-French education laws in some provinces in the years leading up to the First World War, had exacerbated these differences. What is more, the pre-war militia had made little effort to involve French-Canadians, who participated even less in the small Permanent Army.[43] Symbolic of the general situation was the decision of the federal government not to create any French-speaking units when it organized the First Contingent of the CEF in 1914. Public outcry in Quebec eventually led to the creation of the 22nd Battalion (French-Canadian) for the Second Contingent, but prejudice ran deep in the military hierarchy; the

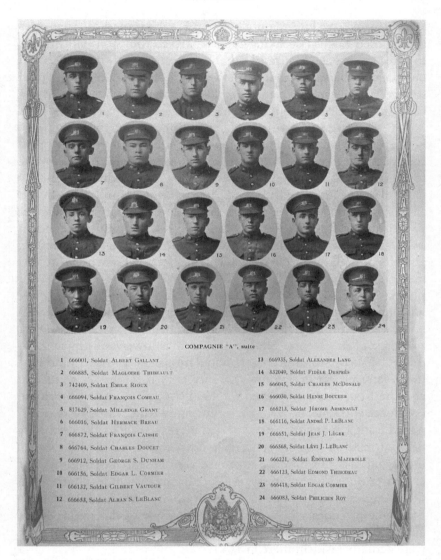

Figure 0.1 Page from the 165th photograph album

Commanding Officer of the 22nd later described the oppressive weight and scrutiny of representing an entire "race" as the only French-language battalion in the entire British Expeditionary Force.[44] Officials authorized only a handful of other CEF French-speaking units during the course of the war, none of whom reached the front.[45]

Historians have long maintained that French-Canadians lagged far behind their English-speaking counterparts in voluntary enlistments. In a recent article, Mourad Djebabla repeats the oft-cited figure of only 35,000 French-Canadians in the CEF, just 5.6 per cent of its total strength.[46] Robert Brown and Donald Loveridge calculated that across Canada, about 12 per cent of the military age group – defined in 1911 as males 15 to 44 years of age – had enlisted in infantry battalions. However, in Quebec, the figure fell to 5 per cent. Desmond Morton speculates that lower enlistments for francophones were in part due to the lack of effort to recruit them where they lived (which was largely in rural areas) and in part due to their tendency to marry early and stay on the farm.[47] Brown and Loveridge agree, pointing to a smaller proportion of single males of military age in the French-Canadian population, a national tendency to concentrate on urban recruiting, and the already mentioned legacy of neglect of French-Canadians in the pre-war military.[48]

C.A. Sharpe looked beyond the infantry to examine the entire CEF. He found that across Canada, around 31 per cent of the eligible population signed up for military service of some kind, compared to just 15 per cent in Quebec. Sharpe agreed that lower enlistment rates related, in part, to larger rural populations, as he also found that there were proportionally fewer recruits in rural parts of Ontario and the Maritimes. However, total enlistments from the Maritime provinces and Quebec went up significantly when those were determined using birthplace instead of current residence; in Quebec, those figures rose from 15 to 21 per cent. In other words, many young, single men from eastern Canada had moved west in search of employment and later opted for military service. Sharpe concludes that "more Quebecers enlisted than is generally acknowledged."[49] Curtis Mainville provides a New Brunswick example of this trend: of the almost 1,100 CEF volunteers originally from Queens County, just 313 were actually resident there in 1911.[50]

Jean Martin conducted a thorough review of French-Canadian rates of voluntary enlistment. Like previous scholars, he found that French-Canadians, about 30 per cent of the entire Canadian population, represented just 5 per cent of the first two contingents of the CEF recruited in 1914 and 1915. However, when he examined the birthplaces of *all* of the recruits concerned, he found that English-Canadians did not do much better. Instead, the majority of the soldiers were recent immigrants from Great Britain. Only the 22nd and 26th Battalions (French-Canadian and New Brunswick respectively) had at least 70 per cent Canadian-born members at the time they were sent overseas.[51] In fact, before conscription integrated new cohorts of Canadian-born men beginning in late 1917, more than half the members of the CEF were born outside Canada. The Canadian-born "had demonstrated much less interest in serving." Martin added that where French-Canadians were members of minority communities (which describes the Acadians) – they were more likely to sign up, partly because they were more likely to be at ease with the English language and partly because they felt more pressure from the English-speaking majority.[52]

Steve Marti examined minority communities in detail for his PhD dissertation on voluntary enlistment in Australia, Canada, and New Zealand during the First World War. He writes that many French-Canadians "rallied to support the war as a means of securing protection against further marginalization" but also, in a more positive light, "to assert and protect their cultural identity." Acadians, like francophones in northern Ontario and Manitoba, wanted to distinguish themselves from their English-speaking neighbours as well as from French-Canadians raised in Quebec.[53] Major Legere, the Deputy Commanding Officer of the 165th Battalion and later a company commander with the CFC, emphasized this point in one of his letters to the New Brunswick Attorney General J.B.M. Baxter. Legere commented on the "difficulty" and "embarrassment" that came from having to explain the differences between French-Canadians and Acadians to colleagues and comrades.[54] It is striking, then, that French-Canadian minorities in other parts of Canada sometimes employed to their own advantage the negative discourse directed at Quebec by anglophone elites.

The Acadians, as well as other ethnic minorities, eventually found some support from the government for the creation of their own distinct units. Across the Dominion, enrolments had fallen to just 10,000 per month by June 1915, yet on 1 January 1916, Prime Minister Robert Borden announced that the CEF would be expanded to 500,000 men.[55] The 165th Battalion (Acadian) was one of thirty-nine "special identity" battalions authorized with a view to boosting the numbers. Few of these units ever reached full strength, and most were disbanded before long.[56] Marti suggests that anglophone recruiters tended to monopolize local efforts and that some communities actively opposed French units recruiting in their midst.[57] However, most anglophone special units suffered a similar fate. Terry Copp relates that the 199th Battalion (Irish Rangers), recruited in Montreal, initially reached its complement thanks to a large number of British- and Irish-born immigrants, but by November 1916 nearly three hundred men were away due to medical conditions or absent without leave.[58]

The Acadian battalion did not reach full strength in part due to competition with other regional units – there were six units recruiting in southern New Brunswick in 1916.[59] There were relatively few Acadians from Prince Edward Island in the 165th Battalion because the newly formed 105th Battalion had just conducted a successful recruiting drive.[60] Léger's most recent study, of the 132nd Battalion (North Shore), found hundreds of Acadians from northeastern New Brunswick in its ranks. This is particularly significant since the 132nd and the 165th had been created at the same time and in direct competition with each other among francophone communities.[61] As we will see, Acadian notables from southeastern and northeastern New Brunswick did not always get along. What is more, and to the consternation of the unit's officers and supporters, official promises to allow Acadians already serving in other units to transfer to the 165th fell by the wayside. An editorial called attention to this problem as early as March 1916.[62]

Jean Martin contends that Acadians and other francophone minorities should be included when calculating the total rate of French-Canadian voluntary enlistment in the CEF. This would considerably increase the previously accepted figure of 35,000 soldiers, which was an estimate for the number of French-Canadian volunteers and conscripts from Quebec originally proposed by Elizabeth Armstrong. However, it would be a monumental task to examine closely all francophone minority communities across Canada. Martin offers a variety of innovative methods to address this challenge, including a sampling method using family names beginning with the letter B as well as estimates gleaned from French-Canadian family names found on war graves. His proposal that the number of French-Canadian soldiers (both volunteers and conscripts) in the CEF be doubled to 70,000 has not been widely accepted by military historians.[63] Although his results seem more suggestive than conclusive, he is certainly correct that we have systematically underrepresented French-Canadian participation in the CEF by ignoring minority communities in Atlantic Canada, Ontario, Manitoba, and elsewhere.

This study of Acadian soldiers will certainly contribute to the debate surrounding French-Canadian enlistment in the CEF. We identified virtually all of the 165th Battalion volunteers and additional samples of Acadians serving elsewhere, linking them to multiple records including official censuses that do confirm language and ethnicity. This allowed us to differentiate between French-speakers and others caught up in the 165th by error or chance. Offering a new conclusive figure for French-Canadian participation across the CEF is beyond the scope of this book; we can, however, say something about Acadian enlistment rates. Acadians volunteered for military service at rates similar to those of other Canadian-born residents of the Maritime provinces: approximately 25 per cent of the eligible male population. I offer the figure of 5,000 Acadian soldiers as a reasonable (low) estimate based on our research. The details of this analysis are offered at the end of chapter 2. If nothing else, this study of the 165th Battalion should remind readers that francophone minorities outside of Quebec made their own distinct contributions to the CEF and deserve recognition. French Canada, much like English Canada, was not a monolith.

REJECTED AND UNDERAGE SOLDIERS

The centenary of the First World War inspired a number of new studies examining forgotten or somewhat obscure historical actors. Another way in which this study of Acadian soldiers contributes to the broader history of Canada's First World War relates to the inclusion of volunteers ultimately rejected as medically unfit. These men have often been excluded from traditional unit histories because they did not stay in their units or go overseas; nevertheless, they constitute a very significant group of willing volunteers deserving our attention. Nic Clarke's foundational study on this subject identified two principal groups: men rejected from the start (and thus lacking any military documentation), and those initially accepted but later discharged (usually leaving an attestation paper and perhaps medical records). Clarke writes that CEF medical examinations "were hindered by a number of interrelated factors: the inexperience and/or professional arrogance of some individuals tasked with conducting examinations; the sheer number of men needing to be examined; recruiting practices; and the willingness of recruits, military authorities, politicians, and medical officers to subvert the medical examination for their own ends." Across Canada, between 5 and 15 per cent of the men enrolled during the first two years of the war were later deemed unfit to serve, and this figure rose to nearly 25 per cent in 1916 according to one government report.[64]

The results for the 165th Battalion indicate a similarly high figure, approaching 20 per cent: 237 volunteers were medically discharged from the unit before it went overseas. A review of the attestation papers reveals that doctors should never have accepted some of them in the first place because they did not meet the minimum physical requirements. For example, thirty of the recruits were not tall enough, and more than two hundred were not sufficiently broad through the chest in accordance with military regulations.[65] Clarke's analysis suggests that this was typical of units recruiting in 1916, that there was pressure to accept more marginal men, and that doctors were not always thorough in their evaluations.[66] Léger emphasizes that the 165th Battalion officers faced significant pressure to find enough recruits and thereby fulfil the unit's nationalist vision.[67]

Undoubtedly, these results point to the youth of many of the soldiers; perhaps the initial medical examiners reasoned that they might fill out during the training. For example, Aubin Gallant of Egmont Bay, Prince Edward Island, stood just over five feet tall and had a chest measurement of only twenty-eight inches. He was seventeen years old and thus underage at the time of enrolment. However, not all short recruits were underdeveloped adolescents. Romauld Gauvin of Madawaska County, New Brunswick, was a thirty-two-year-old labourer when he enlisted at five feet one and a half inches tall and with a thirty-two-inch chest measurement. He may simply have been short; military authorities authorized the creation of "bantam" battalions like the 143rd Battalion (British Columbia) in order to permit men like this to enrol, although they too struggled to fill the ranks.[68] General health and nutrition might also explain a smaller girth. One CEF study suggested that many soldiers had only a barely adequate diet before enlistment due to their economic circumstances; those who did not suffer debilitating injuries actually experienced noticeable weight gain during their military service thanks to the plentiful, if not always appetizing, food.[69]

Military historians are well aware of the presence of underage recruits in the CEF, but they often pay little attention to them in regimental histories. Twenty-five years ago, Desmond Morton wrote:

> Historians have overlooked their service because it has been difficult to distinguish them from their older comrades, since

most of these young soldiers lied about their age in order to enlist. A sense of adventure, peer pressure, and fierce patriotism impelled young and old to serve. Most underage soldiers who enlisted were 16 or 17 (and later 18 when age requirements were raised to 19), but at least one cheeky lad enlisted at only 10 years old, and a 12-year-old made it to the trenches.[70]

Historians taking the military attestation papers at face value have calculated that about 3 per cent of the CEF, or twenty thousand soldiers, were under the required age of eighteen when they enlisted.[71] This is certainly too low, since it does not include those recruits who lied about their age, either with or without the coaxing of recruiting officials. Increasing pressure to recruit and diminishing enlistments in 1916 may have influenced units across Canada to accept more underage volunteers. The attestation papers for the 165th Battalion certainly bear this out; more than 150 of the recruits were officially not yet eighteen but were nevertheless permitted to enrol. While some of these men were seventeen and not far from their next birthday, others were considerably younger. Fifteen-year-old Joseph Albert of Gloucester County, New Brunswick, was one of thirteen volunteers eventually discharged for being underage. That left sixty-five others, including another fifteen-year-old, Alex Chiasson of Inverness County, Nova Scotia, to complete their training and head overseas. Fortunately, by linking soldiers to their census records, we can also identify underage soldiers who lied about their age. The results are staggering. Fully one in four of the 165th Battalion volunteers were not eighteen when they enlisted. This is a good example of how this innovative methodology challenges conventional views of CEF history and could be applied to other units.

Instead of celebrating the plucky and determined youths who made it to the front, perhaps we should be taking a harder look at propaganda, social pressure, and family situations. As we will see, many of the Acadian youth who enlisted in the army did so as part of a broader pattern in which teenagers left home in search of wages to contribute to their families and to gain professional experiences. They were also subjected to repeated calls to enlist from trusted community leaders, including priests, who talked about duty, service, and other masculine ideals. This combination of economic and patriotic pressure proved potent.

Volunteers who were too old could also be found throughout the CEF.[72] Officially, there was just one in the 165th Battalion. Basil Johnson of Kent County, New Brunswick, was a fifty-seven-year-old customs officer. Standing over six feet tall, he was initially accepted on condition that he become a bandsman. He was later discharged for various ailments including poor eyesight and arteriosclerosis. Johnson was determined to go overseas, however, and re-enlisted with the Nova Scotia Forestry Corps in May 1917, claiming that he was only forty-five. He served in the 71st Company of the Canadian Forestry Corps (CFC), suffered during the influenza pandemic from what would become known inaccurately as the "Spanish flu" in October 1918, and was discharged in March 1919 just shy of his sixtieth birthday. Once again, our longitudinal analysis revealed additional cases. For example, Octave Cormier of Caraquet, New Brunswick, claimed to be forty-five years old when he enlisted with the 165th but was actually nearly sixty. A widower with no living children, he was fit enough to be selected for service with a pioneer unit, but six months later he was ruled out by a different doctor and discharged in Halifax.

Although the official reason for the transfer of the former 165th Battalion soldiers to the CFC was the apparent familiarity of some Acadians with the lumber industry, only sixty of the volunteers had declared an occupation related to forestry when they enrolled, such as carpenter, sawyer, or lumberman. Most of the recruits were demonstrably *not* woodsmen. It seems more likely that military authorities observed the many underage, overage, and less than fit soldiers arriving in England and factored this into their decisions.[73] The British Expeditionary Force required that men serving in front-line units be at least nineteen years old. While the need for manpower was high at the front, support formations like the CFC and railway troops also needed men. By the end of the war, more than 31,000 soldiers and attached labourers were working in the CFC.[74] These men were deemed less suitable for combat but still capable of helping in the war effort. This book will take a closer look at the volunteers, compare different groups – for example, those going overseas and those left behind – and offer a more comprehensive view of the recruiting campaign by including those ultimately rejected for military service. These results can be found throughout the first half of the book, with a detailed look at the overseas contingent in the third chapter.

DESERTION AND DISCIPLINE

As mentioned earlier, some topics have received scant attention in the historiography, in part because of concerns about being disrespectful to veterans and the war dead. Nevertheless, in recent years there have been some important studies of military justice. During the First World War, twenty-five Canadian soldiers were executed by firing squad for desertion on the battlefield, including one Acadian, Eugène Perry (Poirier), serving with the 22nd Battalion.[75] In 2001, these soldiers received official pardons from the Canadian government, and their names were added to Parliament's *Book of Remembrance*. Hundreds of other soldiers received less severe punishments for desertion from their courts martial. Thousands more faced summary justice administered by local commanders, receiving minor punishments for absence without leave from their units, drunkenness, and other infractions. The general conclusion is that discipline was a continual challenge and that soldiers did leave their units, especially when the fighting was at its most brutal. However, the military justice system proved flexible enough to deal with a variety of situations, ensuring that soldiers could express their concerns, while maintaining authority and reintegrating minor offenders to keep up unit strength.[76]

We know virtually nothing about those who simply abandoned their units before they ever departed Canada. Thousands of men volunteered for military service but then changed their minds at some point along the way. Studies of this phenomenon of desertion while still in Canada are "practically non-existent."[77] Morton claims that units routinely lost one-quarter of their strength to desertion.[78] Unit histories have highlighted the impact of these losses and the instability and frustration they produced. In one extreme case, the 41st Battalion lost six hundred of one thousand recruits in this way.[79] Indeed, the loss of only one in six recruits to desertion in the 165th Battalion seems comparably quite commendable.

Who chose to desert, and why? A register of deserters for the 165th Battalion enables us to learn quite a bit about this group (see chapter 2).[80] Some were rounded up or arrested relatively quickly, but most were simply struck off the unit strength and disappear from the records. Dramatic stories of escape on trains or across the border to the United States occasionally appear in local newspapers or have been preserved in family oral traditions. A few unlucky souls would ultimately be conscripted into the CEF or by the Americans.

Discipline was a fundamental part of life in the military. It influenced operational effectiveness, engaged and troubled military authorities, and shaped soldiers' wartime experiences. As such, issues surrounding discipline deserve our attention. This study will tackle those issues for the soldiers of the 165th Battalion who did go overseas, with the help of the personnel files and routine orders of the 5th District of the CFC. The records reveal that in addition to absence without leave, disobedience as well as violence such as brawling were common issues. Alcohol was often a factor. Soldiers suffered field punishments, fines, and, in some cases, detention. Local commanders tried to deter future crimes and to rehabilitate those who had offended through corporal punishment and public humiliation. A read-through of the routine orders shows the extensive attempts made to regulate nearly all aspects of work and life in the lumber camps, subsumed into a larger military culture. The details of this analysis are presented in chapter 4, which focuses on the 165th Battalion volunteers overseas.

DEMOBILIZATION AND POST-WAR TRANSITION

Claude Léger writes that "after the war, the soldiers and officers of the 165th returned home and most of them returned to the anonymity of their pre-war lives, like the vast majority of other CEF members."[81] In this, he strikes a somewhat different tone than the foundational studies of Desmond Morton and Glenn Wright, who highlight the many difficulties veterans experienced in reintegrating into a Canadian society that was ill-prepared to receive them. Morton writes that veterans "would have to make their own way in a world that had little time for their stories and even less for their problems."[82] Other scholars have added to the general portrait of former soldiers struggling with physical and mental injuries, unemployment, difficult government bureaucracy as they sought support, and, ultimately, disillusionment. Jonathan Scotland writes that they "may have won the war but now veterans struggled amidst a pessimistic and troubling reality."[83] Some, though, have suggested that there were potential benefits to military service, at least for those not critically injured or killed. Carl Bouchard and Michael Huberman found that French-Canadian soldiers in Quebec, especially volunteers, had gained valuable professional skills that translated into higher salaries and better jobs after the war; another team of scholars found that the general health of the men improved due to a more regular diet and better access to medical and dental services while in uniform.[84]

This book presents one of the first detailed studies of the post-war transition with the help of the 1921 Canadian Census. In essence, we find these men and their families after the war, bringing them out of anonymity. Reintegration into civil society was difficult for many veterans of the CEF. What prospects awaited Acadian soldiers upon their return to Canada in 1919? Many of them did go home, at least at first, just as Léger suggested. Some married quickly and settled down nearby. Others found themselves back at home with their parents, their place in the household and the local economy having been taken by siblings and neighbours during their absence. With limited prospects for work or marriage, a significant number of these men quit the region entirely, heading south or west to seek their fortune. The United States had long been a popular option for young Acadians looking for work, and Acadian communities had existed in Maine and Massachusetts since the nineteenth century.[85] We found that former soldiers were even more likely to cross the border than other young Acadians. A few pursued military service or lumbering as a career, a direct application of the skills learned abroad. The Canadian West also attracted its share of former soldiers. Others opted for a life at sea, continuing to travel the world.

Some of the former soldiers fit the general narrative of struggle, while others clearly benefited from their time in uniform. While we found clear evidence of increased salaries in 1921, even after correcting for inflation, there was also high unemployment in certain sectors and regions. Our results also confirmed an average positive weight gain; however, closer examination demonstrates that this was reserved almost exclusively to adolescents reaching physical maturity and so not directly attributable to military service. A detailed discussion of our research into the post-war transition can be found in the fifth and final chapter of this book. The findings suggest the enormous potential in using census and other records to more comprehensively study demographic, health, and socio-economic outcomes for veterans and their families; this potential will only increase with the release of the 1931 Census.

TOWARDS A MORE COMPREHENSIVE HISTORY OF THE FIRST WORLD WAR

Mark Humphries has called for new research bringing together social history and military history in order to go beyond studying the war simply as a nation-building event to be commemorated.[86] This book is, in part, a response to this appeal: I have leveraged my training and years of experience working in social history to realize a different kind of unit study. The soldiers themselves are front and centre, with a scope stretching from 1911 through 1921; we have attempted to reconstitute their lives across linked records in censuses, military files, newspapers, and personal correspondence. Like Robert Rutherdale, who examined community responses in Trois-Rivières (Quebec), Guelph (Ontario), and Lethbridge (Alberta), I employ "locally situated evidence" to explore how ordinary people experienced the war.[87] Detailed comparisons with the soldiers of the 22nd Battalion (French-Canadian) and the 26th Battalion (New Brunswick) provide important insights into what may have been distinctive about this Acadian national unit.[88] Tackling controversial topics such as discipline and desertion, and adding forgotten volunteers who were discharged as medically unfit, gives this book a more inclusive scope.

Behind these choices is a larger conviction about the importance of the concept of agency for the study of soldiers and their families. Quantitative and qualitative analysis can help us better understand the choices made by these volunteers to sign up, to go overseas, to desert, to resettle at home, to start families, to go abroad after the war. Desmond Morton talked about idealists and idlers and thought that there were more of the former than the latter in the CEF.[89] In her study of French-Canadian volunteer enlistment during the Second World War, Caroline D'Amours similarly suggests that unemployment was not the main driver.[90] Detailed reconstitution and longitudinal analysis enable us to restore human dimensions to our group of more than one thousand Acadians, to retrace their family and community backgrounds and explore their potential motivations.

To close this introduction, I offer an example of the rich documentation and complex life courses of some Acadian volunteers. Aldéric "Aldei" Gallant of Shediac, New Brunswick, joined the 165th Battalion in February 1916, six months shy of his eighteenth birthday. On this basis, he should not have been accepted. The son of a civil servant, Gallant was too young to have a job listed in the 1911 Census, but he declared his occupation as "millman" at the time of his enrolment and had apparently moved to Moncton in search of work. He had a difficult time with the 165th, contracting gonorrhea while in garrison at Saint John. Gallant was discharged due to urinary tract complications from that disease in March 1917. He had taken the train to Halifax with the rest of the unit but was barred from boarding the ship for England at the last moment. Almost six months later, he re-enrolled at Sussex, New Brunswick. He had apparently grown three inches taller and gained three more inches of breadth through his chest since his initial enrolment. This reminds us of how young and physically immature many of the volunteers had been when they first signed up. Now fit for duty, Gallant was sent to England as a member of the CFC based in Southampton. He later answered a call for volunteers to go to the front because of the Allies' desperate need for reinforcements. Gallant was assigned first to the 13th Battalion (Reserve), then to the 44th Battalion (New Brunswick). Gallant reached the front in September 1918 and took part in the Hundred Days offensive that ultimately forced the Germans to sign the Armistice.

Unfortunately, Gallant would not live to see that day. In the early morning of 1 November 1918, he took part in the 10th Brigade advance towards Valenciennes, a French city near the Belgian border that had been held by the Germans since 1914 and was the vital ground for its surrounding defensive network. Gallant's unit advanced towards Marly along a tributary of the Scheldt called the Rhonelle. The 10th Brigade was held up by heavy machine gun fire and low-flying air raids coming from its right, and Gallant was killed in action. The city of Valenciennes fell the next day, greatly accelerating the collapse of the German positions. Although a large proportion of the Canadian Corps was involved in the offensive, it suffered only eighty deaths and another four hundred wounded during the two-day battle. In short, Gallant's death was a footnote to what was otherwise considered an important victory. He may have been the last Acadian killed in action during the First World War.

Was Gallant a hero for dying in battle or simply unlucky? Did he die believing that he had helped Canada, or Acadie, or both? His story, as well as the experiences of his comrades in the 165th Battalion, invite us to problematize our assumptions and take a detailed look at the meaning of war and military service. This book will raise and answer new questions, as well as identify a host of new challenges that traditional military studies are simply incapable of undertaking. We can offer a detailed socio-economic and geographic profile of who signed up. We can reconstitute aspects of their military service and offer insights into its consequences for their own lives and for their families. We can refine our understanding of the problems veterans faced as they sought to reintegrate into Canadian society. This will not be a history of bombs and bullets and it will not end in white marble monuments, although some of the 165th Battalion volunteers, like Aldei Gallant, did ultimately arrive (and die) at the front. My goal is to write a more human history of the war, one that will resonate particularly for those interested in Acadie and Atlantic Canada, but also more broadly for those wanting to know more about the ordinary people who volunteered to serve Canada abroad in the CEF. Many of the methods used here could easily be applied to other groups and even further expand the potential of this social turn of the new military history.

WHAT'S AHEAD ...

This book has five chapters. The first, "Creating an Acadian Battalion, November 1915–June 1916," covers the initial recruitment campaign and examines what we might call the 165th Battalion originals. The second, "Training, Preparations, and Completing the Battalion, July 1916–March 1917," surveys the rest of the time in Canada and tackles the question of desertion in some detail. Next, in "Heading Overseas, March–June 1917," we explain the end of the 165th in England, review and compare the principal characteristics of the overseas contingent with those of other groups of soldiers in the CEF, and consider the possible impact of military service on the families left behind. The fourth chapter, "Life in the Canadian Forestry Corps, May 1917–November 1918," takes a deep dive into overseas service with the help of the daily routine orders for the units in the Jura region of France. We will also consider Acadians serving with other units. Finally, with "Demobilization and Post-War Transition," we follow the former members of the 165th Battalion through the end of the war and their return home into the 1920s.

I

Creating an Acadian Battalion

November 1915–June 1916

ACADIAN RENAISSANCE

The First World War broke out during an important period of Acadian nationalism. The creation of an Acadian battalion was an obvious manifestation of that movement; the same political elites who largely led this "renaissance" were intimately involved in the call for a separate Acadian unit.[1] For example, Pierre-Amand Landry of Memramcook was a kind of elder statesman. He had served in provincial and federal politics and later as a judge named to the Supreme Court of New Brunswick. Throughout his career, he had championed bilingualism; notably, he had presided over the first three Acadian National Conventions beginning in 1881. At these events, an Acadian national day, flag, motto, and hymn had all been chosen, serving as important symbols of unity. Demographic growth and the greater electoral power that came with it offered new hope for a better future. Although in poor health by 1914, Landry was still a prominent leader and was widely recognized as such by both Acadians and anglophones. Notably, he publicly supported the war effort, and two of his sons enlisted.[2] He was among those who met in Moncton to discuss the creation of an Acadian battalion. Clerical elites also supported the war. The newly appointed Bishop of Saint John, Édouard A. LeBlanc, in his first public speech, exhorted New Brunswickers to enlist in defence of Great Britain: "Young men of New Brunswick, we ask you to not allow that Great Britain, to whom we owe our civil and religious liberties, our just laws, the protection and prosperity that we enjoy, cease to exist without raising our arms for its defence. Tonight, beyond the ocean, we hear the call of our motherland."[3]

The strength of the Acadian renaissance was buttressed by new regional and national organizations. For example, post-secondary institutions, such as the Collège Saint-Joseph in Memramcook, besides playing a critical role in education, helped build a distinct Acadian consciousness among young people. These were religious colleges, and the Catholic Church generally pushed a conservative vision of Acadie, one based on farming, faith, and traditional family values. The emergence of the Société de l'Assomption, the progenitor of today's Société nationale de l'Acadie, served as a sort of "mini-government" claiming to represent all Acadians.[4] French-language newspapers distributed the views of these elites. For the first time, a political culture in French operating throughout the Maritime provinces seemed possible.

Some historians caution that we should not exaggerate the unity of this movement. Sheila Andrew points to the regional differences and personal rivalries that prevented the Acadians from voting together and limited the influence of traditional elites even after the national conventions.[5] The newspapers were similarly divided: *Le Moniteur acadien* regularly espoused conservative ideals, while the more liberal *L'Évangéline* covered controversial topics such as women's suffrage. Michel Roy emphasizes the significant internal tensions generated by poverty and inequality across the rural communities where most Acadians lived.[6] Demographic growth had only exacerbated these structural challenges: there was not enough good arable land to go around. Emigration became a serious issue; community leaders despaired as they watched their young people leaving for job opportunities in cities, especially in the United States. To summarize, Acadians were a "complex society" in which there were divergent views on everything from language and culture to industrialization.[7] The growing Acadian community in Moncton found employment opportunities with the Canadian National Railway as well as in factories and service industries in the city. Rural Acadians remained focused on agriculture, fishing, mining, and lumbering.

While the Acadians in Moncton were slowly developing a sense of political identity,[8] many Acadians, including women, began seeking jobs in New England. This spurred church leaders and patriarchs to promote a new "colonization" policy that called for more agricultural communities in New Brunswick's interior in order to keep people employed at home. For them, nothing was more terrifying than the thought of single young women being corrupted by exposure to

American culture. More broadly, they worried that families moving to Maine and Massachusetts would lose their language and their faith in a sea of anglophone Protestantism. Unable to convince all Acadians to stay put, missionaries and French organizations followed them to the United States. Scholars emphasize, however, that notwithstanding the fear mongering of conservative elites, this emigration largely involved entire families within proscribed social networks, rather than an exodus of young, independent men and women.[9] Indeed, so many people moved to the United States that one of the Acadian national conventions was held in Waltham, Massachusetts, in 1903. A year later, at another assembly, delegates created the Société mutuelle de l'Assomption to ensure access to insurance, financial services, and health care for Acadians outside the Maritime provinces.

French-Canadian migration from Quebec to the United States has received considerable attention from scholars, but still more work is needed to improve our understanding of the causes and consequences of temporary and permanent relocation from Acadie.[10] In districts like the Madawaska, cohesive communities on the two banks of the Saint John (Wolastoq) River were artificially divided by the international boundary. By the early twentieth century, some young Acadians were travelling to family members living in the United States in search of temporary work as a way to support their households and gain professional experience. Maine and Massachusetts were not far away, especially given the maritime and railway routes that were already well-established. A study of the mobility patterns of Acadian women from Kent County in southeastern New Brunswick found significant movement from rural communities to cities like Moncton and Saint John, as well as entire families moving to the United States.[11] The key point is that these movements were within the larger Acadian diaspora and fit regional demographic and economic patterns.

Confronted with a growing, increasingly mobile population, Acadian elites sought to strengthen economic development, the French language, and representation in the Catholic Church. The expanding Acadian population in Moncton won a new parish, Notre-Dame-de-l'Assomption, and began construction of the church in the summer of 1914. Acadian national conventions continued to attract participants from across the larger diaspora.[12] The Acadian renaissance wielded considerable influence and brought together many historical actors who shared similar concerns even if they had different solutions in mind. It also led to a greater national consciousness as well as the creation of committees focused on specific challenges such as French-language education.

After the First World War broke out, many Acadian notables expressed support for Canada and Great Britain. It is difficult to ascertain how many Acadians signed up in the early days because the military did not record information about language or ethnicity in the attestation papers. At first glance, one would think there was limited opportunity for francophone recruitment in the Maritime provinces. In New Brunswick, as in most parts of the country, the government's recruiters worked in English and focused on more densely populated urban areas. Most Acadians lived in rural counties. Throughout the war, just 13 of the 275 authorized battalions were francophone, and of these, only the 22nd Battalion was sent to the front.[13] The 165th Battalion, the only francophone unit in the Maritime provinces, was not created until December 1915.

We have several indications that Acadians did enrol in significant numbers before their national unit was established. In his brief account of the early years of the 165th Battalion, its Commanding Officer, Lieutenant-Colonel Louis-Cyriaque Daigle, wrote that "many hundreds of Acadian soldiers" had previously signed up for the First Contingent and that by November 1915 there were more than one thousand Acadians serving at the front with twelve different units, including the 22nd and 26th Battalions. He gathered these figures from lists of names published in newspaper articles.[14] Even a hostile editorialist writing in December 1915 acknowledged that at least 600 Acadians were already overseas.[15] Our own sample of one hundred Acadian volunteers enlisting in 1914 and 1915 indicates that they joined more than twenty different units representing various branches of the CEF, including the infantry, the artillery, and the mounted rifles. Only two of these men had joined francophone units in Quebec; the rest signed up in anglophone units of the Maritime provinces, including the 55th Battalion (New Brunswick and Prince Edward Island) and the 25th Battalion (Nova Scotia).[16]

It is difficult to evaluate this early contribution to the CEF because we lack detailed recruiting figures by year and by linguistic group for each province, but thanks to the work done by several scholars to calculate manpower and enlistment rates more generally for the First World War, we can get a sense of the importance of that contribution. The total population of New Brunswick, Nova Scotia, and Prince Edward Island recorded in the 1911 Canadian Census was 937,935.

The population identified as of French origin was 98,975, or just over 10 per cent. In his official history of the Great War, Colonel Duguid calculated the number of males eligible for military service in 1914 (i.e., between eighteen and forty-five years of age). For the three Maritime provinces, this provided a total of 208,578 who would have been eligible for military service. Sharpe reduced this figure by eliminating foreign-born men who were ineligible for enlistment, resulting in a figure of 180,681. Richard Holt further revised the available manpower pool down to 84,232 after estimating the proportion of men in the general population who would have been declared unfit for overseas service.[17] Assuming that the Acadians were roughly as healthy as other residents of the Maritime provinces, Holt's figure includes about 8,500 Acadians. If Daigle was correct that around 1,000 Acadians were already serving overseas by the end of 1915, then more than 10 per cent of eligible, fit Acadians had already enlisted.

One of them was Joseph Ulric LeBlanc of Cap-Pelé, New Brunswick. A corpus of fifty-two letters written by him to his parents is conserved at the CEAAC. LeBlanc enlisted in the CEF on 25 November 1914. He was the first Acadian from his area to sign up, and just nineteen years old. Typical of many CEF recruits – and certainly those whom we will find in the 165th Battalion – LeBlanc was single and looking to make his place in the world. He had moved to Boston in the hopes of finding work as an auto mechanic. The son of a prominent doctor, Hilarion LeBlanc, perhaps he enlisted out of a sense of family duty; at least one of his brothers would follow him into service. After training at Camp Valcartier and in England, Ulric was assigned to a transport unit in the Canadian Army Service Corps. Samuelle Saindon has completed a detailed reconstitution of LeBlanc's movements during his career as a driver, which extended to the Allied occupation of Germany in 1919.[18] He took part in the Somme offensive of 1916, one of the bloodiest campaigns of the First World War, and viewed his time in the trenches as his coming of age as a man.

Having integrated quickly into anglophone Maritime units like the 26th Battalion (New Brunswick), Acadians did not stick out during parades, on postcards, or in press coverage during the early days of the war. Most people believed that few Acadians had enlisted "and did not hesitate to say so publicly."[19] Daigle complained that "many of our friends the English proclaim loudly that the Acadian French are not enlisting." Daigle adds that he had learned that Sam Hughes, a fervid Orangeman, had publicly disparaged Acadian voluntarism at the funeral for former premier Sir Charles Tupper held in Halifax in November 1915.[20]

These slanted popular views greatly frustrated Acadian leaders. It is not a coincidence that the first serious meetings to discuss the creation of an Acadian national unit were held soon after Hughes's remarks were published. The attendees wanted to prove Acadians' loyalty to Canada. This was probably a naive desire. How many Acadian enlistments would it have taken to quiet these voices? Five thousand? Ten thousand? Just as in our own day, the hateful and ignorant do not need logic or reason to maintain their beliefs. Even overwhelming proof of large numbers of Acadian enlistments would not have swayed those already convinced by their own prejudices. Sharpe makes a similar point about the debate over French-Canadian enlistment in Quebec, both during and after the war: "How many Quebecers would have had to enlist to make the controversy go away?"[21]

Yet Acadian elites believed they could make a difference, and they followed a traditional path to do so, one that would reinforce their prominent role in society. Organizing committees and public meetings chaired by notables, they sought to create interest and action, in the same way that previous assemblies had decided on national symbols and the creation of institutions like the Société mutuelle de l'Assomption. They envisaged a universal Acadian battalion, quickly rejecting the vocabulary "Canadiens-Français de Moncton" proposed by the recruiting officer for New Brunswick, Captain L. Tilley.[22] Led by Acadian officers and ministered by a Catholic chaplain, this unit would be another manifestation of the renaissance and another opportunity for promising young men to make their careers through public service. The battalion would be a living symbol of Acadie.

The 165th Battalion originated with a specific group of Acadian notables, most of them residing in southeastern New Brunswick. These men shared a vision founded on their religious faith and on their shared experiences in education, such as through the Collège Saint-Joseph in Memramcook. The provision of Catholic spiritual care was at the top of their list of reasons for creating an Acadian unit, and they could count on general support from the pulpit. They believed that their region could become the anchor of a larger Acadian national movement; that was why they wanted the unit to be more than a locally raised contingent. Initially focused on New Brunswick, they soon expanded their project to encompass the Maritime provinces as a whole. Unsurprisingly, these men proposed Moncton as the site of the unit headquarters. The first location would be the Brunswick Hotel, across from the CNR's main train station.[23] This group dominated the critical meeting held 3 December 1915 at the parish hall; notables from other regions largely declined the invitation to attend. Among those who did participate were military officers like Lieutenant J.L. Melanson of Shediac, lawyers like A. Robichaud of Cocagne, and clerics such as the abbé J.E. Ouellet. Significantly, the assembly included two newspapermen – Clément Cormier of *L'Acadien* and R.A. Arsenault of *L'Évangéline*.[24]

Acadian newspapers played an important role in promoting debate in society. Not all of them were immediately keen to support the idea of a national battalion. *L'Évangéline*, based in Nova Scotia, gave little space to the idea, and *Le Moniteur acadien* pitched different notions such as raising local Acadian companies within larger Maritime battalions. Predictably, the Moncton-based newspaper *L'Acadien* was the first to embrace the idea of a completely Acadian unit. In an editorial published on 12 November 1915, it emphasized the honour and prestige that would flow from such a project. A more detailed text printed two weeks later related several possible advantages. For example, an Acadian battalion would demonstrate loyalty to Canada and also ensure that the volunteers received spiritual guidance from French-speaking Catholic chaplains. Striking to the core of the issue, the author noted that many Acadians were already serving in other units and that "we have received no credit for it." An Acadian battalion would refute the unjust claims of anti-French opponents and, "incontestably, would be a powerful asset in our hands for later" – a direct allusion to how this project could help strengthen the Acadian renaissance.[25]

Returning to the 3 December meeting: Alphonse Somary, a medical doctor and former Liberal provincial deputy from Shediac, presided over the committee. Pascal Poirier, like Pierre-Amand Landry, an elder statesman of the Acadian national movement, opened the discussion. Poirier was the first Acadian selected for the federal Senate (in 1885) as well as a writer, lawyer, and public official. Elected president of the Société nationale l'Assomption in 1913, he had devoted much of his career to increasing the public visibility of Acadian leaders, especially in political life.[26] Poirier now argued that Acadian participation in this "almost universal war" was a question of national importance. If the Acadian contribution was not yet widely recognized, it was because "our soldiers have been lost in the crowd." Everyone took a turn to speak, and while some of the orators took up the ideas echoed by *Le Moniteur acadien* advocating the more modest goal of creating Acadian companies for Maritime battalions, they soon reached a unanimous decision:

- Given that the Acadians of the Maritime Provinces assembled at Moncton this third day of December 1915 have expressed their desire to create an Acadian Battalion commanded by Acadian officers and under the spiritual guidance of a chaplain of their race;
- Given that, at a recruitment assembly held at Moncton on 9 November last, Captain L.P.D. Tilley suggested the creation of a battalion, with the promise that all Acadians enroled [*sic*] from that date on could be transferred and integrated into this batallion [*sic*];
- Be it resolved that the request be sent to the Honourable Minister of the Navy, to ratify the proposal of Captain Tilley and authorize the creation of such a battalion in the Maritime Provinces.[27]

This would be a national Acadian battalion, and, crucially, all Acadians enlisting in the CEF would have the opportunity to join it.

The resolutions include several interesting details. While Daigle simply recorded that the decision was to be telegraphed to Hughes, the journalist Arsenault specified that the assembly wanted their wishes communicated to the Minister of the Navy. John Douglas Hazen was a former premier of New Brunswick (1908–11), and the Acadians probably surmised that he would understand their situation better than Hughes, especially given the latter's anti-francophone sentiments. Later in the same text summarizing the assembly's deliberations, Arsenault listed Hughes, Hazen, and Robert Borden, the prime minister, as recipients of the resolutions. Undoubtedly, Poirier and the other experienced political men knew that a telegraph could sit on one person's desk a long time if they were not inclined to help. Sending their request to all three top-ranking officials improved the chances of a quick and affirmative response.

Another detail Daigle left out, but duly recounted in the newspaper article, was that the assembly issued an additional resolution expressing regret that there were no Catholic chaplains in the 26th (New Brunswick) and 55th (New Brunswick and Prince Edward Island) Battalions that were already overseas. Deprived of the sacraments, "our brave soldiers" were in mortal peril for their lives and souls. Today's secular society might pass quickly over these kinds of statements, but they reflected heartfelt concerns for those who truly embraced their faith. As we will see, many of the soldiers in their letters home wrote about religious ceremonies, prayer, and the consolation they took from their faith that God would look after them in the next life. In this, they were not unlike those many young Canadians who were motivated, at least in part, by a sense of religious duty. Indeed, some of the members of the 165th Battalion kept up a regular correspondence with their parish priests. However, the Church's powerful role in the Acadian renaissance meant that it wielded considerable *political* influence as well, and it would soon play a key role in encouraging enlistments.

This Acadian assembly of notables did not have to wait long for an official response. Just three days later, Hughes announced in Ottawa that a new battalion would be formed from the French-Canadians of New Brunswick, and on 8 December 1915 he sent an official telegram indicating that "we will be glad to accept an Acadian battalion." Borden responded even more enthusiastically, noting that this was another "demonstration of the valiant loyalty of the Acadian population."[28] Military correspondence followed confirming the assembly's original intention; the Officer Commanding 6th Division based in Halifax relayed that the minister had authorized "the immediate formation of the 165th Overseas Battalion to be recruited from Acadians in the Maritime Provinces." The telegram concluded with a request for recommendations with regard to a commanding officer and the place of mobilization.[29]

Poirier, Somary, and the other notables quickly responded, calling another assembly for the following evening. Many leaned towards Captain Arthur T. LeBlanc, a native of Campbellton and an officer with fifteen years' experience who was already serving overseas with the 26th Battalion, but after much debate, the vote was won by Louis-Cyriaque Daigle. The reasons why are not entirely clear. Some felt that LeBlanc's affiliation with the Liberal Party made him a potentially unpalatable choice for the Conservatives Borden and Hughes. But they also passed over other Acadians already serving in the army, such as Captain M. Cormier of Edmundston and Lieutenant C. Gallant of Halifax. It appears that the assembly wanted one of their own, that is, someone from southeastern New Brunswick. This had clear consequences for the Acadian battalion's prospects in northern New

Brunswick, for the Liberal-leaning newspapers there would eventually become Daigle's implacable enemy. Most Acadians recruited from the northern counties in 1916 opted for the 132nd (North Shore) Battalion; only one Acadian from that region would eventually transfer to the 165th Battalion.[30]

In his unit history, Daigle simply noted that he briefly addressed the assembly, saying that "although the task may be difficult, he would apply all of his energy and all of his learning to make the Acadian battalion a success."[31] In fact, Daigle had little knowledge of military matters; he had pursued agricultural studies at the University of Guelph before returning to his home town of Saint-Louis-de-Kent. The 165th Battalion would be as much a political as a military endeavour – it was important that the CO understand this and be responsive to the imperatives of the cause. At least some of the newspapermen agreed with the choice; *Le Moniteur acadien* commented that Daigle was "well known throughout the province" and that with his selection "the success of the battalion was assured."[32] This goodwill would come under pressure later, as the 165th struggled to fill its ranks.

The creation of the 165th Battalion (Acadian) drew considerable support from the regional press. *L'Évangéline* reversed its previous attitude and provided extensive coverage of the early efforts to organize the unit, launching a call for all Acadians capable of bearing arms to join up. After a brief appeal to general patriotism, this text identified the minimum physical qualifications (age, height), with an interesting comment that the medical exams "are not very rigorous." This writer went on to discuss the salary, separation allowance, and pensions offered by the army. From the beginning, there was an understanding that some potential volunteers and their families would be driven by their economic situation. In addition to the monthly salary of $33, as well as room and board, a $20 separation allowance for the wife or widowed mother could make military service much more appealing. The same article promised pensions for injured soldiers who were unable to work after returning home, as well as for the widows and children of those killed.[33]

Anglophone newspapers noted these events with interest. While some were quick to criticize the French minority; others engaged in a kind of exoticism around the "descendants of the Acadians race, immortalized by Longfellow."[34] The reference to Henry Wadsworth Longfellow is, of course, an allusion to the author of *Evangeline: A Tale of Acadia*, an epic poem published in 1847 that had popularized a romanticized vision of the deportation in 1755 and characterized the Acadians as a simple and devout people. Yet even after this pivotal symbolic moment, there were implicit suggestions that the Acadians were slow to do their part. One editorial, while approving of the "energy" of the men who led this initiative, thought that the Acadians should still be doing more. Citing recruiting officers in the province, he calculated the New Brunswick Acadian population as about 93,000 (a significant overestimate, as this figure is close to the total Acadian population of all three Maritime provinces, according to the 1911 Census cited earlier). The author went on to claim that in France, 11 per cent of the population was in the army, and if the Acadians "were to provide recruits as France has done its share would be a little more than ten battalions."[35] The Acadians could only fall short of such ludicrous expectations. The many English-language newspapers in the region would continue to follow the 165th Battalion with equal measures of encouragement and condescension.

RECRUITING THE 165TH BATTALION

Sam Hughes authorized the 165th Battalion to recruit throughout all three Maritime provinces, an exceptional mandate given that most units targeted a specific town or county. This offered multiple possibilities for finding Acadian volunteers, but it also meant that Daigle and his officers faced significant competition from other units. For example, the 145th Battalion (Kent and Westmorland) operating out of Moncton targeted the same outlying communities in southeastern New Brunswick, and the 132nd Battalion (North Shore) drew from the largely Acadian counties in the north of the province.[36] Daigle noted in his unit history that initially it proved impossible to organize assemblies in Prince Edward Island, because the Acadian notables there were already fully engaged in recruiting for the 105th Battalion.[37] The army had created five new battalions in New Brunswick alone; the local press commented on the "healthy and helpful spirit of competition" among the officers as they set out to fill up their units first.[38] The hope was that the appeal of an Acadian national unit, with its Acadian officers and chaplains and French as its primary language of instruction, would draw forward men who had avoided enlistment up to that point. Daigle quickly established recruiting and training depots in Caraquet, Edmundston, Meteghan, and Antigonish. The idea was not only to create outreach across several Acadian regions

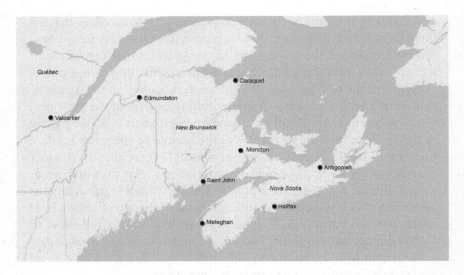

Figure 1.1 Key locations for the 165th Battalion

but also to initially allow recruits to work near their home communities. Bishop LeBlanc nominated Jean Gaudet, parish priest for Adamsville, as the unit chaplain early in the New Year, and Gaudet actively participated in the recruitment effort. The confirmation of his appointment, with the rank of captain, arrived from military authorities in May.[39] Religion was clearly important; the 132nd Battalion also chose a Catholic chaplain, Benedict Joseph Murdoch, in large part to appeal to Acadian and Irish volunteers.[40]

LCol Daigle expressed confidence that the recruiting campaign would go well. Speaking in Halifax in early January 1916, he affirmed that "the French-Acadian people have enthusiastically taken up the idea of raising a Battalion solely among themselves and I anticipate little difficulty in raising the 165th Battalion to strength this winter." He already had a clear plan of where to find his recruits: "the boys on the Caraquet shore are fishermen, hardy fellows who will make great fighters. The Acadians of Moncton and Digby belong to the farming classes, but they come of a fighting stock."[41] Upon returning from preliminary meetings in Ottawa later that month, Daigle laid out his plan to complete the unit in three months. He expected that the recruiting effort would be "relatively easy," since he would be drawing strong, healthy young men from rural parishes not often visited by anglophone units.[42] However, he would quickly learn that the enthusiasm of

Acadian notables living in southeastern New Brunswick was not necessarily shared by the popular classes across the Maritime provinces.

L'Évangéline became especially devoted to the recruiting campaign.[43] Regular reports on recent enlistments and upcoming parish assemblies ensured that everyone knew where to find Daigle and his team of recruiters. Some of the editorials strained credulity with their accounts of the patriotism and military heritage of the Acadian population. Under the pseudonym Vercingetorix, one writer described Acadians' enthusiasm for combat: "in every household there is talk of the great war, and of great feats of arms." Young men spoke only of fighting, he claimed, and of continuing a proud tradition dating back to the Gauls. In one particularly vivid scene, an elderly grandfather takes down his sword dating back to pre-Deportation Acadie from the mantel above the fireplace (and below the Crucifix) and knights his grandson as a champion of justice and defender of the weak:

> Rise up and take this sword; I no longer have the strength to fight, but at your age I held it fiercely. I retrieved it from the battlefield, near Port Royal. The blade was still lodged in an enemy's chest, but my dead grandfather gripped the hilt so tightly that I could not pull it free. Take it [and] go support your brothers in the trenches. Go fight, and if God allows it, return and console me in my old age by telling me how you did your duty.[44]

This editorialist is striking a very different tone from the traditional depictions of peaceful, unassuming farmers found in Longfellow's epic poem and in later scholarly accounts of how Acadians pursued a policy of collective neutrality during the colonial period. What is more, the math does not add up: even if the grandfather had been 100 years old, Port Royal fell to the British for the final time in 1710.

Not to be outdone, the priest F.M. Lanteigne published a song dedicated to the soldiers of the 165th Battalion complete with lyrics paired with the melody of "La Marseillaise." Here is the third of four epic stanzas, which evokes a return to France as well as an appeal to honour and the future:

> Bientôt vous saluerez la France
> Soldats, qui n'envie un tel sort?
> C'est aussi pour sa délivrance
> Que vous allez vous battre fort. [bis]

C'est l'ancienne Mère-patrie
Qui vous ouvre aujourd'hui les bras.
Allez combattre ses combats
Pour votre honneur et pour sa vie.
Debout Peuple Acadien! En avant pour l'honneur!
Pour vous, (bis) pour vos enfants assurez le bonheur.[45]

There is considerable irony in the choice of the French national anthem, composed during the French Revolution, which had been strongly condemned by the Catholic Church for its anticlerical tendencies. These imagined and rebranded links to France and the colonial past remind us of how history can be transformed to serve present ends. This does not mean, however, that this version of the past resonated with everyone. In his account of recruiting in Wentworth County in southern Ontario, Jonathan Vance reminds us that the social pressure from the pulpit, the press, and public assemblies paled in comparison to personal relationships as a factor in getting people to enlist. We will see that this proved to be the case in Acadie as well. Community leaders who became officers, chaplains, and sergeants played decisive roles in recruiting friends and relatives.[46]

The recruiting campaign proved to be a kind of travelling road show, often led by Daigle in person, usually including Gaudet, and featuring Acadian officers from the area who were already serving with the CEF. Although other battalions similarly sent officers to recruit in outlying areas, the geography to be covered by the 165th Battalion created unique challenges.[47] After an initial recruiting assembly held on 28 December 1915 in Moncton, which netted 11 volunteers, the group travelled first to the Madawaska region, where it held assemblies in Edmundston and Saint-Léonard.[48] Next, it was an extended tour of the many small Acadian communities on Cape Breton. After returning briefly to his home in Kent County, Daigle visited the Acadian peninsula in Gloucester County, followed by Halifax, and, finally, toured the Baie Sainte-Marie region of southwestern Nova Scotia. He related that they were always welcomed, noting that most of the parish priests actively supported the project, while those who were less inclined to promote military service "kept an honourable neutrality."[49] There were regional variations: Georges Sirois writes that some parish priests in Madawaska actively opposed voluntary enlistment, fearing that they would lose young men crucial to their plans to expand francophone settlement and holding a healthy disdain for the French Third Republic.[50]

What were these assemblies like? *L'Évangéline* provided detailed coverage of the one held in Halifax on 23 January 1916. Once again, prominent figures in the Acadian renaissance took centre stage. Jean Muise, president of the Halifax branch of the Société nationale l'Assomption, hosted the event. The newspaper reported a large crowd, and the journalist who attended seemed surprised there were so many French-speaking families in the city. The chaplain Jean Gaudet provided the opening discourse, declaring that all Canadians had a common obligation to aid France and England. He spoke about his hope to bring all of the soldiers home in the same condition as they had left. Captain Arthur LeBlanc then presented a more specific appeal to the Acadians of Nova Scotia to join the 165th Battalion, emphasizing the strength of the British navy and the tenacity of the French army overseas. The strategy of these speakers was clear; they emphasized obligation but also the strength of the Allies to build confidence that military service would not be a death sentence. Daigle, for his part, spoke humbly about his previous desire to enlist as a simple soldier, and how honoured he felt to command the 165th Battalion.

The Reverend Foley now took the stage, and spoke about his previous travels to France. This time, in contrast to the Franco-Prussian War, "it would be France that crushes Prussia." Captain Beique, representing the 69th Battalion (Canadien-Français) from Quebec and already well known in the Maritime provinces for his fiery speeches, drew comparisons with past French-Canadian heroes, including Dollard des Ormeaux, Frontenac, and Montcalm. It seems that Beique did not understand that he was speaking to Acadians, who would not have shared those historical references. The time was now, he added: "We need men. And you are men, enlist then!" For Beique and many others, shared ideals of masculinity trumped potential ethnic and linguistic divisions. The journalist concluded that the assembly had been a great success and that there was no doubt Halifax Acadians would sign up in large numbers. In this, he would be proven wrong: only one Acadian living in Halifax at that time (and one other who had been born there but had since moved to Cape Breton) ultimately joined the 165th Battalion. We will see this trend elsewhere during the recruiting campaign – outward public support but less than remarkable concrete results.[51]

The Halifax assembly was noteworthy for the participation of Québécois officers, city officials, and a broad cross-section of people. Most of the recruiting events, though, were held in rural communities across the Maritime provinces. These were local, parish events during which the recruiters appealed to local concerns and the participants were keen to demonstrate their nationalist zeal. A good example was the visit of recruiting officers to Prince Edward Island in June 1916. *L'Évangéline* declared that the inhabitants of Tignish wanted to "prove" their interest in the 165th Battalion. Once again, a fierce desire to prove slanderers wrong was obvious – Acadian masculine honour was under attack. For example, Lieutenant Aimé Léger spoke about his pride in proving "that the Acadians are not slackers and that the Acadian battalion is formed from men of character and national pride, not homeless people as some misinformed and rude members of the other nationality have suggested." Local leaders, including Joseph Arsenault, Sylvain Gaudet, and Joseph Chiasson, then spoke directly to the young men in the hall, exhorting them to enlist. Surrounded as they were with so much popular pressure and enthusiasm, it should come as no surprise that "a good number of young men affirmed their intention to enlist" – crucially, however, only "after the spring labours and fishing season are completed."[52] Two islanders had joined the 165th earlier that year, but no new enlistments followed this commitment. As with the assembly in Halifax, we should not be too quick to assume that public statements matched private sentiments. Indeed, the honest response of the Tignish men that they could not enrol until after they had met their family responsibilities reminds us that military service competed with work and other obligations.

That most of those willing to sign up had already done so by 1916 reflected a national trend. Ian Miller similarly found for Toronto that recruiting bottomed out that summer and that the press quickly turned to blaming French-Canadians.[53] This is not to say that nothing came of the recruiting events; small groups of young men did enlist, and the considerable efforts of Daigle and his team ensured that the Acadian national battalion was in the public eye throughout the Maritime provinces. However, it seems clear that these events were above all political performance opportunities for local leaders, including priests. The priest at Petit-Rocher, writing on behalf of his parishioners, evoked the motto of the Acadian renaissance in thanking the officers for their visit: "At this time when more than ever *l'union fait la force*[54]; at this time when the principles of humanity and events demand our unity and our independence, you, officers and members of the 165th Battalion, remain for us a granite block in this large unit of Acadians who know only victory or death."[55] The assembly netted three volunteers, one of whom was the ill-fated Alphonse Melanson, who died in hospital later that year.[56] Ten individuals from the parish of Petit-Rocher eventually joined the unit.

Parish involvement was not limited to letters of thanks; many assemblies featured speeches of "homage." References to Acadian national identity were common here as well. In Caraquet, for example, the *curé* spoke of *le Grand Dérangement* in his account of the battalion's origins: "Themselves persecuted and victims of flagrant injustices, the Acadian people understand perhaps better than any other people the meaning of oppression and the disdain of human rights. This is why, in a great spirit of bravery and courage, they want to enter, as a people, in this great European conflict to fight the Germans, enemies of the rule of law, of equity, and of humanity." The importance of the 165th Battalion for Acadie was clear: "On the battlefield, you will represent the soul, the devotion, and the bravery of an entire people."[57] Although only a handful of men signed up after the assembly, the town had already provided several recruits. In fact, a total of 34 volunteers for the 165th hailed from Upper and Lower Caraquet. Clearly, local priests could have a strong influence on enlistment numbers.

Key to the recruiting effort were unit bands (*fanfares*), which were thought to raise patriotic sentiments by playing stirring military music. Overseas, bands helped lift soldiers' morale before they went into battle. In March 1916, a public fundraising appeal to purchase instruments generated many donations. This was another way for individuals, especially local leaders, to demonstrate their commitment to Acadie; both *L'Évangéline* and *Le Moniteur acadien* reported regularly on the fundraising.[58] The unit band accompanied the recruiters for the first time in May.[59] Instruments cost money to purchase and maintain; some of Daigle's correspondence concerned soldiers' appeals for reimbursement for out-of-pocket expenses right up to 1918.[60] It is noteworthy that even the unit band had its roots in the Acadian national movement. The Assomption Band had existed for some time, and three of its members joined the 165th. A proud and tearful concert was held in Shediac to celebrate their enlistment, with the military bandmaster, Sergeant Labbadie, assuring everyone that they would be well looked after in Europe.[61] When the unit left for Camp Valcartier at the end of June, unit musicians performed along with the Moncton Citizens' Band and the City Silver Band to see them off.[62]

Daigle and his officers did not intend to rely solely on new volunteers to fill the ranks. Military authorities granted permission to Acadians serving elsewhere to request transfer to their national battalion. Confirmation of this policy was published in February 1916, and the newspapers appealed not only to those soldiers but also to their parents to ensure that transfers were requested promptly.[63] Less than a month later, however, journalists expressed dismay that so many Acadian soldiers had not yet received their transfers and demanded action from the government. As long as these men served in other units, they would be "lost or submerged in the English majority."[64] COs of other units seemingly ignored repeated orders from the Militia Department directing them to grant transfers to the 165th Battalion.[65] Daigle expressed frustration that by the end of June, only a few transfers had arrived, chiefly from the 112th (Nova Scotia) and 85th (Nova Scotia Highlanders) Battalions.[66] The competing units recruiting in New Brunswick largely refused to permit the departure of their hard-won volunteers, undoubtedly because they themselves were struggling to achieve full strength. The military authorities eventually transferred a significant number of Acadian volunteers from the 145th and 140th Battalions, but these were medically unfit men left behind when their units went overseas. Many of them never actually showed up at the 165th, and those who did lacked clothing and equipment, which created an administrative nightmare for Daigle and his team. For example, one list relates that of the eighty-five men left behind by the 145th Battalion and intended for the 165th, forty-three had since deserted, a few had been discharged, and just eight were actually training.[67]

With only 708 of the required 1,000 men boarding the trains for Camp Valcartier at the end of June 1916, Acadian nationalists needed people to blame for their apparent failure to complete the unit. Rival COs refusing to transfer Acadians already serving in their units were a persistent target. Steve Marti relates a similar story for Manitoba's 233rd Battalion (Canadiens-Français du Nord-Ouest). Many French-Canadian soldiers from that province had already enlisted, and their commanding officers denied transfer requests from at least 150 Franco-Manitobans. The 233rd was unable to get to full strength. The 600 officers and men were absorbed into the 178th Battalion (Canadiens-Français), headquartered in Quebec's Eastern Townships. Thus, they lost an identifiable contribution from their communities in western Canada – the goal of the endeavour – and struggled to integrate with their Quebec-based counterparts. And they were broken up yet again once they arrived in England.[68]

Another common complaint was that the recruiters from the Militia Department paid little attention to the 165th Battalion. This left the work to Daigle and his officers at a time when they needed to focus on training the new volunteers.[69] Of course, it comes as no surprise that the recruiters, who had rarely visited Acadian parishes since the beginning of the war, continued this behaviour. Increasingly, Acadian writers also held the anglophone press guilty of harming the recruitment campaign. For example, one writer for *L'Évangéline* accused these newspapers of dissuading young men from signing up when they pointed to the supposed lack of experience of the Acadian battalion's officers.[70] Of course, there was an element of truth to this, beginning with Daigle himself. Journalists at *Le Moniteur acadien* expressed indignation at the "insults" launched at the unit in general and its CO in particular. They portrayed the CO and his officers not as political appointees but as brave and competent leaders.[71]

Given the obvious exaggerations appearing in the francophone newspapers about the supposed patriotism and martial spirit of the Acadian population, one might wonder about the accuracy of the above explanations for the recruiting campaign falling short. Did rival units really jealously hoard valuable Acadian recruits, or did the repeated calls for family and parents to get involved imply that many of those recruits never actually asked to transfer to the 165th Battalion? One Acadian whom we have already met, Joseph Ulric LeBlanc, wrote to his parents in July 1916 saying that he had forgotten about requesting a transfer to the 165th because he figured that the unit would be broken up anyway.[72]

Even the most fervent boosters of the Acadian national unit sometimes concluded that the biggest obstacle might be an unwillingness to sign up in the first place. However, the journalists couched these observations in gendered language that blamed Acadian mothers for clinging too tightly to their sons. In one lengthy appeal, a writer in *L'Évangéline* beseeched Acadian mothers to be as brave as their counterparts in France, noting that there was nothing to worry about because the officers of the battalion treated their soldiers like family. The unit's imminent departure for training at Camp Valcartier should not worry them; instead, mothers should remind themselves of their sons' opportunity to work with their Quebec "brothers" and to experience military life, which had unique "charms." The editorial further noted that unit officers were organizing at least two visits during the upcoming summer training period to allow families to visit the volunteers while they were in Quebec.[73]

The criticisms of the 165th Battalion's officers deserve some attention, given that few had any combat experience, starting with Daigle. The transfer of Captain J. Arthur Legere from the 26th Battalion to the 165th went some way to address this lack of military experience; notably, he had led a grenadier company in the trenches. He was also a skilled orator and a passionate Acadian nationalist. Léger clearly received more respect in the anglophone press than Daigle on account of his years of service in the militia and overseas.[74] Originally from Richibucto, he was also a member of the southeastern New Brunswick elite, like most of the other officers in the battalion. In May 2016, the military authorities also transferred Major J.F. Bissonnette from the 150th Battalion (Carabiniers Mont-Royal) to the 165th, where he would serve as second in command.[75] The *Daily Gleaner* noted that Bissonnette was a native of Quebec and "is an officer of much experience." Similarly, the *Saint John Globe* stressed his "long military career" dating back to 1901; although not yet at the front, Bissonnette had completed several training courses and contributed to the creation of two other French-Canadian units.[76] Both Legere and Bissonnette seemed ideally suited to help Daigle complete recruitment and training.

The junior officers of the 165th Battalion had diverse backgrounds, and criticisms of their lack of experience were not entirely justified. Twenty-two of the twenty-seven officers identified in our database came from the militia, most of them from local regiments, including the 73rd (Northumberland) and 74th (Brunswick Rangers) in New Brunswick and the 93rd (Cumberland) in Nova Scotia. Placide Boucher of Springhill, Nova Scotia, had served thirteen years in the latter regiment by the time he enlisted. Arthur Cyr was born in the Madawaska region but had since moved to Meteghan in Nova Scotia; he had served several years in the 67th (Carleton Light Infantry) and 74th Regiments, rising in the ranks from private to sergeant before being commissioned as a lieutenant in 1913. Daigle, who listed "dairy superintendent" as his occupation on his attestation papers, was one of only five officers who lacked military experience. The importance of unit leadership was indisputable; Desmond Morton writes that the 41st Battalion (Canadien-Français), created in 1915, "was especially handicapped by the near-total absence of military experience on the part of almost all of its officers." After the unit struggled for months with desertions and a serious lack of discipline, a court of inquiry ordered it broken up.[77]

Richard Holt has emphasized that the quality and quantity of militia training varied widely across Canada before 1914. We know that a few of the officers appointed to the 165th Battalion did not make the cut.[78] Lieutenants Joseph Barrieau and Jean Dugas, both from the 73rd Regiment, were released in June 1916 because of "never giving any indication which would warrant him being retained as an officer."[79] Major Bissonnette recommended the discharge of two other officers soon after the unit's arrival for training at Camp Valcartier. He described Lieutenant François Arsenault as "slovenly in dress and appearance, and does not take the interest in his work which is expected from an efficient Officer." Arsenault may not have travelled to Valcartier – his file indicates that he resigned on 24 June, so Bissonnette's letter of 8 July may simply have reflected a *fait accompli*. The major added that "I have also heard in Moncton, that he had no intention of proceeding Overseas with this Battalion, and his wife is also very anxious that he return to civil life."[80] Regarding Lieutenant William Turgeon, Bissonnette advised that "he has shown no indication of the spirit and energy which is essential in an efficient Officer." However, Bissonnette was concerned that Turgeon "might hurt recruiting" if sent home to Edmundston, where he was well known and "popular on account of his being a good baseball player."[81] Meanwhile, Lieutenant Leo Richard transferred in from the 85th Battalion (Nova Scotia Highlanders), proof that at least some Acadians did make a successful transition to the new national unit.[82] Army life was not for everyone; Lieutenant W. LeBlanc resigned his commission part way through the training.[83] Bissonnette himself may not have integrated well with the Acadian battalion; he returned to his militia unit in Quebec after the summer training period.[84] Jonathan Vance similarly found quite a bit of shuffling around of officers with various levels of experience in southern Ontario.[85]

When we include those discharged as unfit for service and those who deserted, we find that the officers of the 165th Battalion enticed 827 men to sign up before the end of June 1916. They were part of a larger group of Canadians encouraged by the creation of 86 new CEF battalions in the fall of 1915, and 58 more during the following winter, after Prime Minister Borden announced that the CEF would be expanded to 500,000 men. Morton estimates that between

October 1915 and May 1916, the CEF signed up almost 186,000 recruits.[86] Where did these men come from? Even in Canada's biggest cities, voluntary recruitment had begun to dry up by the summer of 1915. Militia Minister Hughes focused on locally raised battalions, many with special identities. This included other ethnic groups such as Icelanders, African Nova Scotians, and Poles.[87] Nearly all of these units failed to completely fill their ranks, just like the 165th. Of the 39 "special identity" battalions, 6 were quickly disbanded and only 10 reached full strength. After the initial push, recruiting nationally fell to just 10,059 for the month of June 1916 and to less than 5,000 each month by the end of the year.[88] It seems that volunteering had come to an end, and besides that, scholars point to the growing industrial production in support of the war, which "cut deeply into the potential manpower supply for military service."[89] In the end, conscription would be necessary if the federal government hoped to grow and sustain the CEF overseas. Acadian recruitment closely followed these national trends.

PROFILE OF THE 165TH BATTALION ORIGINALS

Claude Léger found that more than half the initial volunteers resided in the Moncton area, along with most of the officers. Not surprisingly, most of the others came from the towns where the unit had established recruiting and training depots – Meteghan, Antigonish, Caraquet, and Edmundston.[90] These contingents were split fairly evenly, from a high of seventy-four recruits from Meteghan to a low of forty-nine from Edmundston, which suggests that the hope for a unified Acadian battalion representing the entire Maritime provinces was not completely without basis, even if southeastern New Brunswick dominated the endeavour. By delving into the attestation papers of these men, we can gain additional insight into their backgrounds and their motivations for enlisting.

With regard to age, it is little surprise that 87 per cent of the volunteers were under thirty. Perhaps more surprising is how many of them were under eighteen. This was officially against the rules. While forty-one of them were three months or less from that important birthday, thirty-four others declared themselves to be under seventeen. Indeed, three were only fourteen: John LeBlanc of Little River, Inverness County, Nova Scotia, Edgar Joseph Cormier of Caraquet, and Cécime Maillet of Saint-Norbert, Kent County, New Brunswick.

None of them would go overseas. The unit left LeBlanc behind when it embarked for England in March 1917, and a month later doctors ordered his discharge. Officers sent Cormier home from Valcartier in August 1916 for being underage; Maillet deserted that same month. The personnel file on Melbourne Doucette, barely fifteen years old when he volunteered for the 165th Battalion, illustrates the mobility of young men seeking work in the Maritime provinces. Born in Yarmouth, Nova Scotia, he had since moved to Saint John, New Brunswick, where he worked as a bellhop at a hotel. At just four feet, ten inches tall, and with a chest measurement of twenty-eight inches, Doucette was far from physical maturity, which raises the question of why the recruiters accepted his enlistment in the first place. When the unit came under more scrutiny at Camp Valcartier, Doucette, like Cormier, was discharged as underage. He re-enlisted in 1918, falsifying his birthdate, as he still had not reached eighteen. Assigned to a depot battalion, he never left Canada, but served until demobilization in April 1919.

Were these adolescents inspired by the patriotic call to serve in the Acadian national battalion, or were they simply marginalized youth with few other options? With regard to the CEF as a whole, Desmond Morton wrote that "then and now, one can only guess why most men enlisted. Social pressure, unemployment, escape from a tiresome family or a dead-end job, self-respect, and proving one's manhood have motivated soldiers through the ages." However, Morton also suggested that while the army attracted men from different backgrounds, "idealists were more common than idlers. Most of the men who joined in 1915 left good jobs behind them."[91]

The three Acadian fourteen-year-olds were all still living at home when they volunteered. Consulting the 1911 Canadian Census, we learn that Maillet came from a family of eight children, including two older brothers. While his father declared farming as his principal occupation, the fact that the census also records that he supplemented his income with temporary full-time work doing odd jobs for the paltry sum of seventy-five dollars per year suggests that the family had trouble getting by. The army was a way for Cécime to contribute to the family or, at the very least, to be looked after. Melbourne Doucette was the only son of a widowed mother, who in 1911 was running a boarding house. With his sisters working at a nearby cotton mill – along with most of the boarders – Melbourne needed to contribute and also make room. This may explain his departure at such a young

Table 1.1
Declared age at enrolment

Age range	Number	Proportion (n=827)
Under 18	138	16.7%
18–20	306	37.0%
21–9	275	33.3%
30–44	96	11.6%
45+	9	1.1%
Unrecorded	2	0.2%

Table 1.2
Declared occupation at enrolment in the 165th Battalion and the CEF[1]

Sector	Number	Proportion % (n=827)	CEF % (n=616170)
Agriculture	178	21.5	19.8
Student	22	2.7	2.4
Fishing/sea	71	8.6	0.7
Labourer	306	37	24.8
Mining	18	2.2	3.0
Professional/official	19	2.3	4.8
Clerical/sales	35	4.2	8.6
Trades/transportation	145	17.6	18.7
Forestry/woods	24	2.9	1.9
Other/unknown	8	1.0	15.3

1 Morton, *When Your Number's Up*, 245. Morton did not separate mining into a separate category. Current research has raised the total number of enlistments to about 630,000, of which about 424,000 deployed overseas. These CEF figures include volunteers and conscripts (after 1917).

age for Saint John: the Army offered another opportunity. However, it seems that not all of these adolescents were hard-luck cases. Edgar Joseph Cormier was the son of Joseph C. Cormier, a merchant in Caraquet according to the 1911 Census. The family employed a servant, and Cormier had a number of employees. He was also one of the few heads of household from the database to hold a robust life insurance policy. The Cormier family, then, more closely fit the profile of local notables wanting to be seen as doing their part for the Acadian national battalion – Morton's "idealists."

We know that most of the recruits were single (just 123 of the 827 recruits declared a wife, and three others were widowers). However, the attestation papers provide little information about the economic situation of the recruits. The military did not appear particularly interested in their work experience.

More than one-third of the Acadian volunteers simply indicated labourer as their occupation, a much higher percentage than for the CEF as a whole. There is no further information on whether they worked in agriculture, in a forestry camp, or in a factory. A further one in five declared a farming background, although this also lacks precision. Identifying as a farmer was common practice for rural dwellers, so we cannot know if the family farm was large, small, or non-existent. While workers often (though not always) indicated their annual salary, farmers did not indicate their revenue, so there is no way to measure how prosperous they were.[92] The rest of the volunteers emerged from various sectors led by skilled trades such as carpentry, fishing, and clerical work. Given that the 165th Battalion was later assigned to the CFC, it is worth noting that less than 3 per cent of the original volunteers declared forestry as their previous principal occupation. Of course, some of the labourers may have had experience in this sector. Particularly for those living in coastal regions, there existed a seasonal cycle of work: fishing in the summer, woodcutting in the winter.

The 165th Battalion volunteers included a small but important group of merchants, professionals, and public servants. Unsurprisingly, several of the officers came from this group – they left good jobs behind them, to use Morton's expression. Lieutenant Rufin Arsenault of Adamsville, New Brunswick, was one of the editors of *L'Évangéline*, and Lieutenant Arthur Cyr practised law in Meteghan, Nova Scotia. Joseph Amédé Charest was postmaster for the community of Saint-Jacques in Madawaska County, New Brunswick. He rose rapidly through the ranks of the 165th and overseas in the CFC, first as a pay sergeant and then as a company sergeant major (CSM). Thomas LeBlanc of Chéticamp, Nova Scotia, and Joseph Landry of Burnsville, New Brunswick, were schoolteachers. As we will see in chapter 4, educated men were frequently selected as non-commissioned officers (NCOs). They would become the backbone of the new unit, playing a crucial role in training and discipline.

The Acadian recruits included farmers, tradesmen, and students in proportions similar to those of the CEF as a whole. The Acadians, however, were somewhat more likely to be unskilled labourers and fishermen and less likely to be from clerical and professional (white-collar) jobs. These results reflected Acadian society as a whole. The majority were farmers, or they worked in natural resource sectors such as fishing, mining, and forestry; that said, the pull of urban centres also drew young men into the manufacturing, skilled trade, and transportation sectors.[93] For example, several of the recruits were employed by the railways, while others came from mills or worked as teamsters. At this early stage of the twentieth century, some Acadians were benefiting from new education opportunities, especially in French, but the relative isolation and poverty of the population was also on display. Michel Roy characterized the period as one of "misery, exodus, and proletarization." The resource economy remained vulnerable to cycles of boom and bust, and urban employment depended on anglophone entrepreneurs.[94] Most Acadians continued to rely on family-based household production, which often entailed young people leaving home to seek wage work. High mobility was not necessarily a sign of misery; since the mid-nineteenth century, Acadians had been moving around the region, including to the United States, in search of education and employment opportunities. It was entirely normal for young men to leave home for temporary wage work – indeed, many would have embraced the opportunity to have new experiences. Military service fit very well into this tradition, especially since these men would be able to send part of their salary – and, often, a separation allowance – directly to family members.[95]

The overwhelming majority of the men in the 165th were New Brunswickers. There were few enlistments from outside Atlantic Canada – just fourteen from Quebec and eleven from the United States. According to the 1911 Census, around 60 per cent of francophone Maritimers lived in New Brunswick, and New Brunswickers accounted for nearly three-quarters of the 165th Battalion recruits.[96] As we have seen, there were few Prince Edward Island Acadians in the 165th. The recruiters for that battalion did not even travel to PEI until June 1916; Daigle reported that more than four hundred Acadians had already signed up for the 105th Battalion (Prince Edward Island).[97] This latter unit, also created in December 1915, headed overseas more quickly, although it was similarly disbanded upon arrival. This underscores that there was at least some reason to be discouraged by the apparent slow pace of enlistment in the 165th.[98]

The largest group of volunteers, some two hundred men, declared residence in the greater Moncton area, in Westmorland County. The two southeastern counties of New Brunswick provided nearly half the recruits. Recruitment efforts in Nova Scotia, particularly among

Acadian communities around the Baie Sainte-Marie and on Cape Breton, also bore fruit. In fact, after Moncton, Meteghan (near Digby) provided the largest number of recruits from a single community (fifty-four). Enlistments from the Madawaska and Antigonish regions lagged in comparison. In general, beyond the large group residing in Moncton and the cluster from Meteghan, the declared residences of the volunteers reveal the dispersed, rural settlement pattern of much of Acadie. Caraquet (twenty-eight) and Richibucto (twenty-one) were the next most important towns, and after that, smaller groups of ten to twenty men emerged from a variety of places. In some ways, then, the vision of a unified national battalion representing all of Acadie was being realized.[99]

The idea behind special identity battalions like the 165th was that community-based units would attract people sharing common characteristics who wanted to serve together. Obviously, in the case of the Acadian national unit, these characteristics included language and religion (here, French and Roman Catholic); however, Daigle and his team did not enjoy the advantage of being able to concentrate their efforts on a single geographic area. By following the recruiting assemblies and examining the enrolment statistics, we can determine the correlation between the campaign and enlistments as well as the degree to which friends from the same towns and parishes joined up together.

In addition to the results depicted in figure 1.2, forty-two volunteers enlisted in 1915. These were successful transfers of Acadians from other units to the 165th Battalion. The initial response to the call to arms was underwhelming: just over fifty enrolments during the month of January. The first recruiting assemblies, held on 6 and 7 January 1916 in Edmundston and Saint-Léonard respectively, enticed precisely no one to enlist. Despite the enthusiastic media coverage of the large event held in Halifax, only a single recruit materialized from there. The chaplain's visit to Cape Breton netted a single coal miner. In fairness, the slow start is also attributable to the time it took to form the recruiting team. Daigle himself spent much of early January in Ottawa, and Captain A. Legere and other key figures did not arrive until later. In fact, the only success story for the entire month of January emerged from Meteghan, Nova Scotia, where thirty-nine men volunteered. This achievement was due not to an official visit or a large event but rather to the efforts of Émile Jean Stehelin, a prominent local notable who signed up himself on 4 January 1916 at the age of forty-five.

Table 1.3
Declared counties of residence of 165th Battalion originals

Community	Volunteers	Proportion (%)
Westmorland, NB	252	30
Kent, NB	140	17
Gloucester, NB	111	13
Digby, NS	83	10
Madawaska, NB	51	6
Inverness, NS	43	5
Richmond, NS	28	3
Other/Unknown	119	14

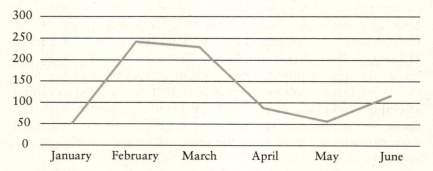

Figure 1.2 Enlistments by month in the 165th Battalion, January–June 1916

Stehelin provides a case in point of the importance of local elites for drumming up enlistments. He had a unique connection to the war in that he was born in Alsace, a region claimed by France but held by Germany since 1871. France would not regain the contested territories of Alsace and Lorraine until after the First World War, yet Stehelin indicated on his attestation paper that his birthplace was in France, and he reported one year of experience in the French army as an artillery officer before his family moved to Canada in 1892. By the time of the 1911 Canadian Census, Stehelin was well established at Pointe-de-l'Église (Church Point), not far from where the Université Sainte-Anne stands today. He had married an Englishwoman, Anne-Marie Baldwin, in 1895, and become a British subject in 1906 (Canadian citizenship did not exist before 1947). They had four children, and he declared his occupation as lumbering. He was in fact the owner of a large forestry business employing many workers. His relative wealth is suggested by his $2,000 life insurance policy and the size of the family home.[100]

It seems that Stehelin threw himself to the war effort, as did many first-generation immigrants from France and Great Britain. Despite his age, he rose in the ranks from lieutenant to acting major, and he would ultimately command a forestry company in France. While it is unclear whether the men who signed up from the Meteghan area were his employees – only two indicate an occupation related to lumbering – his example clearly inspired others. The majority of the volunteers signed up together, on 17 and 18 January 1916. They included four brothers – Joseph, William, Paul, and Frank Saulnier – between the ages of 18 and 28. Although they declared themselves to be farmers, the 1911 Census indicates that they were working for their father, a shipowner, as sailors.[101] It seems that Stehelin motivated men of all ages to sign up, from teenagers to men in their forties.

Recruiting in New Brunswick took off in February, with the help of Captain Legere and various notables in the southeastern part of the province. Thirty-one volunteers from Moncton signed up on 5 February 1916 alone, with many more to follow. Most of the Moncton contingent had enlisted by the beginning of March. The momentum spread to other regions, particularly around Caraquet and through Kent County. Here we can finally see the results of the travelling recruiting campaign. Five men from the small community of Petite-Aldouane signed up together on 10 March 1916, and five more emerged from nearby Richibucto three days later. Meanwhile, recruiting on Cape Breton also began to pick up, with twenty-six men enlisting on 18 March 1916 from several communities, including Chéticamp and D'Escousse. It proved more difficult to break through in the Madawaska region, although small groups did sign up beginning in April. For example, three men from Saint-André enrolled on 7 April and four more from Edmundston on 10 April. More emerged in June, in the wake of renewed calls to find more volunteers and complete the ranks before the unit's imminent departure for Valcartier.[102] Here, the newspapers betray their resort to propaganda – the claim made by *Le Moniteur acadien* that more than fifty new recruits had emerged from the Madawaska region bore little resemblance to reality. The true number was closer to twenty.[103] June did see a small uptick for voluntary enlistments generally in the 165th Battalion, particularly in Gloucester County. Daigle and his team had to hope that more would follow in the coming months if they were going to reach one thousand.

Recruiting often remained tied to the influence and commitment of local leaders. For example, Daigle promoted John H. Devine, of Cap-Pelé, to sergeant and appointed him recruiter for the area, based in Shediac. Devine was a skilled tradesman and prominent head of household. In just six weeks he enlisted fifty-seven men, forty-five of whom ended up in the 165th Battalion. An article about him in *Le Moniteur acadien* reveals part of the reason for his success: he had employed Alban LeBlanc, a twenty-year-old factory worker in Moncton, to assist him.[104] Young people then, just like today, were more likely to enlist if encouraged by their peers, and LeBlanc was among a cohort of mobile young men looking for work who might be convinced to sign up. Devine's sudden death from influenza on 31 March 1916 undoubtedly stymied the local campaign; just six more volunteers had turned up from the Shediac area by the end of June.

Adamsville, New Brunswick, provides the most obvious example of the importance of prominent local people in recruiting drives. This tiny parish of about one hundred souls was the home of the unit chaplain, Captain Jean V. Gaudet; remarkably, it supplied fourteen recruits to the 165th Battalion. Five of them were underage, and eleven were younger than twenty. Scholars have pointed out that one reason why French-Canadian enlistments were lower across the country was that men in that group tended to marry young and quickly set up their own households.[105] This also appears to be true of the Acadians: it was unmarried young men who were most likely to be able to leave home, and they often were already looking for work and willing to travel. In fact, most studies of enlistment rates assume that single men were the primary recruitment pool for all CEF units. Brown and Loveridge suggest that the smaller size of this pool in the Maritimes and Quebec went far to explain the lower enlistment rates there.[106]

Jonathan Vance and C.A. Sharpe contend that enlistment rates based on residence can be misleading in many ways. Vance notes that the enlistment rate was comparatively high in Manitoba (about 54,000 in total throughout the war), but that many of the men who enlisted from there were actually from northern Ontario and the United States. To what degree, then, were these recruits Manitoban? Quebec inhabitants from the Gatineau region crossed into Ontario to enlist in Ottawa, and some from the Gaspé region travelled to nearby northern New Brunswick. In fact, birthplace, residence, and place of enlistment varied the most in the Maritime provinces, reflecting the high degree of mobility in the region – mobility due at least in part to limited job prospects but also to family networks and the larger Acadian diaspora.[107] As mentioned in the introduction, Sharpe hypothesizes that an examination of birthplace rather than residence might significantly raise the enlistment rate in Quebec and lower the rate in the Prairie provinces.[108] Indeed, adding the birthplace of the volunteers reveals a little more diversity in the 165th Battalion.

For example, forty-two of the Acadian recruits were born outside Canada. This group included three men originally from Saint-Pierre and Miquelon, the two small islands in the Gulf of St Lawrence that still belong to France. The Acadian diaspora crossed international boundaries, across which there was frequent trade and movement. John Joseph Burt moved to Sydney, Cape Breton, with his father sometime between 1911 and 1916 and was just nineteen years old when he enlisted. It is clear that he was educated, for he worked as a telegraph operator. Daigle promoted him to sergeant in July 1916, a rare promotion for a man so young. Burt seems to have been especially eager to serve; while most of the unit ended up in the CFC, he transferred to the 26th Battalion (New Brunswick) at the front, where he served as a sapper. Although he contracted influenza, he survived the war. Along with Stehelin, three other French nationals signed up, including Auguste Dauverchain and Joseph Vervoke. These older men, like Stehelin, also were born in areas by then occupied by the Germans. Dauverchain worked in Moncton, but his wife lived in Adamsville – an additional link to Captain Gaudet. Another man from a border region, Joani Michel, had moved to Quebec but tried to sign up with the 165th Battalion in June 1916. Soon discharged as overage (he was forty-nine), Michel may have tried the Acadian unit after being rejected by local Quebec-based units.

This small group of Frenchmen is perhaps exceptional. The thirty-one volunteers born in the United States provide additional evidence of the Acadian diaspora at work and the pull of the Acadian national movement. Although beyond the scope of this book, the enlistment of Acadians in the US Army during the First World War would be worth exploring. Drawn primarily from families in Maine and Massachusetts, the American men who signed up for the 165th Battalion were part of a larger body of Acadian migrants seeking better employment opportunities.[109] This trend clearly worked both ways; many of the volunteers born in the United States had moved back to Canada even before the war, and some had moved back and forth several times. Families in the Madawaska frequently crossed into Maine and back; this was part of a broader historical movement along the Saint John River.[110] Railways and shipping routes made it relatively easy to move long distances, from New Bedford, Massachusetts, to Moncton, or from Worcester to Yarmouth.

We also find evidence of Quebec residents, particularly from the Gaspé region, travelling to New Brunswick in order to enlist, just as Vance has suggested. In addition, several men born in the Magdalen Islands signed up. Settled by Acadians during *le Grand Dérangement*, these fishing communities were part of Quebec but maintained close contact with the Maritimes. A few of the Quebec-born volunteers had travelled long distances before the war. For example, Arthur Lavoie was born in Montreal, had lived in Hartford, Connecticut (where his brother still resided), and was working as a labourer in Edmundston when he signed up on 10 April 1916. His military file reveals that he served for five years with the US Army (1905–10), two of them with the artillery (in Mississippi) and three with the infantry (13th Regiment). A thirty-three-year-old bachelor, Lavoie may have been a restless spirit, for he soon transferred to the 4th Pioneer Battalion. We might wonder how Wilfred Boulay, a tailor born and residing in Montreal, ended up in the 165th Battalion. It turns out that he first enlisted with the 22nd Battalion at the end of 1914, was found to be underage, and was sent to the new 64th Battalion for training at Camp Sussex, New Brunswick. He was detained briefly for an unknown infraction in Halifax and ultimately discharged. He ended up in Amherst, Nova Scotia, and may have been attracted by the chance to serve with a local francophone unit. However, he seems to have had a last-minute change of heart about going overseas; he deserted just before the 165th departed for England.

The most significant trend gleaned from this comparative analysis of residence and birthplace is that just 37 of the 203 men who declared Moncton as their residence at the time they enlisted were born there. Three-quarters of this group had moved to Moncton only recently, from the surrounding rural parishes in Westmorland and Kent Counties. No single area stood out. Twelve of the volunteers were born in Bouctouche, eleven in Shediac, and ten in Sainte-Marie, and there were smaller groups from nearly every Acadian community in the region. Phyllis LeBlanc notes that the population of Moncton grew nearly 400 per cent between 1871 and 1941 and that the proportion of French-speakers more than doubled from 15 to 34 per cent over the same period.[111] Anglophones came to Moncton as well, but Acadian migrants outnumbered them. The city attracted young people – men and women – looking for employment, but only some stayed permanently. Others returned home after making some money, particularly when they were ready to marry or when it was time to take over the family farm from aging parents.

Kenneth Sylvester reminds us that across Canada in the early twentieth century, industrialization had not fractured rural household patterns or drawn everyone to the cities; indeed, it rather strengthened traditional demographic practices by offering steadier wages and enabling larger geographic networks.[112] R.W. Sandwell highlights the enduring rural component of the Canadian population: throughout the 1930s, more Canadians were employed in agriculture than in any other occupation. She describes how many rural households supported themselves with three economic pillars – self-provisioning, waged work, and the sale of commodities. They were not peasants or the proletariat, but something much more complex, something that shifted in response to life course and regional conditions. In the Maritime provinces, trade and natural resource extraction were important sectors that offered many work opportunities centred on a burgeoning transportation infrastructure that connected rural households.[113] The young Acadian men already moving around before the war, particularly those who had travelled even farther afield across provincial and international boundaries, were strongly represented among the 165th Battalion volunteers.

Using the 1911 Census, we can delve more deeply into the family backgrounds and situations of the 165th Battalion volunteers. Not surprisingly, there are clear signs of their rural origins. While about one-third of Canadians declaring an occupation in 1911 worked in agriculture, nearly half the Acadian households represented here were led by a farmer. What is more, the families supplying recruits tended to be quite large by Canadian standards. The average size of Canadian households in 1911 was 4.8 persons, while for these Acadian families it was 8.3, and almost 60 per cent of those households had eight or more persons. Sandwell writes that rural households tended to be more complex than their urban counterparts: there were more stem families (parents living with their married children) as well as multiple families co-residing in the same household. And when extended family members did not live in the same home, they were often not far away.[114]

With the help of a study by Stacie Burke on New Brunswick in 1901, we can compare household structure among the families of the Acadian recruits with that of the population as a whole.[115] The volunteers were more likely to live in nuclear families (56 compared to 48 per cent) and also more likely to live in complex households with extended family and/or lodgers (34 compared to 21 per cent). This reflects the rural character of Acadian society and also suggests that life course played a role in enlistment. Farming families with many children still at home and supporting members of the extended family – most often elderly grandparents – were the most likely to provide recruits. They were near their peak size and productivity, and perhaps they were struggling to support everyone. Newer families as well as those headed by widowed or older parents were less likely to have a member enlist.

We also looked at the number of sons in each household and the birth order of the 576 recruits who declared *son* as their relationship to the head of household in the 1911 Census. On average, these young men had three other brothers still at home (the census does not always allow us to identify older siblings, who may have already left home). Just 10 per cent of these recruits were the only son at home as reported in the 1911 Census. Most often, the volunteer was a middle son (about 40 per cent), although eldest sons were also well represented (31 per cent). These results reinforce the impression that military service was one available means for unmarried adolescents and younger men to contribute to their families' upkeep, as was expected of them. With a few exceptions – notably the four Saulnier brothers of Baie Sainte-Marie in Nova Scotia – it was rare to find brothers and other relations enlisting together in the 165th Battalion. We identified forty pairs of brothers and a few father–son duos – less than 10 per cent of the group as a whole. This does not, however, exclude the possibility that other family members were already serving with other units. Lionel LeBlanc enrolled as an officer with the 165th; we have already met his older brother, Ulric, who was among the first Acadians to sign up in 1914.

Examining the next of kin declared by the volunteers further highlights mobility and broad, shifting family networks. For example, nineteen soldiers indicated that their next of kin lived in Massachusetts, but only three of these men were residing in the United States at the time of enlistment. Indeed, three men declared that they had wives in Massachusetts, despite living and working in Moncton. Philias Léger was a thirty-eight-year-old bricklayer, Éric Bourque was forty and worked as a shoemaker, and Valérie Richard was a new husband at twenty-one: he had left his wife Blanche behind while he sought employment as a carpenter. Valérie appears to have been another man particularly focused on getting to the front. He did not go to the CFC but instead moved to the 22nd Battalion and was killed in action at Passchendaele on 21 July 1917.

A few soldiers had contacts even farther away as well as more complex family situations. For example, Joseph Chenard declared his stepbrother, Joseph Pinet, to be his next of kin. Pinet lived in Saskatchewan. According to the 1911 Census, Chenard was one of four Acadian children adopted by John Morrison, head of a farming family in Caraquet. Similarly, Larry Desjardins, a barber in Sainte-Anne, Kent County, New Brunswick, declared his brother, who lived in Wisconsin, as his next of kin. We know that John Patrick Maillet's parents had died. His brother Frank lived on Long Island, New York. These and other stories suggest that many volunteers were neither idealists nor idlers; rather, for them, military service fit comfortably within broader patterns of employment and migration.

CONCLUSION

In many ways, the 165th Battalion originals were similar to their counterparts across the CEF. As Ian Miller has written about volunteers in Toronto, the public expression of patriotic enthusiasm "was the result of hundreds of private decisions, prompted by the needs and aspirations of each individual."[116] However, each "home town" had its own version of an encounter between "official" and "vernacular" cultures that attempted to combine local interests with larger national and international concerns.[117] When prominent Acadians made speeches or published editorials in favour of recruitment, they engaged in language that resonated with their own goals of order and advancement for their group, evoking common cultural references such as Catholic piety and *le Grand Dérangement*. The creation of the 165th inspired men already engaged in the Acadian renaissance to integrate their cause with that of the young Dominion and the British Empire.

Unmarried men not yet 30 years old formed the majority of the volunteers, while local notables and skilled tradesmen provided the backbone of officers and NCOs. The 165th Battalion differed from most other units not just because of its French-speaking, Catholic character but also due to the high proportion of volunteers born in

Canada and the prevalence of men from rural backgrounds. Some specific Acadian family strategies related to mobility, employment, and life course emerge from a deeper analysis of data from military attestation papers and census records. In the following chapter, we will follow the 165th to Valcartier and then to winter quarters in Saint John, New Brunswick. The recruiting campaign continued, and we will add these latecomers to the demographic analysis and determine whether their profile and motivations were different. Other units created at the end of 1915, like the 105th Battalion (Prince Edward Island) and the 145th (New Brunswick), travelled overseas and were broken up to provide reinforcements at the front. Some units, including the 104th Battalion (New Brunswick) and the 112th (Nova Scotia), were broken up and assigned to reserve battalions before they even left for England. Acadian leaders worried that the same fate awaited their national unit, while anglophones observed that the military authorities seemed to be holding the 165th back. It was a tense period at home, with the news from Europe revealing the increasing death and destruction wrought by the war. Against this backdrop, the 165th would ultimately fall short of its stated goal of one thousand men.

2

Training, Preparations, and Completing the Battalion

July 1916–March 1917

Filling the ranks and getting the soldiers ready for deployment overseas would prove to be no easy task for Louis-Cyriaque Daigle and the other officers of the 165th Battalion. In his short history of the unit, the CO referred to "the numerous inherent difficulties in such an important enterprise, challenges of organization in a new sphere, challenges of effective supervision of a large body of men assembled in haste." The soldiers departed for Camp Valcartier on 28 June 1916, and Daigle reminds us that up to this point, they had not trained together but instead remained in regional depots.[1] After six months of local work, this was a key moment in the recruits' commitment to continue in military service. It was one thing to show up for simple lessons and administration with their friends, quite another to begin real combat training away from home.

Fortunately, public enthusiasm sped them on their way. The volunteers from Meteghan and Antigonish joined up with the contingent of soldiers and officers in Moncton, where a large gathering sent the unit off with much "admiration" despite the torrential rain.[2] According to one newspaper, "hundreds were present to wish the boys Godspeed and on all sides the men were heaped with dainties, prepared for them by the good ladies of Moncton."[3] The train stopped in Caraquet before continuing on to Rivière-du-Loup, where the Edmundston contingent met up with them. We can imagine the excitement and anticipation in the air as men from different parts of Acadie came together to constitute the 165th Battalion as a whole (less the party, including the band, left behind in Moncton to continue the recruiting campaign). The packed train sped them towards their new life in the CEF.

THE ACADIAN BATTALION
AND CAMP VALCARTIER

First impressions of the training grounds were largely positive, according to Daigle, but he was not actually there – he was finishing officer training in Aldershot.[4] Soldiers' letters home relate stories of cold and austere conditions. Alphée Langis of Cocagne wrote shortly after his arrival: "It is very healthy, always in clear air, but the worst is that we freeze at night, we lay down on the ground and we are short of blankets."[5] Before long, the volunteers would be complaining about working through the day during the "very hot and sultry" July weather. A serious fire broke out 13 July in a nearby forest tract, ultimately requiring the mobilization of 30,000 soldiers and several hours of work to contain it.[6] There were other, more positive distractions, such as sporting events organized among the many New Brunswick units training together at the camp. For example, the 145th Battalion fielded a baseball team that soundly trounced their counterparts from the 165th, twenty-five to five. The newspaper article concerned described the coaching of one of the 145th officers, a former baseball star, and the fact that other ballplayers had joined his unit since its arrival at Valcartier.[7]

The French-language newspapers that had committed so fully to the recruiting campaign published little about the 165th Battalion during its three months of training in Valcartier. Perhaps there was little to tell; training could be monotonous, and there were few accomplishments to celebrate. Or perhaps newspapers were muzzled by official censorship; Jeffrey Keshen describes explicit directives in 1916 to prevent the media from reporting on adverse conditions during training at Valcartier and other camps.[8] In addition, Acadian journalists had little access to the unit at this time. This was long before the modern practice of embedding reporters with military units. While one of the unit officers, Lieutenant Rufin Arsenault, had been an editor with *Le Moniteur acadien*, his request to resign his commission in November 1916 suggests that his experience of the 165th was not positive.[9] What coverage did emerge largely concerned ceremonial events, including general reviews – military parades conducted for honoured visitors – that emphasized the good conduct and martial bearing of the unit. A short letter home from Dismas Daigle, published on 1 August 1916, emphasized his pride at serving in the 165th, that the work was not too hard, and that Prime Minister Robert Borden

Figure 2.1 Photo of 165th lines at Valcartier

had told them their unit was the finest in Canada.[10] A stonemason from Petite Aldouane, Daigle had enrolled at the end of June, and he must not have enjoyed military life that much, for he deserted a month later. Editorials periodically reminded their readers of the desperate need for new recruits to help the Acadian national battalion complete its ranks.

Some of the volunteers took to military training very well and expressed genuine pride. Figure 2.2 shows a postcard featuring three Acadian soldiers at Valcartier. Their brief, scrawled text mentions their "swords" (bayonets) and their physical fitness. They had become "so terribly lean" (that is, thin) that they resembled "the devil."[11] The bonds among friends certainly played a role in keeping the unit together. Daigle and his team had divided the men into subunits in an attempt to maintain regional identities. A Company was composed almost entirely of men from southeastern New Brunswick; B Company, from North Shore communities; and C Company, from Nova Scotia.

The 165th Battalion joined three other New Brunswick units – the 115th, the 132nd, and the 145th – as the 4th Brigade at Camp Valcartier. Located at the northern end of the camp, about one and a half miles from the central camp headquarters, the unit lines stretched on either side of the main road and down to the banks of the Cartier River.[12] The weather could be a considerable concern; heavy thunderstorms in July "illuminated the interior of the tents and kept a large portion of the camp awake for a considerable time." In general, the first two weeks in camp were not too demanding; the New Brunswick brigade would only start "all day training" in late July, and even that

Figure 2.2 165th Battalion postcard from Valcartier

was complete by 5 p.m. Field kitchens accompanied the soldiers and provided hot beverages and meals throughout the day. Visitors "expressed delight at the splendid and artistic way in which the various battalion lines had been laid out and decorated."[13] Indeed, there were many visitors, including parents, spouses, and children, who added to the social atmosphere.

Some of the officers and NCOs received advanced training in musketry, mortars, and grenades. The daily routine for most of the soldiers seems hardly to have been arduous, given that as civilians they had been accustomed to working long hours on farms or in factories. Morton describes long periods of waiting, such as for the issuing of kit or medical exams and vaccinations, during which the soldiers had little to do.[14] As the summer progressed, the unit leaders devoted much of their time to preparing the soldiers for ceremonial reviews. The highlight was undoubtedly the visit of the Governor General in August. Prince Arthur, the Duke of Connaught, would inspect more than 15,000 soldiers in a camp-wide parade, as well as visit individual units.[15]

As the training wound down at the end of summer, various reports detailed the success and good reputation of the 165th Battalion. For example, a 4th Brigade document cited by one newspaper congratulated the officers of the 165th for "showing wonderful control ... regarding attention and clean grounds. The eating area was left almost perfectly clean without the use of a fatigue party. On the whole this battalion has been an example in discipline and good behaviour."[16] Specific details about combat training are harder to come by. One article relates that the 165th had an excellent machine gun squad that was considered the best at Camp Valcartier. The officer in charge, Lieutenant Melanson of Bathurst, New Brunswick, was appointed a lead instructor at the machine gun range.[17] French-language newspapers were quick to point out that although the unit would not be going overseas in the fall, as had been planned, this was due to the request to keep it back so it could finish recruiting, rather than any issues with training. The Acadian national unit "had become one of the best battalions in the entire camp."[18]

Of course, this emphasis on ceremonial and deportment was not particular to New Brunswick units and media. Historians have long made note of the anachronistic approach to the military generally and war fighting in particular that prevailed during the First World War. Many contend that this partly explains why senior commanders were so slow to adopt innovative tactics in the face of improved firepower and defensive works and continued to emphasize costly frontal assaults. The summer of 1916 witnessed futile offensives on the Western Front in which entire battalions, such as the Royal Newfoundland Regiment, perished in a single day.[19] The 26th Battalion (New Brunswick) suffered serious losses at Mont Sorrel in June, and the casualties during the difficult Somme campaign that began that July shocked Canadians. No doubt, the casualty lists planted seeds of doubt in some recruits and their families, particularly those who might already have been wavering in their desire to continue in military service. However, the media minimized these setbacks and continued to laud the traditional view, describing gallant men in formation successfully confronting a demonized enemy.[20] The coverage of the Acadian national unit continued to add cultural references to this equation, such as the "descendants of Evangeline and Gabriel" fighting against "the Hun."[21]

The soldiers of 4th Brigade, which included the 165th Battalion, left Valcartier on 1 October and boarded the train for Saint John, New Brunswick, where they would spend the winter. Some soldiers must have been impatient to get to France, while others likely welcomed the news that they would be closer to home and safe for several more months. In the words of one journalist, the soldiers would be proud of their accomplishments at Valcartier, "happy to return and renew their patriotism through contact with their native soil."[22] LCol Daigle described the enthusiastic welcome: "the city was covered in flags, the streets filled with people."[23] Many accounts emphasized the special lunch for all the soldiers, which had been prepared by the "ladies" of the city at the armoury. Organized by a coalition of social groups including the Women's Canadian Club, five chapters of the Daughters of the Empire, and the Young Women's Patriotic Association, the lunch featured fresh coffee, sandwiches, doughnuts and other treats. The mayor, for his part, hosted a banquet for the unit officers. Music featured prominently throughout these events; it included the unit band, now twenty-five members strong, as well as impromptu solos and group renditions of patriotic songs. Meanwhile, the soldiers were "mixing in the various features of our community life."[24] After months living in tents, the restaurants, taverns, shops, and cafés must have seemed all right.

THE 165TH BATTALION IN SAINT JOHN

At first, there was little sign of linguistic or ethnic hostility towards the Acadians in the English-language newspaper coverage afforded the 165th Battalion during its stay in Saint John. Instead, there was a certain pride about "their" local French. The *St. John Standard* described them as "Men of Action," while *The Daily Telegraph and Sun* reported that the "the great majority of the men are splendid physical specimens" and contrasted the 165th band favourably with that of the 69th Battalion, a French-Canadian unit from Quebec that had earlier spent time in the city.[25] In a letter written to his brigade commander against the idea of combining the 165th with other French-speaking units, Daigle stated that "the French Acadians are a distinct people from the French Canadians both in character and temperament."[26] Some anglophone journalists listened to these kinds of affirmations and attempted to educate their readers about Acadian history. In one article, the author explained that the Acadians had little to do with other French-Canadians until after Confederation, in part because of their "expatriation" (that is, the deportation) but also because of their close association with the English-speaking majority. Furthermore, there "is plenty of fighting blood in their veins, as those who are familiar with the history of Acadie can testify."[27] At least temporarily, the Acadians benefited from enthusiastic, if sometimes ill-informed, support.

Eager to describe the military activities in the city, the local newspapers continued to provide extensive coverage of the 165th Battalion alongside that of several other units. The 165th soon settled into a regular routine of physical training, drills, and route marches. For example, the schedule announced for 7 October included an hour of physical training, followed by section drill (small groups of eight to twelve soldiers), extended order (on parade), a short lecture and rest, platoon drills (larger groups of thirty-five to forty soldiers), and, finally, an afternoon route march in the city. The next day featured lighter duties, including cleaning up the quarters and an afternoon holiday.[28] Before long, some of the Acadian officers were leading more specialized training. For example, Lieutenant LeBlanc conducted bayonet-fighting exercises, which featured dummy figures representing Germans and public displays of what the "French Acadian boys of the 165th Battalion intend to do to the first 'sausage' they meet on the western front." Meanwhile, Lieutenant Michaud instructed on throwing grenades and bombs.[29] Others soon arrived to bolster the NCO corps, including Sergeant Marcil of the Royal Canadian Regiment, a veteran of twenty-four years.[30] Captain Scott, an officer from Ottawa, wounded at the front and returned to Canada, arrived to teach modern trench warfare, while Captain Johnston, previously of the 5th Brigade in France, took over the bomb training.[31]

With several units scheduled to pass as long as six months in the city, the military leadership became even more ambitious about conducting realistic training. Perhaps the latest battles and casualty rates in Europe and the need for proficient reinforcements had galvanized these officers. Some probably hoped to shorten the final training necessary in England once the directive to travel overseas arrived. Others may have simply realized that to maintain the morale of the soldiers in garrison, they needed to vary the daily regime. The 165th Battalion took on the construction of full trenches in the area around Courtenay Bay. The plan involved "a trench front of some three hundred yards" and intricate earthworks built precisely like those on the Western Front, "which have been, for many months holding back the German hordes and withstanding their artillery fire."[32] By mid-December, the trenches were extensive enough to accommodate an entire company in training. A visiting instructor from Halifax commented on the fine work and, in particular, on how the bombing specialists could now practise building their positions and lobbing the mock incendiaries.[33] The onset of snow initially halted the training, but an early thaw in February brought the 165th out to resume their practice. By now, the training ground extended towards Westmorland Road and could accommodate the entire unit of about eight hundred people at one time.[34]

Periodic inspections, ceremonial reviews, and social events also punctuated the life of the 165th Battalion soldiers in garrison during the winter of 1916–17. For example, on 7 November at the Imperial Theatre, the unit performed a fundraising concert in partnership with the Young Women's Patriotic Association (YWPA). The "very large and most appreciative audience" included the Lieutenant Governor and Brigadier General McLean. After opening remarks delivered by newly promoted Major Arthur Legere, the concert presented the 165th Battalion band. The program opened with "God Save the King," followed by "La Marseillaise" as an obvious allusion to the French war effort (perhaps the soldiers sang the lyrics written specifically for the Acadian battalion). The theatre projected pictures of Lieutenant-Colonel Daigle and the other officers of the Acadian battalion onto a large screen during the playing of the French national anthem, which generated rounds of applause. Quartets, duets, and soloists followed, performing favourites like "Adieu mon soldat" and "When the World Has Peace Again." Romantic tunes like "Drink to Me Only with Thine Eyes" were mixed with humorous ones like "The Wedding o' Lauchie McGraw." Apparently one of the biggest hits of the night was the comedy act of Leo "Frecco" Leger, one of the battalion drummers, "who was attired as a Jew" and performed several encores.[35] We will see "Fricot" again, as his misadventures while in France were the subject of a soldier's personal notebook. The concert also included an impassioned "recruiting sermon" and patriotic readings from members of the YWPA, as well as a dance number called "The Madawaska Shuffle." There was even a demonstration of trained dogs. The concert raised $451.10 to help fund the unit's messes, canteen supplies, and other sundries for the soldiers.[36]

Public events deliberately reinforced social hierarchy and gender roles. A reception and ball given by the officers of the 165th Battalion at the Knights of Columbus Hall attracted three hundred guests – a cross-section of senior military officers in dress uniform and civilian elites in formalwear.[37] There were plenty of other diversions for the ordinary soldiers. For example, Christian organizations like the YMCA and local parish associations provided entertainment. These events, which became more frequent in the lead-up to Christmas, featured music, literature, and refreshments, and typically were held at the city's armoury, where they could be closely supervised. Journalists emphasized the prominent role played by women, who "entertained the boys" as a kind of patriotic duty, all under the watchful eye of male authority figures including the mayor, priests, and senior military officials.[38] Ian Miller similarly describes how women became increasingly involved in recruiting and fundraising events in Toronto. Their participation reflected traditional gender roles; even so, their presence and encouragement could exercise a powerful influence on young volunteers.[39]

Sporting events remained popular, just as they had at Camp Valcartier, but now they drew enthusiastic spectators. The city sponsored a military hockey league, and in the first game, held on 19 January 1917, a team from the 165th Battalion narrowly defeated their counterparts from the Field Ambulance Corps, 4–3. The match "was fast and hotly contested from start to finish, but like all early season games there was a glaring lack of team work."[40]

As both a diversion and an expression of unit pride, Daigle arranged the printing of a unit photo album with the Mortimer Company, based in Ottawa. Mortimer contracted the Reid Studio in Saint John to take the photographs, beginning in November 1916. A few soldiers visited the studio each day; the manager reported to Daigle that he could only reserve an hour each morning for the 165th Battalion because of the "Christmas Rush."[41] By March 1917, some 662 photographs had been taken, half of which had been delivered to the Mortimer Company for the album. The manager wrote to Daigle assuring him that they would do everything possible to finish the work before the unit went overseas.[42] They failed to meet that goal, and frustrated soldiers who had paid up front wondered what had happened. In 1918, Captain Malenfant wrote to Daigle from France about the outstanding books, commenting that everybody had ordered at least one copy and that some of the soldiers suspected they had been cheated.[43] However, the books did eventually arrive, and many families have conserved them in their family records.

Leave was another important aspect of military life. Most soldiers of the 165th Battalion could easily travel home by train or through the port of Saint John. The officers granted leave on a rotating basis, and the newspapers often mentioned the departure or return of individual soldiers. Half the battalion would be home at Christmas, the other half would receive time off at New Year's. The unit observed its own holiday traditions, putting on special meals for those not with their families.[44] In addition, the military authorities released the soldiers so that they could return home to vote in the provincial general election of 24 February 1917.[45] This was undoubtedly an appreciated opportunity to visit family and friends as well as engage in social revelry.

During its stay in Saint John, the unit also celebrated weddings, which were officiated by its chaplain. According to military regulations, a soldier "who wishes to marry must first obtain the consent of his colonel."[46] Charles Blinn, from the small community of Grosses Coques, Nova Scotia, was one of the first to enlist in the 165th Battalion, and he had named his sister Celeste as his next of kin. He married Josephine Boudreau on 12 February 1917. It seems that neither bride nor groom had their immediate family present for the ceremony; however, a "dainty breakfast" was served afterwards for all of the guests, and the newlyweds received "numerous presents."[47] Similarly, Hilarion Hebert and Elinore Chase married in Saint John, relatively far from home. They both hailed from Kent County, the groom from Bouctouche and the bride from Sainte-Marie. Elinore had her sister Regina present, while Private Alphé LeBlanc, a chum from the same region, witnessed for the groom.[48] However, this story takes a tragic turn. Hebert deserted the unit just before it left for overseas in March. He must have gone home first to gather some belongings, because he would later be charged with breaking and entering a shop in Bouctouche. Police captured him in civilian clothes while he was attempting to flee to the United States. A judge sentenced him to five years in Dorchester Penitentiary for his crimes.[49]

Of course, the men of the 165th Battalion faced some less happy events during their time in Saint John. Accidents, injuries, and illnesses were quite frequent. Private Joseph Gallant, from Egmont Bay on Prince Edward Island, while out late one night in March 1917, was struck by an automobile while on his way back to the armoury. He suffered contusions and "a general shaking up," and required hospitalization.[50] The injuries must have been minor, for he deployed overseas with his battalion just a few days later. Major Emile Stehelin barely escaped injury after a panicked horse threw him from a moving cart.[51] Antoine Nowlan of Upper Pokemouche, in Gloucester County, was not so lucky. The eighteen-year-old, while returning from home leave a few days before the unit was to depart overseas, fell from a train near Caraquet. Lance Corporal Telesphore Richard was with Nowlan in the front passenger car of the train, and reported:

> The car gave a slight jolt and the said Antoine Knowlan's feet slipped from under him and he fell feet first off of the platform of the car and his feet struck the hard snow-bank along the side of the track and he was thrown back against the car and went out of my sight under it, and I shouted that he had fallen off and others also called out and men immediately put on the brakes and stopped the train and I got off to go and see him, but was ordered to go back in the train and did so, and I did not see the said Antoine Knowlan afterwards.[52]

Corporal Asade Arsenault spared Richard the sight of his friend crushed by the train, but two other soldiers, a priest, and a doctor stayed with Nowlan, who died later that day.[53]

Three other soldiers – Onésime Babineau, Alphonse Melanson, and George Doucet – died of pneumonia over the winter. Illnesses were certainly common; some of the officers went on medical leave for a few weeks, and contagious diseases could spread quickly among the men, as happened with the 132nd Battalion (North Shore), which suffered an outbreak of measles that delayed its departure overseas.[54] Daigle reported that on the eve of their departure in March 1917, the health of the soldiers was good. However, the training must have taken a toll on joints, tendons, and muscles, for he also noted widespread issues with rheumatism (inflammation).[55]

Saint John's Chief Constable wrote to Daigle congratulating him on the "model conduct" of his battalion, but inevitably, some of the soldiers had run-ins with the law.[56] Apparently, some of them liked to gather near the railway station to drink with other residents of the city. That group included Private William "Willie" Melanson, originally from Sainte-Marie-de-Kent, and his friend Edmund Cormier. When a railway policeman ordered Cormier to clear out, Melanson "interfered, threatening to assault him, and when placed under arrest made a threat to bring down the 165th and mob the place."[57] According to his military service record, this was the first of several disciplinary issues involving Melanson and alcohol.

Authorities were also concerned about prostitution. As so often happened in that era, the courts criminalized and blamed the women rather than the men. In January 1917, municipal police raided a "bawdy house" on St. Andrew's Street, not far from the armoury, that had opened shortly after the soldiers arrived in the city. The proprietors, two women, were sentenced to six months in jail and fined for managing "a place of ill-repute." At the same time, the unnamed two soldiers found using their services were "given their freedom," likely due to the presence and testimony of Captain Leo Richard, son of Ambroise D. Richard, a former MLA for Westmorland County (1895–99). Clearly, the military looked after its own. The court seemed particularly scandalized by the attempt to bribe detectives during the raid and by the fact that the women had husbands at the front.[58] The YWPA was also concerned about prostitution and advocated for the city to recruit female police "to deal with the problem of young girls on the streets at night."[59] We will examine the issue of venereal disease in more detail later, as this was a serious problem for the entire CEF.

In general, though, garrison duty in Saint John was a positive experience for the volunteers of the 165th Battalion. Training improved and expanded with the help of new facilities and expert instructors. At the same time, winter conditions limited what could be accomplished, and there was plenty of time for recreation and visits home. The unit sought to maintain morale and ensure discipline by keeping things organized, including sporting events, concerts, and church parades. Inevitably, a few soldiers got into trouble, but this is not surprising given the large number of single young men, their regular pay, and the availability of alcohol. The battalion's leaders worked closely with the municipal authorities and patriotic associations to provide and supervise approved entertainment.

The local press seemed genuinely interested in highlighting the Acadians, and this balanced the anti-francophone sentiments expressed elsewhere. Unfortunately, not everyone welcomed the Acadians. One member of Saint John City Council "made violent objection" to the proposal to entertain the 165th Battalion officers, "took occasion to denounce the 69th Quebec Battalion which spent last winter" there, and "pitched in to the French generally."[60] The provincial election provided an opportunity for some Tories to vociferously denounce what they viewed as a French "conspiracy" against enlistment, although the physical presence of the 165th provided counter-arguments against this claim, as the Acadian elites had hoped.[61] Although the Liberal Party, supported by Acadian and Irish Catholics alike, pulled out a surprising win in 1917, Andrew Theobald reminds us that New Brunswick remained divided along linguistic and religious lines, and that divide would only intensify over the course of the polarizing national debate around conscription.[62] It is also worth noting that the Acadians countered anti-French slander in part by throwing their French-Canadian brethren in Quebec under the bus. For example, Daigle resisted the proposal that the 165th be folded into other French-Canadian units,[63] and Major Legere contrasted those units with the "readiness" of the Acadians, who benefited from an engaged elite and dedicated (militia) officers. The anglophone press was quick to adopt this theme. For example, the *St. John Standard* remarked that if Quebec had lieutenants "more like those who have led the Maritime Acadians, the young men of Quebec might have made a showing equally as good as their brothers in these provinces."[64]

Not all New Brunswickers were convinced of all this, as Acadian women conducting a "tag day" in Moncton in February 1917 soon learned. A tag day was a local fundraiser in which charitable organizations went door to door and gave tags to donors, which could then be displayed. Ian Miller writes that tag days in Toronto, which began in the summer of 1915, were examples of women's greater role in recruiting and fundraising efforts for the CEF.[65] Alice Comeau wrote a lengthy editorial for *The Moncton Times* in which she highlighted some of the slanders she had heard about Acadian soldiers, including that they were "cowards" and "lazy loafers." One lady reportedly told her to "go collect among your own." A pharmacist went further, saying that "he would like to see every one of the 165th shot down one by one." Comeau emphasized that many prominent Moncton families refused to donate and that some, including the wife of a city official, heaped abuse and then slammed the door in her face. Comeau was horrified by these unjust responses, pointing out that her brother, Arthur, had been the first Moncton resident to lose his life overseas. The tag day brought in $220 for the 165th, and the editors of *The Moncton Times* suggested in a postscript that "the ladies who conducted the sale should not take the few discourteous ones as representative when so many bought freely." Indeed, $220 was a genuine success, the equivalent of over $4,000 today. The editors of *L'Évangéline*, who republished Comeau's text in English and French, expressed concern at the anti-Acadian sentiments reported by the collectors and hoped that the story would "wake up" those not fully aware of the problem.[66] In a letter of thanks written on board the ss *Metagama* while the unit was crossing to England, LCol Daigle asked to be informed of the names of all of the collectors who had experienced this abuse so that he could thank them personally.[67]

Finally, in March 1917, the orders to depart for England arrived.[68] If the initial plan to keep the 165th Battalion back was to allow it to recruit up to strength, the military authorities must have finally realized that the unit was actually losing almost as many men as it was gaining with the delay. Richard Holt writes that the wait to deploy overseas had been getting longer for all CEF units in 1916 and especially in 1917, due to the difficulties in recruiting but also because of the limited facilities for training and holding reinforcements in England. On average, battalions embarking in 1917 had waited forty-three weeks in Canada. The Acadian volunteers of the 165th had waited even longer, about fourteen months.[69]

RECRUITING FALLS SHORT

While the local anglophone press provided extensive coverage of military activities and events in their city, including those related to the 165th Battalion, Acadian newspapers were relatively quiet about the unit's time in Valcartier and Saint John. They remained focused on recruiting for the Acadian national battalion, but their impassioned pleas soon shifted to expressions of disappointment. The turning point may have been a public assembly held in Moncton on 21 December 1916. Daigle and other members of the Acadian elite who had supported the project since the beginning, such as Senator Pascal Poirier, convened this event to re-energize recruitment and make a final push in the New Year. After the discharge of unfit soldiers and

Figure 2.3 Officers of the 165th Battalion at Saint John

the loss of some volunteers to desertion, the unit required three hundred more men. Although it had been announced in several newspapers, including *L'Évangéline* and *Le Moniteur acadien*, and through a circular letter to parish priests and politicians, the event flopped, attracting only 10 individuals. One front-page article had "hoped" that the battalion's friends were "more numerous" than this and decried those who absented themselves "by design or by indifference." The journalist enjoined all who had agreed to create an Acadian national unit in the first place to live up to their commitment. However, in a postscript, the editors struck quite a different tone. They regretted that certain people had criticized the battalion and its commander out of political partisanship and announced that in these "difficult circumstances" they would refrain from further debate about the battalion and redirect their efforts to "more important matters."[70]

L'Évangéline also published a final salvo in support of the recruiting campaign with the message "finish what we started." However, in a comprehensive editorial published on 3 January 1917 under the pseudonym Sellig, the tone shifted to resignation and blame. The author highlighted the popular opposition to military service and, in particular, the fears of parents that "going to war or running towards death had become the similar things." He argued that the 165th Battalion was supported by strong and capable officers. Perhaps knowing that his arguments would ring hollow, Sellig went on to shame those parents who prevented their sons from enlisting. By depriving the Acadian national unit of its full complement, they would be the cause of its disappearance, leaving the hundreds who had already signed up to be dispersed among anglophone units. Not only were they denying the Acadians their chance to win glory on the battlefield, but much worse, the recruits they were abandoning would lose their faith while scattered among people of "foreign religions." Only the 165th, with its dedicated Catholic chaplain and devout officers, could ensure the spiritual well-being of these brave souls.[71]

This final flurry of editorials signalled the end of the media campaign in support of recruiting. Those editorials also bear witness to the very real divisions within Acadian society regarding the war and military service. Only a handful of articles published in 1917 concerned the 165th Battalion, and they focused on the departure of the unit for England in March. Around this time, the anglophone newspapers commented on the battalion's failure to recruit enough men and openly speculated about the consequences. As early as August 1916, some commentators raised questions about the 165th as well as the 140th and 145th Battalions, including about whether they would be able to go overseas at all.[72] The fact that other battalions besides the 165th were struggling to reach their recruitment goals indicates that this was not specifically an Acadian issue.

Orders issued from Ottawa after the resignation of Sam Hughes in November 1916 directed that those units that could not reach their full complement would be broken up as drafts to reinforce other CEF units.[73] Historians have noted a dramatic reduction in voluntary recruitment nationwide by the end of 1916. Some 169,621 soldiers joined the colours across Canada in 1916, but enlistments had fallen from a peak of 33,960 in March to just 4,930 in December.[74] The press was keenly aware of this trend. For example, the week ending 18 November 1916 saw just sixty-four enlistments in the entire province of New Brunswick, and "for the first time in the recruiting history of the province seven counties report[ed] no recruits" at all.[75] In fact, these enlistment trends mirrored those of the entire Dominion.[76] Daigle attempted to put a positive spin on the renewed recruiting campaign mentioned earlier, claiming another hundred or so volunteers from the beginning of January through mid-February 1917.[77]

However, we have identified just sixty-two men during that time, and while this did represent a brief improvement, it was nowhere near enough of one, and it soon trailed off.

THE 165TH BATTALION RECRUITS: ORIGINALS AND LATECOMERS

In chapter 1, we examined the unit "originals" who left for Camp Valcartier together. Here, we briefly examine those who signed up after this point – 182 additional volunteers for the Acadian national battalion during the period from July 1916 to March 1917. These numbers do not include those who had enrolled earlier with other units and later transferred to the 165th. As we will see a bit later in this chapter, many of these transfers concerned absentees or men left behind by other units when they went overseas, so they do not necessarily concern individuals choosing to serve with the 165th. The goal here is to ascertain whether the latecomers differed from those who had responded more quickly to the call to serve in the Acadian national unit.

Our examination suggests that there was little to differentiate the groups: there were similar proportions of recruits under 18, in their twenties, or older, and little change in terms of their declared birthplaces and residences. There were relatively fewer enlistments from Nova Scotia, and a few more from Quebec. New Brunswick Acadians continued to dominate the ranks of the 165th Battalion, but there were some shifts in regional origin. The proportion from the southeast dropped from 47 to 33 per cent, while that from the northern counties of Gloucester and Madawaska rose from 19 to 28 per cent. Regarding Gloucester communities like Bathurst, Caraquet, and Petit Rocher, this was likely due to the departure overseas of the 132nd Battalion (North Shore) in October 1916, which meant it was no longer competing directly with the 165th.[78] As we have seen, there was also a renewed effort to recruit in the north.

The occupational profile of the latecomers was also largely unchanged, although there were somewhat fewer agricultural labourers and white-collar professionals and somewhat higher proportions of miners and general labourers. The key observation is that the recruiting campaign failed to diversify beyond its initial appeal and recruitment base. Although every region of Acadie sent volunteers to the national unit, the eastern half of New Brunswick continued to provide the most leaders as well as soldiers.

QUALITY AND QUANTITY

Unfortunately, many of the volunteers proved to be unfit for military service. An anonymous volunteer of the 165th Battalion wrote (in English) to Prime Minister Robert Borden in November 1916 advising that medical staff at Valcartier had pronounced at least fifty of the original recruits, including himself, physically unfit. He wanted to know why he could not receive his discharge since keeping him on was "just using the government's money for nothing. For my share, I'd sooner be home, than here, I could get better wages and would not be on the government's charge." The same letter indicated another problem: the 165th had received between twenty-five and thirty men transferred from other units who were similarly unsuitable for military service. While it is unclear whether Borden read the letter himself, it clearly raised concerns in Ottawa. Major General W.E. Hodgins, the Acting Adjutant General of Militia, immediately wrote to the No. 6 District Commander in Halifax directing him to investigate and "take prompt and drastic action" if the statements proved "well-founded." When the correspondence reached LCol Daigle, he was quick to respond that they had discharged any men declared unfit as soon as possible and that none of them had made the trip to Saint John. He received support from his brigade commander, Brigadier General McLean, who reported that the 165th had indeed received 144 men from other units, but that 42 of them never actually turned up, while others were in hospital. He referred to the "shocking state" of the paperwork sent over by the units concerned; many files had simply been lost, so that medical boards needed to be repeated.[79]

More correspondence soon reached Hodgins's desk, including a letter from a concerned New Brunswick citizen claiming that the 165th Battalion had recruited more than 2,750 men but still had not reached full strength. The implication was clear: the army had spent considerable time and money recruiting Acadians but few if any of them were actually fit for service. The author pointed out that other units, including the 145th Battalion, had gone overseas much more quickly. Called upon once again to explain what was happening in his brigade, an evidently frustrated McLean advised his superior that "all of these reports and statements regarding this Battalion are only tending to defeat the end to which it was kept in Canada, namely, to recruit up to strength. There has been a satisfactory improvement in this Unit."

McLean enclosed a letter from Major Legere providing detailed numbers. This document indicates that a total of 890 men had enlisted directly into the 165th Battalion, while 91 transfers and 147 "casuals" – that is, men left behind – from other units brought the total to 1,128. Legere then subtracted 113 deserters and 174 medically unfit men from the original volunteers, as well as 96 deserters and unfit men received (in fact, never actually received) from other units. He reported a parade strength as of 18 December 1916 of 745 men. However, of these remaining men, another 39 were in hospital or absent without leave. The unit DCO was confident they would get up to full strength owing to the support of "clergymen and influential parties"; he was likely thinking of the upcoming public assembly in Moncton that would turn out to be so disappointing. Significantly, Legere also pointed out that the number of deserters and medically unfit, while considerable, was "less than in other units." He concluded that the letter writer had engaged in "gross exaggeration" and that these views, if circulated, "will prove disastrous to the Battalion and detrimental to recruiting." Legere declared the author to be "an enemy to this Unit and I request that his name be made known to me."[80]

Clearly, a few favourable stories in the local Saint John press could not counter the prevailing view among many anglophones about Acadians, French-Canadians, and military service. What is more, as reported by French-language newspapers, there clearly was reticence on the part of some Acadians to enlist, in addition to problems in the organization of the 165th Battalion. However, as both McLean and Legere pointed out in their responses, issues around recruitment, desertion, and fitness were common across the CEF and certainly among the other Maritime units. Ultimately, just 57 per cent of the 165th Battalion volunteers would deploy overseas; it is striking that this proportion was the same among the originals and the latecomers. In other words, there was no apparent qualitative difference between these groups of volunteers. Indeed, Nic Clarke has found considerable continuity in the reasons why CEF volunteers across Canada were declared medically unfit. The most common included substandard eyesight, poor teeth, varicose veins, varicocele, hernias, and heart problems. He points out that most of these conditions would not have been obvious to casual observers or recruiters.[81]

McLean knew that Ottawa would be disappointed that the plans for an Acadian national unit were not coming to fruition. The District Commander, Major-General Benson, advised the Militia Council that

McLean "cannot account for the great falling down in numbers, except on the supposition that the Unit was carrying on its strength a lot of absentees whom they were showing on their returns as on parade. In any case I had not information that the Unit had fallen down so badly in numbers until they arrived on the Dock."[82] We have identified about 550 soldiers from the 165th Battalion who went overseas together in March 1917. However, on the eve of their departure, one newspaper account indicated that after the medical exams held in Saint John, there were still 658 fit men in the ranks.[83] Other factors must have accounted for the additional losses; last-minute desertions were among them.

DESERTION IN THE 165TH BATTALION

The above-mentioned correspondence about the effective strength of the Acadian national unit offers a rare glimpse into desertion, which remains a little-studied and misunderstood aspect of military life during the First World War. Although desertion was a common problem in all CEF units recruiting and training in Canada, officers at the time were naturally reluctant to highlight it, believing rightly that it could reflect badly on their leadership. We just saw an exchange where Major Legere was angered by false accusations that the 165th Battalion had lost more men than it actually had. Desmond Morton connects the abysmally high desertion rate in the 41st Battalion (French-Canadian) with the inexperience and ineptitude of the unit's officer corps.[84] At the same time, publicity about desertion could damage recruiting efforts as well as the reputation of the unit as a whole. It is no coincidence that the French-language newspapers never specifically mentioned desertion in relation to the 165th, although they obliquely referred to certain "points faibles."[85] They might complain that parents refused to allow their sons to enlist in the first place, but there was no public comment about families that welcomed deserters home. English-language newspapers similarly avoided the topic, although we can find a few references to noteworthy escapes and court cases. For example, one unnamed repeat offender from the 165th hid in a lavatory and then jumped from a moving train, eluding the accompanying Dominion Police constable. The news story related that this was his fourth time fleeing custody.[86] As we have seen, the federal government moved quickly to apply pressure on newspaper editors to avoid publishing stories that would reflect unfavourably on the war effort.[87]

Military authorities wanted deserters to be apprehended and punished swiftly as an example to others.[88] However, CEF units training in Canada had few resources to chase them down. The Dominion Police – Canada's first federal police force, which would be merged with the North-West Mounted Police in 1920 to form the Royal Canadian Mounted Police (RCMP) – had been assigned the task of tracking down and arresting deserters and draft evaders, but this proved to be an impossible assignment for such a small and patchwork force.[89] Once a soldier had been gone long enough, a unit board would be convened and the man would be declared "struck off strength." This stroke of the pen excised the soldier from the ranks and denied further pay and benefits, but it also removed him from the historical record. Desertion trends certainly merit our attention as we develop a better understanding of the origins and motivations of CEF volunteers. However, they are very difficult to study. Claude Léger notes that the 132nd Battalion (North Shore) reported 1,998 recruits in the period up to April 1916, which included 550 men ultimately declared unfit for service. However, in the same month, the unit nominal role identified just 1,052 men. What happened to the other 400 men? Official records are silent.[90] Fortunately, for the 165th Battalion, Daigle conserved a unit register of deserters. We can also identify a few other cases from military records and newspapers. In total, we have identified 240 deserters among the roughly 1,200 members of the 165th – including non-francophone recruits.[91]

In addition to the source challenges, as mentioned in the introduction, historians have been reluctant to discuss topics like desertion because they can be considered inappropriate, even disrespectful to our veterans. This shows a lack of discipline in our scholarship and methods, which typically reference desertion only in passing. Richard Holt's study devoted to CEF manpower mentions desertion exactly twice, once with regard to imprisoned deserters being approached to rejoin the CEF, and once with regard to increasing desertion rates when units faced long waits before deploying overseas.[92] Yet desertion influenced operational effectiveness, engaged and troubled military authorities, and was at the heart of the experiences of ordinary soldiers. Some left and others thought about leaving. Glossing over or leaving out discussion of this topic does veterans and today's readers a profound disservice, especially since issues around retention and discipline continue to plague the modern Canadian Armed Forces.[93]

There are exceptions; in recent years a handful of studies have focused on military justice. During the First World War, twenty-five Canadian soldiers were killed not by their adversaries but by their fellow soldiers in firing squads because they had been found guilty of desertion on the battlefield.[94] This was an extreme exercise of justice in the name of deterrence. Recognizing the arbitrary and cruel nature of these sentences, these soldiers received official pardons from the Canadian government in 2001, and their names were added to Parliament Hill's *Book of Remembrance*. During the war, hundreds of other soldiers were court-martialled for desertion and received less severe punishments. Thousands more faced summary justice and minor punishments for being absent without leave from their units.[95] Patrick Bouvier has demonstrated that French-Canadian soldiers were no more or less likely than their anglophone colleagues to desert. He studied battlefield desertion and concluded that courts martial found only sixty-one French-Canadians guilty of this charge over the course of the war.[96] Maxime Dagenais writes that the 22nd Battalion (French-Canadian) did have a higher rate of summary trials and courts martial for a variety of military offences when compared with other CEF battalions at the front. However, he also found that this was due to transitions in leadership and the heavy losses and subsequent reconstitution of the unit during the Battle of the Somme.[97]

Studies of military discipline confront a variety of archival and methodological challenges. A higher number of cases could indicate problems with discipline, or it could indicate greater diligence or better record keeping within the unit being studied. Of course, the study here is not about desertion on the battlefield but rather about those who left military service during the training of new units back in Canada. If we know a little bit about deserters overseas, we know virtually nothing about this phenomenon at home. Thousands of men volunteered for military service, then changed their minds at some point along the way. Yet studies of this phenomenon remain "practically non-existent."[98] What can we say about these men and what motivated them? Jonathan Vance observes that "there were likely as many reasons for deserting as there were for enlisting in the first place and we can't claim to understand why men took the step, because they may not have fully understood themselves."[99]

This section delves into the incomplete documentation and compares the characteristics of the deserters with those of the volunteers who stayed and ultimately went overseas. There were no glaring differences. However, recruits from southeastern New Brunswick who had already moved before the war in search of employment were among those most likely to leave. The results suggest that Acadians were no more prone to desertion than any other group in Canada. Indeed, many CEF units in the Maritime provinces and elsewhere lost an even larger proportion of their recruits in this way. The total desertion rate for the 165th Battalion – 240 deserters from approximately 1,200 total volunteers – was only 1 in 5, or 20 per cent, so somewhat less than the general trend of 25 per cent Morton identified. So to be clear, this section about desertion in the 165th Battalion (Acadian) has nothing to do with criticizing a particular linguistic or ethnic group. Instead, the exceptional documentation that survived from this period permits additional analysis that would be valuable for other CEF units but is not always available to them. Even without a unit register, it would be possible to find out more about deserters elsewhere by studying samples of volunteers via their military records available online at LAC. Deserters are clearly indicated in these files, usually as "struck off strength" shortly after being reported absent.

The 165th Battalion register of deserters covers much of 1916, beginning in March and ending around Christmas. For the early months of 1917, we can identify some additional cases from individual military personnel records. Unsurprisingly, desertion was connected with key events. After arriving at Camp Valcartier, some of the volunteers soon realized that army life was not for them. Sixty-two of the seven hundred originals (nearly 10 per cent of them) quit in July and August 1916. Eight recruits left the unit on 13 July alone. Four of them were from the village of Bouctouche, in Kent County, New Brunswick. Small groups of friends often enlisted together, so it should come as no surprise that they also deserted together. Eventually, police apprehended three of the eight escapees from that day, and they rejoined the unit in late August, apparently without incident or punishment. There were more desertions in November after the unit returned to New Brunswick. Three young men from Acadieville, also in Kent County, had enrolled together and then quit together, leaving on 5 November. Martin and Emile LeBlanc, two brothers from the small community of Saint Bernard in Digby County, Nova Scotia, similarly signed up together and then abandoned the unit on the same day, 7 November. The reasons for these desertions are unclear. Onésime Babineau died of pneumonia on 1 November, and the soldiers may have feared for their own health, given that they lived in

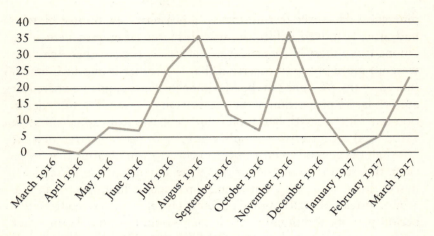

Figure 2.4 Desertions from the 165th Battalion

crowded conditions. At least some soldiers had been disappointed that they had not been sent immediately to Europe after finishing their training at Valcartier.[100] Perhaps the prospect of spending the winter in garrison in Saint John, doing more drill and exercises, was not that appealing. Some may have been yearning to be closer to home.

While seasonal work and temporary absences may not have been unusual for some Acadians, particularly those working in the fishing and forestry sectors, extended time away with no end in sight as well as the dangers of military life may have placed a significant economic and psychological burden on families.[101] Media coverage of the horrific battles in Europe would have weighed heavily on some. Simple pragmatism may explain why some soldiers decided to desert. To give just one example, Willie Daigle of South Tetagouche, Gloucester County, left a wife and at least four children behind when he enlisted in the 165th Battalion. They had always struggled to make ends meet. In 1911, Daigle's family was living with his wife's parents to save money, while Willie worked for meagre earnings in lumber camps. At the time he enlisted in June 1916, Willie was still living apart from his wife and children, working as a general labourer farther north in Restigouche County. The 165th may have amounted to a welcome summer job; he quit in November, probably to head back to the winter lumber camps, where he could earn more money. In 1921, we find him working in a sawmill near Bathurst. He seems, then, to have enlisted for opportunistic reasons, and his doing so fit a broader pattern of seasonal, mobile work. Martha Hanna's study of Manitoba war wives emphasizes that by the winter of 1917, Canadian families were under increasing pressure due to rising prices for food and fuel. At the same time, wages were also increasing, and the Daigles may simply have calculated that they could do better. Relying on extended family for support was also common among Manitoba's war wives.[102]

Not surprisingly, there was a final surge in desertions in the days leading up to 25 March 1917, which was the designated departure date for the ss *Metagama*. Some of these men deliberately or accidently missed the train to Halifax and the unit did not have time to find them. Others appear to have gotten lost along the way. As we saw above, military authorities realized that the 165th Battalion leadership may have failed to declare all their absentees, and some of the men may actually have left much earlier. The large number of desertions in March also relates to the final medical exams, which declared many of the men unfit. The army had created a Special Services Battalion in Halifax to hold on to unfit men for possible future service, but some refused to show after being left behind.[103] This continued the trend we have already observed with volunteers left behind by other units such as the 145th Battalion. Although transferred to the 165th, many of these men simply left. Nic Clarke emphasizes that the psychological, social, and emotional wounds of being rejected for service could be severe and long-lasting. Many such men cut themselves off from society, and a few engaged in self-harm.[104]

The single worst day for desertions in the 165th Battalion merits special attention. This was 21 September 1916, just ten days before the battalion boarded the train to return to Saint John. On that day, eleven anglophone recruits quit the unit together. These men hailed mostly from Saint John and Albert Counties, and it is not surprising that they did not find their place in the Acadian national battalion. We might wonder why they did not simply transfer to another New Brunswick unit. Perhaps Daigle was just as reluctant as other cos to allow transfers, hoping to maintain his numbers. Perhaps these men had been promised transfers if they completed their training, only to discover that they would not be allowed to leave. Other non-French-speaking volunteers were quicker to desert. For example, Laurence Giabbi was an Italian immigrant working in Saint John who enlisted in December 1916 and deserted the following day. In total, nearly 25 per cent of the 240 deserters identified for the 165th were not francophone. Tragically, one of these men, Lorenzo Sawyer, was killed in a confrontation with the Dominion Police.[105]

The rest of this section deals with the remaining 190 deserters. A few men took an instant dislike to military life. Joseph Lefebvre signed up on 9 August 1916 in Meteghan, Digby County, Nova Scotia. He took the train to join the unit at Valcartier, but clearly thought better of it, for he never arrived. He may have discreetly stepped into the crowd in Moncton or at one of the other stops along the way. Onesime Goguen and Jacques Michaud were both twenty-two years old and from the village of Saint-André in Madawaska County. They signed up together in Moncton on 5 April 1916 and left just twenty-eight days later on 3 May. However, the records indicate that these were exceptional cases; most deserters had spent three to six months (28 per cent) or more than six months (52 per cent) with the unit before leaving. Between November 1916 and March 1917, the 165th Battalion recruited 112 new volunteers and lost 78 men to desertion – a net gain of just 34 men. What is more, the newer recruits had little or no previous military experience, while many of the absentees had at least completed the training at Valcartier. Desertion constituted a loss of numbers but also of capability.

The Militia Act of 1904 stated that units should declare soldiers absent without permission after seven days. Government decrees during the war established the penalty for such absences as imprisonment for up to two years. However, very few of the deserters faced consequences for their actions.[106] In the 165th Battalion, the usual procedure was to wait several weeks to see if the individual returned on his own accord before declaring him as absent; perhaps a cursory search would be conducted. The logic here was that many cases involved soldiers heading home on leave and not coming back. With volunteers hailing from the four corners of the Maritime provinces, it could take more than a week to travel and return. Units that recruited from a single town or county probably had more luck tracking down deserters.

Adolphe Gaudet, a student from Yarmouth, Nova Scotia, was initially identified as a deserter but did return, and the register notes that he had simply "overstayed" his leave pass. Military authorities proclaimed a general amnesty in December 1916 for "recruits who for various reasons quit commands" if they came back voluntarily.[107] Twelve men seem to have accepted this offer. However, more than 90 per cent of those struck off strength never came back. An exceptional case was that of Abel Lapointe, who left the unit on 1 September 1916 on sick leave and was declared a deserter three weeks later. He had returned to his parents' home in Saint-Léonard, Madawaska County. A year later, a chance encounter led to his arrest. Brought back by train under guard to Saint John, Lapointe would spend several weeks in jail before facing the courts. His lawyer produced medical certificates and two telegrams sent by Lapointe to Daigle (the CO) explaining his situation. Since he never received a response, the soldier had assumed that he was in the clear. The judge ultimately agreed that he had done his best to contact the unit and that, in any case, he was not fit for duty.

This case is especially interesting for the remarks by several witnesses formerly of the 165th Battalion who were called to testify, for they shed light on how desertion actually occurred. Charles Davidson affirmed that as many as one hundred members of the unit failed to return from leaves permitted while they were training in Valcartier. The unit register records seventy-four such cases for that period. Although the document does not indicate the circumstances of these absences, Davidson's testimony specifies that most absentees had not fled the camp but rather had failed to report back after being granted some time at home. This reminds us of the importance of family support for military service – and, presumably, for desertion.[108] Lapointe's testimony included a statement and baptismal certificate that he had been underage and had not sought his father's permission to enlist, which the court apparently took seriously.[109] Lapointe was not the only volunteer lacking parental approval. Other soldiers may have found that the initial support for their service changed as a result of news about the carnage at the front. We also might wonder whether the increasingly polemical debate around conscription and the anti-French discourse during the provincial election campaign soured local attitudes towards the war.[110] What is clear is that in many cases parents and families welcomed their men home.

Davidson added that to his knowledge, none of these deserters were ever prosecuted. We should not conclude, however, that the men concerned took the decision lightly or that the police ignored the issue. Henri LeBlanc was among those who quit the unit just before it embarked for England in March 1917. He gave himself up to police in Moncton in May 1918 "when he found that they were close on his trail." Although originally from that city, LeBlanc admitted that he had been living in the vicinity of Acadieville since leaving the 165th Battalion "some time ago." He told the court he had lost "30 pounds of flesh in the past few weeks from worry." After pleading guilty to a lesser charge of failing to work, the judge released LeBlanc on his own recognizance, and he eventually paid a fine. This is interesting because at this point conscription was in full swing and we might have expected a harsher penalty. Ultimately, the Dominion Police apprehended just 12 of the 190 Acadian deserters before the unit departed for Europe. These men all agreed to rejoin the unit and thus avoided incarceration.

Among these was Joseph Babineau, a seventeen-year-old from Shediac, New Brunswick. Like many of the volunteers, he lied about his age in order to enlist. Babineau faced a civil court in Saint John, but the magistrate only gave him a "lecture" and a suspended sentence after Captain Leo Richard confirmed that the unit was willing to take him back.[111] The court knew he was underage, but both civil and military authorities seemed willing to avoid enforcing the minimum age requirement. Tim Cook explains that whatever the regulations might state, the army found ways to employ underage youth in reserve units, forestry companies, and other holding places until they were old enough to fight. Richard Holt adds that between August 1915 and January 1917 there were provisions to enlist teenagers as bandsmen. The question of age became particularly difficult once units arrived in England because British military regulations provided that soldiers had to be at least nineteen to go into combat. This left CEF units with numerous eighteen-year-olds (or supposed eighteen-year-olds) short-handed.[112] We will return to the issue of underage soldiers in more detail in the next chapter.

Although many of the deserters simply returned home, at least a few ensured that the Dominion Police would be unable to find them by crossing the border into the United States. Bélonie Beaulieu was one of a small group of volunteers recruited from the Madawaska region during the final recruiting drive in early 1917. He abandoned the 165th Battalion in Saint John on 2 March 1917. Originally from Baker Lake, Beaulieu probably returned home before slipping discreetly into Maine. Border officials recorded a brief return to Edmundston in June 1917, but Beaulieu would later definitively move to Vermont. Alyre Arsenault of Acadieville was one of the larger group that quit the unit after it first moved back to Saint John in November 1916. His record in the 1920 US Census confirms that he immigrated in 1916, and we find him working in a lumber camp in New Hampshire. Willie Frigault similarly crossed in January 1917, and headed to Caribou, Maine, to work with his father. The border was no obstacle to many of these young men; before computers there was no way to have an integrated database of who was on the run. Although Frigault declared his residence as Memramcook when he enlisted, his father lived in Massachusetts. Border officials noted the deserter's American eagle tattoo on his right forearm. These cases clearly demonstrate that family support could be instrumental in helping soldiers escape military life, either initially or by providing a destination and work opportunities.

Things did not work out as well for Edward Bédard, originally from Montreal but living before the war in Moncton. He fled across the border to Massachusetts, then wound up incarcerated at the Gardner State Colony for the Insane. Like many other institutions of this kind, Gardner was an agricultural colony where the inmates worked. Frank Doucet, originally from Rexton, New Brunswick, travelled even farther; the 1921 Canadian Census records him as an inmate at the Essondale Hospital in Chilliwack, British Columbia. These two cases raise an interesting question about whether mental health played a role in discipline and desertion. Those with serious illnesses may have struggled to fit in with military life. Unfortunately, we know very little about mental health in the CEF or in Canadian society generally at this time. We will return to this issue in the final chapter, since military doctors identified a few other Acadian soldiers as suffering from mental illness.

Censuses, border controls, and civil registration archives are far from complete for this period. We often lost track of the former soldiers once they had quit the unit and particularly after they crossed into the United States. Sometimes, though, it is possible to piece together indications of remarkable journeys. Julius Saulnier was born and raised in Saulnierville, Digby County, Nova Scotia. He identified as a twenty-one-year-old farmer when he enlisted at the end of December 1915. He was one of the first Acadians from the Baie Sainte-Marie to sign up for the 165th Battalion. Soon joined by others from the area under the supervision of Émile Stehelin, he completed part of the training at Valcartier, but officers recorded him as deserting on 6 August 1916. In fact, he must have left earlier than this because he crossed the border from Toronto to Detroit on 1 August 1916 by rail. We find him next in San Francisco, where he enlisted in the US Army on 4 December 1917, serving until 15 March 1919. It is unclear why he joined the US Army after quitting the CEF. Saulnier next appears in the historical record in 1945 in Houston, Texas, where he married Althie Mae Howard, who was just sixteen years old (he would have been about fifty years old at this time). They had one daughter, Sylvia Elaine, when Saulnier applied for naturalization as an American citizen in 1949. Saulnier died of an aneurism and arteriosclerosis in a veterans' hospital in Houston in 1961. What made him choose Texas after the war? Where was he between 1919 and 1945? Even when multiple records exist, many questions remain, but Saulnier's exceptional case serves as a reminder that people had options to travel far indeed.

TOWARDS A PROFILE OF DESERTERS

We have identified more than 1,000 Acadian volunteers for the 165th Battalion. Of these, 190 eventually quit the unit. There were deserters among every age group, from every county, and from every professional background. However, when we compare the volunteers who stayed with those who left, several trends are discernible. The next sections refer to "soldiers" and "deserters" as separate groups for comparison purposes, even though, of course, the deserters were also soldiers.

First, we tested for age in order to see if younger or older volunteers were more likely to quit military service. On this point, there was little to differentiate the two subgroups. The average declared age of the soldiers was 22.97 years, while that of the deserters was 23.30. Volunteers sometimes lied about their age, particularly if they were too young or too old according to military regulations. A more accurate profile emerged when declared ages were checked against census records. However, when the average age of the soldiers and deserters was recalculated, there was virtually no difference: the average age was 22.61 for soldiers, 22.64 for deserters.

Next, the cohorts were divided into age groups, and this did reveal some important distinctions. For example, underage soldiers were much more likely to remain with their unit, while those in their mid- to late twenties were much more likely to leave. However, the trend does not continue for older volunteers; those in their thirties were no more or less likely to leave, while those in their forties were much more likely to stay. In general, and perhaps predictably, those who lied about their age because they were too young or too old seemed especially dedicated to sticking it out.

Another possible assumption is that married soldiers would have been more likely to leave due to greater family responsibilities and a stronger desire to return home after an extended absence. Newspaper

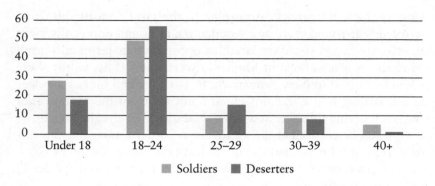

Figure 2.5 Corrected age at enrolment (%) of soldiers and deserters (n=705 and 160)

editorials focused on mothers' perceived unwillingness to let their sons serve, but at least some wives must have been against their husbands going away, even if it did bring a small monthly allowance from the government. Indeed, at the beginning of the war, wives could petition to block their husbands from serving. (By the summer of 1915, they could no longer do so.)[113] Scholars have demonstrated that military pay and separation allowance had fallen behind the cost of living for families by early 1917.[114] At first glance, the results here do not show a strong trend related to marital status; 14 per cent of the soldiers declared that they were married when they enlisted, against 18 per cent of those who ultimately deserted. However, all of the married men who left departed in late 1916 or early 1917, reinforcing Hanna's observation about rising costs.

Further analysis indicates that those who were most mobile were also most likely to desert. Fully one-third of the deserters had already moved at least once to a different county, province, or country prior to enlisting. Only one-quarter of the soldiers fit this description. For example, Maxime Richard had left his family at Mont-Carmel on Prince Edward Island to reside in Moncton, New Brunswick, prior to enlisting at the age of twenty-two. He was one of several deserters who left just before the 165th Battalion departed overseas. Furthermore, Acadian and francophone volunteers born outside the Maritime provinces (including in Maine, Massachusetts, Quebec, and France) were almost twice as likely to desert as other recruits. For example, Maurice McGraw was born in Portland, Maine, but had moved with his entire family to the Losier Settlement in Gloucester

County, New Brunswick. According to the 1911 Census, McGraw worked year-round there as a woodcutter, although upon enlistment the twenty-five-year-old declared his occupation as farming. Joseph Michaud was also born in Maine; however, he left his family there when he moved to New Brunswick. In 1911 we find him as a lodger in a boarding house in Saint-Hilaire, not far from the Madawaska region, working full-time as a general labourer. Five years later, however, when he enlisted at the age of thirty, he had moved again, this time to Saint John. Michaud chose to leave the unit in the fall of 1916; perhaps his contacts in the city made it easier for him to escape detection and leave the area.

The results also show that volunteers from urban centres like Saint John were more likely to desert (38 versus 32 per cent of the remaining soldiers). Of course, what constituted an urban centre was open to interpretation. Volunteers from smaller regional centres like Bathurst, New Brunswick, and Meteghan, Nova Scotia, were actually more likely to stick with the 165th Battalion. What about larger cities? As seen in chapter 1, a significant number of the volunteers had previously moved to Moncton, New Brunswick, in search of work. In the Maritime provinces, Moncton was by far the largest urban centre with a considerable Acadian population. That growing city had emerged as an industrial centre and offered employment opportunities in its railway yards, sugar refineries, and textile mills.[115] That may explain why volunteers residing in Moncton accounted for nearly 30 per cent of the deserters, and only 18 per cent of the remaining soldiers. Gilbert Caissie was a case in point. Born in Saint-Paul, Kent County, he moved to Moncton for work and enlisted when he was nineteen years old. Caissie left the unit in November 1916, while it was in garrison in Saint John. According to the 1921 Census, he was working in that city's shipyard. His healthy annual salary of more than $900 suggests that leaving the army had paid off for him. In a similar vein, Theobald relates that after the 165th was disbanded in 1917 and most of its soldiers were transferred to the Canadian Forestry Corps, some Acadians wondered why they should join the army and cut trees when they could do it for better wages at home.[116]

An analysis of the occupations declared by the volunteers when they enlisted further supports the hypothesis that competing work opportunities influenced desertion. Tradesmen and especially general labourers are overrepresented among the deserters. The term labourer is notoriously vague and could mean anything from helping out

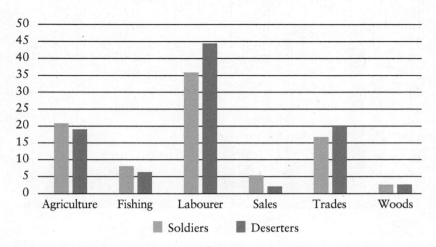

Figure 2.6 Declared occupation (%) at enrolment of soldiers and deserters (n=843 and 189)

around the family farm to wage work in a city, from part-time to full-time, from seasonal to permanent. The trades are not necessarily more specific; someone identifying as a carpenter could be an apprentice or master, build ships, houses, or furniture, do contract work and odd jobs, or be employed in a factory. Fortunately, the 1911 census records say more about wages and employment. For example, the enumerators often recorded a general category such as "labourer" but then added a code to indicate *where* the person was working, such as on a farm, in a mine, or in a lumber camp. However, going back in time reduces the number of volunteers we can study in this way, as many of them were simply too young to declare an occupation in 1911. Others could not be linked to the census because of incomplete information or spelling errors, because they were on the move at the time the census was taken, or because the enumerators simply missed them. All of that said, the census data considerably modify the profiles gleaned from the military attestation papers. Indeed, some trends seem to be reversed, with farmers and fishers more likely to desert and tradespeople more likely to stay. Such results highlight the challenges involved when historical sources are being interpreted. In the span of just five years, two different sources are telling us two different things.

The concept of life course provides a partial answer to this conundrum. People are rarely a single thing throughout their lives. According

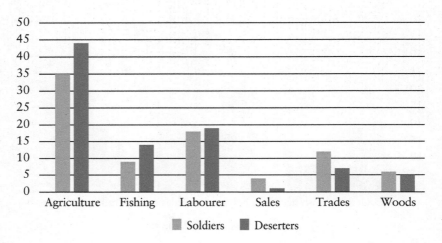

Figure 2.7 Declared occupation (%) 1911 census of soldiers and deserters (n=262 and 59)

to Glen Elder's foundational article "Family History and the Life Course," life course "refers to pathways which individuals follow through age-differentiated roles and events. The timing of an event may be as important for life experience as whether the event occurs at all, and the degree or type of change."[117] For example, marriage can happen once, multiple times, or not at all and at a variety of ages. When and if marriage happens influences other aspects of an individual's life such as employment, where they live, and social obligations. Tamara Harevan explains life course studies as "the reconstruction of a multi-tiered reality – the lives of individual families and their interactions with major social, economic, and political forces ... in short, it represents an effort to understand the interrelationship between individual time, family time, and historical time."[118] Enlistment in the 165th Battalion occurred at different points in the life course for different people, but the majority of the volunteers were young, single men. When we look back at this earlier stage in their life course – the 1911 Canadian Census – most of the volunteers worked on a farm (whether at home or nearby), and many of them were still going to school. Few of the recruits identified a trade, and comparably more identified that they were working in the fishing or lumber sectors, often as part-time or seasonal workers. This is entirely typical of adolescents and young adults in the Maritime provinces during this period.

The pull of cities and wage work is clearly visible in the occupations the men were beginning to declare by 1916. Some of the volunteers had learned trades, and others had moved from agricultural work to manufacturing or service jobs. The individual stories of three teamsters from Moncton have common threads but also demonstrate the range of family situations. Thus, Iréné LeBlanc moved to Moncton from his family farm in Cormier Village. He enlisted at twenty-one, and after leaving the unit he married Maria and settled just outside the city at Fox Creek. He continued in the teamster trade, reporting a robust annual salary of $800 but also that he had been out of work for twenty weeks when the census was taken in 1921. George Caissie was born on Prince Edward Island but his family moved to Rogersville, New Brunswick. The second oldest of twelve children, George and two of his brothers were helping on their father's farm in 1911. By 1916, we find George working in Moncton and married to Elizabeth. He enlisted in May but returned home two months later while the unit was in Valcartier. After the war, George moved back to Rogersville to be with his extended family. Meanwhile, Edward Goguen travelled even more. Born in Cocagne in 1885, he moved to Prince Edward Island, where he married Adeline ("Addie"), who in 1905 gave birth to their daughter, Dorothy. Edward was among the first Acadians to enlist in the 165th Battalion in December 1915. A closer look at his military personnel file indicates that he had previously enlisted in the 145th Battalion and deserted. He left the 165th in September 1916 only to enlist again in April 1918. It seems that for Goguen, the army was a stopgap for those times when he needed income. On both occasions of re-enlistment, he concealed his previous service. He continued to struggle to find work after the war. We find him in 1921 living with his brother in Saint John, still pursuing the teamster trade but out of work for several weeks due to illness. His family stayed in Moncton. We will pick up the analysis of economic outcomes after the war in the final chapter.

These accounts of LeBlanc, Caissie, and Goguen demonstrate that volunteers could be both farmers in 1911 and urban tradesmen in 1916. They were in their twenties when they enlisted and had already gained some experience on the job market and with moving around. Working for the army fit into a broader pattern of migration. Perhaps they never intended to go overseas when they signed up, or perhaps they changed their minds during the long wait up to March 1917, when the 165th Battalion finally left for England. Life course also suggests reasons why those who declared an occupation in the agricultural and fishing sectors proved more likely to stay with the 165th. The tradesmen who left the unit were on average four years older (24.82) than the agricultural workers who stayed (20.86 years). For late adolescents and early adults, four years was a very considerable amount of time during which they would be working, establishing themselves away from the parental home, and possibly getting married. For the volunteers who enlisted directly from family farms, the army was probably their first full-time, waged employment. Travelling with the unit to Valcartier and Saint John may have also been their first experience living permanently away from home. It makes sense that these men would have been less comfortable leaving the battalion, as well as less tempted by job opportunities with which they were less familiar.

These findings nuance the consensus, already discussed in the historiography, that people in the countryside were less likely to enlist. In his social and demographic study of the soldiers of the 22nd Battalion (Canadien-Français), Jean-Philippe Gagnon found that only 5.3 per cent of the French-Canadian volunteers declared an agricultural occupation. Urban wageworkers, especially general labourers, were the largest group in the ranks. Gagnon concludes that unemployment and job insecurity among those lacking trades training or other professional qualifications played a major role in the decision to enlist.[119] In his official history of the CEF, Nicholson wrote that "although fear of being unemployed was, of course, far from being the only motive which impelled men to answer the call to arms in very large numbers, it must be considered a not unimportant factor." He went on to explain that employment prospects and wages had improved considerably by the end of 1915 – exactly when the Acadian national unit began recruiting – which "inevitably" created competing demands for "Canada's manpower."[120] For their part, Brown and Loveridge identified that "a concentration on urban recruiting" in the Maritime provinces accounted for some of the gaps in voluntary recruiting.[121] Jonathan Vance takes this one step further, noting that official statistics tell us where soldiers enlisted but not where they were from. The question of residence could be particularly thorny. He asks, "Have we assumed that most [CEF volunteers] were from the cities because most of them enlisted in the cities?"[122]

Regarding the 165th Battalion, the majority of the volunteers lived in rural areas (62 per cent) when they enlisted, and nearly all of them had been born in the countryside (82 per cent). Following Vance, we might wonder how many of those declaring an urban residence had been there long. Of the eleven recruits who declared their residence as Amherst, Nova Scotia, none of them had been born there and nine had been born in rural parishes. Just three were already living in Amherst in 1911. The largest group of urban residents among the volunteers was, of course, the 202 men living in Moncton. However, just 40 of the volunteers had been born there, and of the remainder, only a handful of the older men were already in the city by 1911. So can we really say that these recruits had urban backgrounds? Official statistics looking only at declared residence at enlistment do not provide the full picture.

This analysis of desertion has revealed several clear trends. People who resided in larger urban areas like Moncton, who declared a trade when enlisting, or who had an agricultural occupation according to the 1911 Census, or who were in their late twenties, were more likely to desert. Life course and mobility thus emerge as significant factors, but a more basic analysis of regional origins provides some of the strongest results yet.

As already noted, volunteers from outside the Maritime provinces were more likely to leave the 165th Battalion, perhaps because they did not fit easily into the Acadian culture, or because it was more difficult for them to be farther from home. Recruits born or residing in southeastern New Brunswick were the most numerous in the unit, but also the most likely to desert, and this by a considerable margin. Those born in Kent County and other parts of Westmorland County, particularly those who had previously moved to Moncton, formed the largest group of deserters. One interesting result is that volunteers residing in Madawaska County were very unlikely to desert, but men born there who had already moved somewhere else were among the most likely to do so. This group included several Acadians who had been working in Maine or Massachusetts or had family there when they enlisted. Volunteers from Gloucester County, notably from towns like Bathurst and Caraquet, were much less likely to desert. Perhaps local competition with the 132nd Battalion (North Shore) meant that those who chose the 165th were particularly dedicated to the Acadian national cause. This might also explain why desertion rates were much lower for the smaller contingents of Acadian volunteers from Nova Scotia and Prince Edward Island. Recruiters had already come through those areas for other local units, which means they had actively chosen the 165th Battalion. Another factor in all of these cases could have

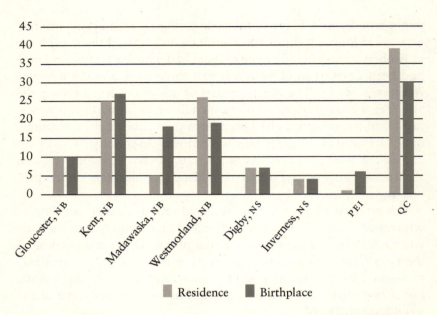

Figure 2.8 Desertion rate (%) by residence and birthplace for select regions

been group dynamics. Friends and family from smaller places like Tracadie, Saulnierville, and Chéticamp could support one another. Also, prominent community members during the initial, local phases of training, like Émile Stehelin in Meteghan, may have helped build cohesion and resilience in their contingents. The 165th may have been led by notable men from southeastern New Brunswick, but the most reliable volunteers came from other parts of Acadie.

Another strong factor in desertion rates turns out to have been socio-economic status. The creation of an Acadian battalion was an important initiative within a larger national movement seeking recognition and respect. Local elites, particularly in southeastern New Brunswick, stepped up to support the cause. So it should not be surprising that of the seventy volunteers who declared a white-collar or commerce-related occupation when they enlisted, only four deserted. One of these was Joseph Lirette, a firefighter from Sackville who had already been discharged once for being underage before joining the 165th Battalion in February 1916. Lirette also had medical problems, and this may explain his unsanctioned absence in the summer of that year. Released as medically unfit, Lirette enlisted for a third time in 1918, only to be hospitalized with the mumps. Now twenty years old, Lirette did eventually reach the front with the 44th Battalion. In general, these prominent members of the community would have faced additional scrutiny of their military service, and furthermore, they would have experienced more difficulty evading capture. When Eugène Roy, a clerk working in Shediac before enlisting, decided to leave the unit, he and his entire family fled to Massachusetts. The 1911 Canadian Census contains additional information related to socio-economic status. About one-quarter of the deserters were illiterate compared to just 15 per cent of the soldiers who remained. In addition, more of the volunteers reporting higher salaries in 1911 (at least $400), ended up staying. The military salary of $1.10 per day, which remained stagnant even as wages rose during the war years, would not have been the primary incentive for these individuals. These results suggest that Morton's idealists may not have been more numerous among the volunteers for the 165th, but they were much more likely to stay.

TOWARDS AN ACADIAN ENLISTMENT RATE

Before continuing our study of the 165th Battalion volunteers with their departure overseas, it is worth looking more broadly at how recruitment for the Acadian national unit was part of a larger Acadian and French-Canadian contribution to the First World War. As discussed in the introduction, there has been considerable debate about this topic for Quebec, and scholars have used various methods to calculate enlistment rates.

First, some demographics. The total population of New Brunswick, Nova Scotia, and Prince Edward Island recorded in the 1911 Canadian Census was 937,935. The population identified as of French origin was 98,975, or just over 10 per cent. In his official history of the Great War, Colonel Duguid calculated the number of males eligible for military service in 1914 (that is, between eighteen and forty-five years of age) and the number of recruits throughout the war for each province in order to determine a general voluntary enlistment rate. For the three Maritime provinces, this provided a total of 208,578 men who would have been eligible for military service. Duguid identified 66,480 volunteers from this region, giving an enlistment rate of 31.9 per cent. This compares favourably with the Canadian national rate of 31.5 per cent.[123] Sharpe offered a revised analysis using a more thorough year-over-year calculation of the eligible male population. He determined a similar Canadian voluntary enlistment rate (31.4 per cent), but his results for the Maritime provinces were not quite as high, at 27 per cent. Sharpe's analysis confirmed the long-standing consensus that recent British immigrants – especially settlers in western Canada and Ontario – fuelled the CEF. Since the Maritimes had the highest Canadian-born population in the Dominion, it is not surprising that their enlistment results were a little lower.[124]

In his study of the 22nd Battalion, Joseph Chaballe suggested that many French-Canadian volunteers were missed because they were distributed among anglophone units in Quebec and elsewhere, including kilted units. However, he had no way to find them with the sources available in 1952.[125] To test this notion, Jean Martin employed a sampling technique using family names beginning with the letter B and compiling data from attestation papers and war graves. This netted an estimate of 7,157 francophone recruits in the Maritime provinces, although he had no way to differentiate between volunteers and conscripts. Our research results expose some of the flaws in this method. For example, Martin calculated a total of just 249 Acadians from Prince Edward Island, but nominal roles indicate that at least 500 of them had enlisted voluntarily in the 55th, 105th and 165th Battalions by the end of 1916. At the same time, however, Martin's numbers seem a little inflated for New Brunswick. His figure of 7,157 might be considered the upper limit of the range. The lower limit of that range counts only men specifically identified by the official record or in our database. This provides about 3,000 men, pulled nearly exclusively from the 165th, 132nd, and 105th Battalions as well as our small sample from the 26th. This number is certainly too low; there were many more in the 26th Battalion, and our separate sample of 100 Acadians recruited in 1914–15 involved twenty different units from across the Maritime provinces.

It is difficult to zero in on an exact figure between these two limits, as this would require detailed work with military and census records across multiple units. However, Major Legere's assertion in December 1917 that there were more than 6,000 Acadian volunteers seems quite feasible, and he would have been well placed to know, given his extensive correspondence and senior position working with regional recruiters. There would have been few additional volunteers in 1918; Acadians joining in that year were likely conscripts. We can also derive an estimate using CEF casualty rates. Nicholson's official history of the CEF established a general mortality rate of 9.3 per cent attributable to military service (including killed in action, by disease, and in accidents).[126] Using the records of the Commonwealth War Graves Commission, Ronald Cormier has identified 417 Acadians buried overseas. Applying the general CEF mortality rate provides an estimate of 4,500 soldiers of Acadian descent CEF-wide. Cormier's figures are incomplete, based again on common Acadian family names and so leaving out others. Meanwhile, Landry and Lang suggest a minimum of 4,200 volunteers, but that is solely from New Brunswick; they had insufficient information to evaluate the contributions from Nova Scotia and Prince Edward Island.[127]

Folding together all of these approaches, we can state with confidence that at least 5,000 Acadians in the Maritime provinces volunteered during the First World War. Following the census ratio and the work of Duguid and Sharpe, the eligible male Acadian population in 1914 was about 22,000 (10.5 per cent of the total Maritime eligible population). This gives us a minimum voluntary enlistment rate of 23 per cent, not far from Sharpe's calculation of 27 per cent for the Maritime provinces as a whole. If there was a gap between francophone and anglophone enlistment in this region, it was not very wide. Acadians volunteered at a similar rate as their anglophone brethren, despite the institutional barriers against French in the army and the limited efforts to recruit in their communities. Indeed, their rate exceeded that of some anglophone rural counties.[128] Ultimately, it should come as no surprise that there were regional differences in national trends and that Acadian voluntarism differed from that of French-Canadians in Quebec and other parts of the Dominion.

Adding this minimum to the tally pushes the total French-Canadian contribution to the CEF from 35,000 to at least 40,000, an increase of about 15 per cent. Ideally, this book will encourage ongoing and new research into French-Canadian minorities in other parts of Canada.[129] Martin may have been too enthusiastic with his proposed figure of 70,000 or more, but he was certainly right that 35,000 was too low.

Does it matter that the true French-Canadian contribution to the CEF was higher than believed at that time or since? After all, we still end up with a gap in voluntary enlistment rates nationally, albeit one much smaller than assumed and better explained by demographic and economic factors. I believe it does matter that we update the historiographical consensus, because so much of what has followed, from the initial justifications for conscription – that ultimate arbitrary exercise of state power – to the bitter nationalist feuds that have divided Canadians throughout the twentieth century, has been built on faulty or exaggerated premises. We are conducting a posthumous fact check of the anti-French polemical discourse. When they repeat older figures and assumptions without reflection – or ignore French-Canadian participation entirely – scholars perpetuate deeply ingrained popular beliefs mobilized against minority communities that continue to have consequences today. There are important reminders here about how beliefs and false information can be used to serve political ends (or to sell newspapers), how petty hatreds can justify violations of freedom, and how historians have to be more careful about simply reproducing conventional "wisdom" and accepting too easily what they find in official discourse and easily accessible archives. The historiography of Canada's First World War might change for the better if we simply jettisoned some of these tired old debates, making space for more meaningful questions that would resonate more with contemporary issues – to give just a few examples, issues such as diversity and inclusion, support to soldiers and their families, the use and misuse of information, the training and development of leaders, and the relationship between military and civil societies at home and abroad.

CONCLUSION

There is no denying that the 165th Battalion (Acadian) fell short of its recruiting target. After some initial success and a spirited campaign supported by local notables and clergy, volunteers proved hard to come by for several reasons. Undoubtedly, those most interested in military service had already signed up by 1916, which left the officers with the difficult task of convincing the rest to enlist, particularly as inflation and better job opportunities at home made army pay less attractive. Indeed, throughout Canada, recruiting had become increasingly difficult by the end of 1916. Furthermore, competition with other local units such as the 132nd Battalion (North Shore) divided what was left of the willing. While newspaper editorialists were quick to blame military authorities for reneging on their promise to support transfers from other units into the 165th, it is not at all clear that Acadians serving in other units wanted this. Most of the soldiers who did make the transfer turned out to be ill, injured, or missing – men left behind by units like the 145th Battalion (New Brunswick). Medical exams eliminated some of the unfit and underage soldiers in the unit, while others chose to leave. Ultimately, only about half of a complete battalion sailed on the ss *Metagama*.

How we frame these results is important. With more than 1,200 volunteers, including around 1,050 Acadians, the 165th Battalion had done well compared to many other new Maritime and special identity units raised during 1916. The unit completed training at Valcartier without major incident. With a few notable exceptions, the 165th maintained good discipline and connected with notables and officials while in Saint John. Social events and leaves offered soldiers a break, and the printing of a photograph album and the concerts put on by the band encouraged pride and bolstered morale. Meanwhile, senior military officers commended the progress in training and the improvement in specific skills such as trench building, machine gunning, and bomb throwing. While desertion was certainly a problem, it seems to have been less prevalent than in many other units. In the end, the soldiers being sent overseas were at least as prepared as any other members of the CEF. The 165th achieved the goal established by the Acadian elites who met in late 1915 – its soldiers gained local and even national recognition for their distinct identity. Prime Minister Robert Borden spoke positively about their contribution and was quick to act when correspondence addressed to him suggested there were problems. Indeed, the District Commander in Halifax and the New Brunswick brigade commander were well aware of the political will for this project to succeed. In the end, the challenges that undermined the 165th and caused it to fall short of its goal were common to all CEF units created around this time.

Most regimental histories quickly pass over this period of training and garrison duty in Canada in order to get to the fighting overseas. However, from a social history perspective, this time at Camp Valcartier and in Saint John is essential if we are to understand the volunteers and the unit as a whole. This chapter has variously examined the addition and integration of "latecomers" to the group of originals; desertions, especially by men from certain regions and age groups; and interactions with the local civilian population. One striking finding relates to the ways that the Acadian newspapers championed the unit at first, but eventually disengaged, even as the anglophone press became excited about the exotic French unit in their midst. What happened during these months would profoundly shape how these Acadian soldiers perceived military service. The demographic findings related to life course and mobility are likely relevant

Figure 2.9 The 165th Battalion on parade in Valcartier, 1916

to many other CEF units, even as they provide a particular snapshot of Acadian society, especially in New Brunswick. In the next chapter, we pursue this analysis for those who did head overseas, delving further into the linked records from military archives and censuses and offering comparisons between the Acadian soldiers of the 165th Battalion and other CEF members.

3

Heading Overseas

March–June 1917

By March 1917, the soldiers of the 165th Battalion knew their departure for England was imminent. LCol Daigle and the other officers proceeded with final preparations. Among other things, Daigle arranged permission from Bishop LeBlanc to send a circular letter to Acadian parishes in his diocese soliciting donations to the regimental fund. The listed expenses included those for printing and stationery, telegram and phone services, postage stamps, desks, and even a barber chair.[1] The city of Saint John rose to the occasion as well. The municipal women's council organized a sock drive and presented 750 pairs to the soldiers, and the merchants of the city contributed $600 – nearly $12,000 in today's dollars.[2] On 24 March, a parade by the departing 165th and 198th Battalions attracted "more attention than usual."[3] One journalist observed: "Canadians to the core, but with the quickening of that firey [sic] blood of their fathers, which once dominated their veins, the boys of the 165th made a splendid showing, in heavy marching order, moving along sprightly and soldierly in the gathering twilight of the spring evening."[4] It is worth noting that the 198th Battalion (Canadian Buffs), recruited in Toronto and associated with the prestigious Queen's Own Rifles, had also failed to reach full strength.[5]

The Acadian community in Moncton, especially those who had lobbied hardest for their own national unit, organized a welcome and send-off for the 165th Battalion when the train stopped in their city. Newspaper coverage emphasized the presence there of the Société nationale de l'Acadie, the Société mutuelle de l'Assomption, and the Knights of Columbus, in addition to providing a complete list of the unit officers going overseas – all of them scions of prominent local families. Military authorities had not made it easy for the soldiers' families to see them off. The train made only a brief stop, late on Saturday night, before continuing to Halifax. One journalist described the gathering, which was impressive despite the rain and which included family members from across the Acadian parishes of New Brunswick, as well as military music played by several bands.[6] François DeGrâce would recount in a letter home that they arrived in Moncton at 2 a.m. He was grateful for the socks and boots brought by family members.[7] Although the media coverage took up the familiar refrain of honour for "l'Acadie toute entière," there were also signs of disappointment and even disengagement. The same journalist remarked that the latest medical exams had been "very severe" and noted that a planned ceremony presenting the unit with its colours (that is, its unit flag) never materialized. A final assembly in early March seems to have been no more successful than the one held the previous December in rallying supporters.[8] After such a long wait, the departure of the under-strength 165th Battalion was hurried and left little time for celebration. Jaddus Lanteigne of Caraquet, one of the embarking soldiers, wrote that this was also a sad occasion – "there were mothers with sons in the regiment, kissing them for the last time and weeping profusely."[9]

This chapter will first consider what happened to those left behind when the 165th Battalion left Saint John in March 1917. We will then describe the unit's voyage to and arrival in England, using accounts written by the soldiers themselves. Letters home and private notebooks offer a series of glimpses into the thoughts and feelings of the Acadian volunteers. From there, we will compare the profile of this overseas contingent of the 165th with that of the 22nd Battalion (French-Canadian) as well as smaller samples of Acadian soldiers serving in other Maritime units such as the 26th Battalion (New Brunswick). Using information about next of kin and the separation allowance, as well as the records from the 1911 Canadian Census, we will partly reconstitute the family backgrounds of the Acadian soldiers and consider how their absence would have affected the household economy. The chapter will conclude with an account of the disbandment of the 165th and the transfer of most of its members to the Canadian Forestry Corps (CFC).

LEFT BEHIND

Most unit histories pay little attention to the volunteers who did *not* depart as planned with their comrades. There were several reasons why not everyone boarded the *ss Metagama* in Halifax. Of the 1,038 Acadian volunteers, nearly 200 had deserted, including some who did not turn up for the final roll call when the transport ship was ready to sail. That leaves about 300 volunteers who had been rejected. The unit officers had already released more than 100 of them for being under (or over) the age for military service or for having some kind of infirmity. This still left nearly 200 men with an uncertain future. Even before the departure of the 165th Battalion, newspapers announced that Major Stehelin, who was too old to fight in the trenches, would be responsible for the "rear guard." This was only a temporary situation; they also shared that Stehelin would be commanding a new forestry company, which would be recruited in Nova Scotia – presumably among Acadians in Digby County. The CFC had more relaxed requirements for service, including allowing men up to age 48.[10] For now, the 200 men left behind would be transferred to a Special Services unit. As one journalist explained, "in the early days of the war, men turned down as physically unfit were immediately given their discharge, but since that time manpower has become a more valuable asset to the nation than ever before."[11] Indeed, the Special Service units, created in July 1916, were meant to employ "invalidated" men and new recruits "who have some slight physical defect or disability." In practice, this included obviously underage recruits who could not yet be sent overseas. The idea was that these men and adolescents could replace soldiers doing guard duty or clerical work in Canada. Minimum standards were relaxed, allowing for shorter and less robust men, those with impaired vision, flat feet, and even amputations in the case of wounded soldiers returning from the front.[12]

The rules for the new company created in Saint John were not relaxed entirely. Several of the men left behind would ultimately be discharged, a few as soon as the end of April, others by October 1917. Some joined Stehelin in the Nova Scotia Forestry Battalion or transferred to a New Brunswick "depot" unit awaiting home duties. Richard Holt writes that territorial depot units were created in August 1917 in order to more efficiently manage reinforcements for the front by organizing smaller drafts of men.[13] Indeed, about forty of the men of the 165th Battalion left behind eventually made it overseas. A few of them had left and then re-enlisted somewhere else.

Some of the men left behind preferred to be discharged as soon as possible. We considered this issue in the previous chapter, when a member of the 165th Battalion wrote to Prime Minister Borden asking why the men declared unfit at Valcartier could not be released to go home. For the second time in a year, the treatment of unfit men from the 165th created political embarrassment in Ottawa. The *Saint John Standard* published a report in May 1917 about the Special Service Company based in Saint John. William Pugsley, a former cabinet minister with the Laurier government and now sitting in opposition, raised the issue on the floor of the House of Commons on 25 May 1917. He "drew the attention of the Minister of Militia" to the fact that "the men of the 165th had not received any pay since last March and had also not been supplied with underclothing ... their condition is such as actually to excite pity." Edward Kemp, the minister concerned since replacing Sam Hughes, declared that he was unaware of the situation and asked for a copy of the newspaper. The government's support to soldiers during wartime was a sensitive issue to raise. The editors of the same newspaper printed a front-page note explaining that they did not believe Ottawa was at fault and that local officers had remedied the problem quickly once informed. Meanwhile, though, Kemp wanted answers.[14]

A senior officer from the Militia Department arrived three days later to inspect the company.[15] A Board of Officers found "that thirty-seven of the men attached to Detachment 'A' 62nd Regiment, awaiting disposition, were found to be covered with vermin and without sufficient clothing to permit them keeping themselves clean." They recommended that new clothes issued to the men be charged to public expense, and that the old clothing "be destroyed immediately to prevent the Barracks from being contaminated."[16] A second inquiry looked into the rest of the clothing and equipment issued to these men; it found that most of the articles concerned were "no longer fit for wear" and that the men did not have the opportunity to procure other clothing from home. Lacking other items to give them, he permitted them to retain the clothing and instructed them to destroy it two weeks after discharge. This raised the ire of the Quartermaster General, who wrote a sharp letter stating that "it should be well known to this Officer that it is totally against Regulations for discharged men to take away Public Clothing."[17] In general, these investigations reveal that the military establishment did not treat the Acadian volunteers left behind very well. For all of the talk of the need for labour, these men lacked supervision, had stopped receiving pay, and were languishing in a miserable state. A lack of leadership allowed a difficult situation to become unhealthy. How many other Canadians pronounced unfit for overseas duty languished and suffered humiliation in similar situations?

ON BOARD THE SS METAGAMA

The departure of the 165th Battalion overseas created renewed media interest in Acadian military service. The editors of *Le Moniteur acadien* wrote: "We will follow closely their progress in this career full of danger and ordeals that they have so nobly and courageously embraced."[18] Certainly, the families were anxious to have news of their loved ones. The voyage was a particular cause for concern since there would be no mail from the men for several weeks. We get a sense of these families' anxiety in a short article advising that the men had safely arrived in England. The writer noted that "all kinds of more or less alarming rumours have circulated concerning the voyage of the Acadian battalion: happily, these rumours [are] without foundation."[19]

The departure was a profound moment for many of the soldiers, judging by what they wrote about it. While most of their private thoughts throughout their military service are lost to us, letters written home, several published by newspapers, provide detailed accounts of the voyage. They summon to us the individual perspectives and motivations behind the sense of collective purpose that had led to the creation of an Acadian national unit. François DeGrâce wrote: "It is not without a certain regret that I must distance myself from Canada's coasts. It is hard to leave one's parents, one's friends: to leave everything in order to go to a foreign country, but it must be done and what a great trip I will undertake. Life in the trenches does not frighten me at all."[20] Iréné Gallant was more prosaic; he advised his parents that he enjoyed seeing the port of Halifax but as soon as they left sight of land, he became seasick.[21] Jaddus Lanteigne expanded on the feelings of sadness and uncertainty, writing with uncharacteristic emotion: "Goodbye dear parents, goodbye dear friends and beautiful Canada, will I see you again? I certainly hope so. But if God calls me to die on the battlefield, I will die content, because it will be to defend that which is most dear to me, my homeland."[22] References to religion appeared frequently in soldiers' letters. The chaplain of the 165th, Captain Jean V. Gaudet, noted in his diary that before leaving Halifax, the officers addressed the entire battalion and he conducted Mass. The choice of hymns, starting with the official Acadian national anthem of "Ave Maris Stella," reflected the patriotic tone of the assembly.[23]

The volunteers described a difficult and at times stressful transatlantic voyage. François DeGrâce hailed from Shippagan, New Brunswick. The son of a woodcutter and the third of four sons in a large family, François appears to have been well educated judging by the clarity of his prose. He had worked as a clerk before the war, and unit officers selected him for promotion to sergeant soon after he enlisted. In his letters, he offered unique insights from the vantage point of an NCO. He described being bunked in first-class quarters with the other sergeants and their duties with regard to maintaining the schedule and sentry lists. He explained that they took the latter task more seriously than in camp or barracks due to the dangers of the voyage. Each day began at 0600 with *le réveil* – a trumpet blast – followed by ablutions and breakfast. Physical drill followed in mid-morning; DeGrâce ironically described the exercises as "physical tortures." Lunch break was followed by more calisthenics – the cramped space on the ship did not lend itself to other kinds of military training. Supper typically lasted from 1700 to 1830, and forced rest for the soldiers began at 2100.

There was clearly some scope for entertainment and downtime. DeGrâce describes a boxing match observed by about two hundred soldiers that tragically resulted in the death of a soldier from the 198th Battalion, who fell from a railing trying to get a better view. This accident, which occurred before the ship even left Halifax, likely led to stronger efforts to organize activities for the soldiers during off-hours, just as we saw while they were in garrison in Saint John. For example, concerts and plays were organized in the dining hall; the latter featured some of the ship's employees as actors. The NCO also indicated that he stayed current on world events thanks to the wireless telegraph on board; all of the first-class passengers received a daily printout. DeGrâce frequently mentioned religious devotions as part of his daily routine. These included prayers and attendance at Mass but also confession with the unit chaplain. The sergeant explained that it was difficult to observe Lent: "We will observe our Lent when we are in the trenches." He related that they still had an open-air service on board the ship, which included hymns and the reciting of prayers with crucifixes in hand. Finishing with "Ave Marie Stella," the soldiers thanked the Holy Virgin for her protection during the voyage. The danger was real; DeGrâce described the vigilance against submarines, the arrival of their destroyer escort as they approached their destination, and the death of one soldier on another transport that struck a mine.[24]

Jean Iréné Gallant of Saint-Chrysostome, Prince Edward Island, offered a different point of view in his letter home. From it, we get a good sense of his misery and feelings of isolation. At first, he was excited to write home about his trip on "le sérieux gros bateau." However, he quickly struck a sombre note as he recounted the death of the soldier watching "the sailors at play." He spent the next several days seasick and worried about the threat posed by German submarines. By the fourth day at sea he was praying for England, and the next day he was too sick to write anything at all. By the end of the week, Gallant could relate that his seasickness had improved, but now he was suffering from a serious cold. The rations were less than inspiring – just a little bully beef at supper – and the soldiers were growing considerably more anxious as they approached land. Gallant recounted that lifeboats were always nearby and ready in case of a submarine attack. The SS *Metagama* picked up speed as they traversed "the worst of the War zone" and met up with their torpedo-boat escort. He seemed fascinated by these small but fast vessels, describing them as moving like "real fish." He expressed genuine relief at being able to set his feet on land and have a good supper, and closed with an appeal for prayers to give him strength and courage.[25]

We are left with the sense that Gallant was not feeling very confident as he began the next part of his military service. Not surprisingly, there were diverse points of view about the voyage and the impending service overseas. For example, Jaddus Lanteigne tried to give his friend Edmond a sense of the soldiers' experiences. He wrote about smoking on deck, the initial days when almost everyone was seasick, how the transport veered off course due to high winds, the anxiety concerning encounters with other ships at sea, the feel of a silver English pound received upon arrival, and being whisked off in a convoy from Liverpool.[26]

Personal diaries often provide unique insights because they were not written as letters home and did not have to pass military censorship. Unfortunately, few of these exceptional records have been conserved in archives. One belonged to the chaplain Gaudet, who sometimes found the experience of military service and providing spiritual support overwhelming. He described the press and confusion of the crowd as well as the grief of families saying goodbye when the train carrying the soldiers had stopped in Moncton on the way to Halifax. He noted that he spent the following day in his cabin late into the night listening to confession for forty-nine individuals. He related being summoned to the scene when the soldier of the 198th Battalion fell onto the deck. He found the soldier, Kerr, with a fractured skull and "lying in his own blood." He gave him absolution before he died and then returned to his cabin to hear more confessions. The following day he noted simply that his sleep had been agitated; the following night he succumbed to seasickness. Gaudet also recorded the sudden death of a sailor, thrown against an iron railing by a strong wave during a storm (an incident, it seems, that the soldiers did not mention in their letters home). The crew commended the man's body to the sea just an hour after the incident. Not everything was hardship; the priest enjoyed the camaraderie among the officers and was fascinated by the account of one man who had been part of Ernest Shackleton's expedition to Antarctica. He also described the music and competitions organized for the soldiers, which included a tug-of-war tournament. Gaudet shared in the soldiers' good humour when they arrived at Liverpool, and expressed gratitude for the "ideal" weather on Easter morning when he delivered a bilingual Mass for eight hundred Catholics and had the opportunity to meet with the more experienced chaplain of the 22nd Battalion.[27]

A small notebook belonging to Ferdinand Malenfant, the son of Jean Malenfant, a senior unit officer and a prominent member of the Acadian elite, provides remarkable details. Joining up was clearly a family decision, since his father and younger brother Robert also enlisted with the 165th Battalion in March 1916. Ferdinand was twenty-two years old and had been working in Moncton as a machinist. He had previously spent two years in the band of the 74th Regiment, a militia unit headquartered in Sussex, New Brunswick. His family status and previous military service undoubtedly contributed to his selection for promotion to sergeant. Ferdinand was unusual among his peers in that he was already married and had two young children. This, and the fact that his father was a unit officer, may have set him apart from other soldiers. For example, his entry for 2 April 1917 related that "the boys are all in the smoking room playing cards and I am here all alone writing this letter story and thinking of my dear little Wife and Baby." The next day, he wrote that while "all the boys are in good spirit ... talk about a lonesome trip and long it seems to me a year I been on this boat." Interestingly, he chose to write in English; some of the soldiers explained to their families that they wrote their letters in English because the military censors could not understand French, but this would not have been a factor for this notebook. As a musician, he was different from the other soldiers in another way: he regularly played for the officers at supper and, no doubt, received extra money and food in return. Still, he undoubtedly shared in the sense of adventure felt by many of the youthful volunteers. He was excited about seeing a shark jumping out of the water – "it was a sight to see it was about 7 feet long" – and impressed by the accompanying armed merchant cruiser HMS *Calgarian*: "She is certainly some boat she rated at 25 knots an hour and has 20 guns on her."[28]

Almost all the soldiers emphasized the threat posed by German U-boats and airplanes. This was their first taste of the adversary and of the danger of being in a theatre of war. A mine strike on the SS *Lapland* was a stark reminder that these dangers were real. Gaudet related that while travelling by train from Liverpool to the military camp at Shoreham-by-Sea, officials briefed everyone about the importance of not discussing military events in public and reminded them that letters would be censored. At dusk, black curtains covered the car windows because the lights from the train might attract airplanes and even zeppelins.[29] Some of the men picked up on other signs of the war. Félicien (Félix) Landry was one of the last volunteers for the 165th Battalion, joining up in February 1917 soon after turning eighteen. The son of a farmer, he noticed right away that times were tough in the English countryside: "All the young men from here have left for the war: only the elderly and girls are left to work the fields and it inspires pity to see them."

Landry also shared that he had met up with Camille DeGrâce, an Acadian soldier on leave in England after being wounded twice at the front. Far from discouraged by this encounter, Landry was excited to learn from Camille about life in the trenches and noted that "he is very big and tall and makes a good soldier."[30] A little more research reveals that DeGrâce was among the first Acadian volunteers for the CEF, joining the artillery in December 1914. He served with the 12th Brigade, Canadian Field Artillery, in France at the Battle of Ancre Heights in the fall of 1916. This was part of the larger and very costly British offensive at the Somme. After more than a month of intense fighting, including repeated German counter-attacks, the British forces made some gains. The German defence included extensive use of lachrymatory agents (tear gas) delivered by artillery shells and mortars. Camille DeGrâce's injuries, including a hospitalization for myalgia (serious pain and weakness in the muscles), had been caused by such a chemical attack. Perhaps due to his excitement at finally arriving in England, Landry did not mention the specific cause of the injuries in his letter.

INTERPRETING LETTERS

Given the emphasis here on soldiers' letters home, it is worth saying a bit more about how this book uses that source. In general, correspondence is a valuable resource, but it needs to be read carefully. Official censorship conducted by designated officers aimed to ensure that sensitive information about unit plans and activities would not fall into the hands of the enemy if the documents were captured. It is also clear that the authorities did not want overly negative sentiments or "discredit" about the CEF to get home, where it could damage public support for the war.[31] Photographs were also banned, and owning a camera was treated as a chargeable offence.[32] In addition to all this, scholars have pointed out that CEF soldiers tended to limit the details in their letters home. They did this for a variety of reasons, including wishing to avoid worrying family members, escapism and nostalgia, and lacking the language to describe their experiences. Also, they knew full well that their letters would be shared and possibly published in local newspapers, so they censored themselves and made a point of using the language of patriotic duty, hope, and faith. That is not to say they never complained, but their complaints tended to be reserved for mundane and completely understandable concerns such as poor weather, unappetizing food, and wanting more news from home. Jessica Meyer, writing about British soldiers in the First World War, explains that "in creating a space in which men wrote both as soldiers and domestic figures, letters home offered an important connection for men between their lives as soldiers and the civilian lives and expectations that they had put on hold for the duration."[33] Samuelle Saindon's study of Ulric LeBlanc's correspondence is a case in point; LeBlanc often wrote about his siblings and cousins, his relationship with his fiancée, Marcelline, and his patriotic duty.[34]

We might wonder, then, to what extent Acadian soldiers wrote differently than other CEF and allied soldiers. French-Canadian letters have received some attention from scholars. Michel Litalien writes that relatively little correspondence from French-Canadian soldiers has been preserved in public archives compared to their English-Canadian counterparts, because families tended to keep those letters private and also because of the challenging political situation in Quebec during and after the war.[35] The letters are often monotonous in their formulation, with short statements thanking family members for care packages and letters, requesting more news, and assuring them that everything is fine and not to worry. There are occasional references to pride in their distinct identity and language, especially among members of the 22nd Battalion, but otherwise, Litalien finds little to differentiate these letters from others written by CEF soldiers.[36]

Bernard Andrès finds more diversity in the French-Canadian letters, noting that humour played a key role in helping soldiers process their experiences and create distance from the horrors of combat.[37] While telling jokes about life in the trenches was a way that many soldiers of all backgrounds dealt with the omnipresence of death, these French-Canadian *poilus* also poked fun at the ambivalence of their allegiances to Great Britain and France and the domination of the English language they experienced while serving abroad.[38] We do not find as much humour of this latter kind in the Acadian letters. Ulric LeBlanc reminds us that the soldiers were well aware that their correspondence might be published in newspapers like *L'Évangéline* and shared widely in the community.[39] Meanwhile, for the former members of the 165th Battalion in the CFC, their distance from the trenches gave them a different kind of experience, and they may have felt awkward making light of their situation when others faced more horrible circumstances.

Similarly, Ross Hebb emphasizes that soldiers from Canada's Maritime provinces wrote letters to keep up sustained conversations with loved ones over years of absence. He was fortunate to be able to consult series of letters, and found that many of them "clearly convey the unique personality of each of their authors."[40] There are certainly plenty of examples of this in the letters written by Acadians. In the following passage, Lionel LeBlanc (Ulric's brother and a former officer in the 165th Battalion) tells his parents he is thinking about applying to join the Royal Flying Corps after cooling his heels for a time with the 23rd Battalion (Reserve) in England:

> I might apply for a transfer to the flying corps before long, it doesn't cost anything and they need the men, altho I admit it's rather adventurous [sic]. I'll see how everything plays out first. There is a very good pay in that and after all we have to die only once. But don't let your shirt fly up your back now I'm not in it yet; *excite-toi pas le poil des jambes* like Ulric used to say. You know when a young imagination has tried everything on land there is nothing else to do but fly.[41]

Figure 3.1 (Above and facing) Wartime portraits of Joseph Ulric LeBlanc

Linguistic scholars like France Martineau have found that letters are excellent resources for the study of regional dialects and expressions. Ulric LeBlanc stood out for his superior spelling and grammar but also for his sense of humour.[42]

It is no surprise that references to nationalism and religion abound in the Acadian letters published in newspapers. In their letters, the soldiers of the 165th Battalion reassured family members that they attended Mass as well as confession, reminded them that military service was a patriotic and religious duty, and declared that they were proud to do their bit for Canada. Victorien Lagacé wrote home to his parish priest from France asking for a benediction. Seemingly grateful for his lot with the CFC, he added: "If God calls me to Him while I am fighting for my homeland, I will be happy to die the death of a brave man."[43] Pierre Vautour, an older recruit serving in a labour battalion and seeking to reassure his goddaughter, provides a particularly eloquent example of religious sentiment and optimism:

> I am near the trenches, and while the birds share their joyous songs, and the sun brings forth, with its warmth, the harvest from the earth, and the trees return to their green foliage, Men are fighting each other and destroying everything that God has made for their service. When will they come to realize their folly and their inferiority before the greatness and wisdom of God? It will be, I think, when the vices of pride, envy, and impurity receive their just punishment. When God reveals someone from the humble masses who will show us the road to victory, which is, undoubtedly, the victory over our own nature. When we have won that victory over each person, the peace of the world will be entirely assured.[44]

Meanwhile, numerous references to the Virgin Mary, singing "Ave Maris Stella," and celebrating the Feast of the Assumption (15 August) – adopted as a national holiday at the first Acadian national convention of 1881 – remind us of specific Acadian traditions. Edmond Barrieau marked the feast day with a letter home about his loneliness but also his hope:

> Since I have left home, about a year ago, I have been rarely troubled. In fact, I am not that susceptible to what some call

le *mal du pays*. But today, August 15th, my thoughts are entirely in Rogersville, where no doubt there is a great feast in honour of the Assumption and of Acadie. And truly I cannot hide it, I cannot prevent myself from feeling loneliness, me so far from everyone who is dear to me, and with whom I would be so happy to be today. I am lost in the upheaval of this great war. But there is one comforting thought that encourages me today; it is that I know that on this joyful day there are hearts thinking of me and sending such fervent prayers that I know the Virgin Mary will hear them and protect me.[45]

Although the published letters represent only a fraction of the correspondence sent home, and were no doubt selected by families and editors to reinforce particular themes of patriotism and religious devotion, they do provide insight into the language adopted by the soldiers themselves to make sense of their experiences and to stay connected. Indeed, many of the letters shared the same "mixture of earnest hope, fateful preparation, and boyish innocence" noted by Rutherdale for a multitude of Canadian communities.[46]

Acadians may not have written more than the French-Canadian soldiers studied by Litalien, but their letters appear to have been more frequently shared and published, yet another indication that the Acadian experience of the First World War was different. The disappointing end of the 165th Battalion and the transfer of most of its men to the CFC adds a further element to many of these letters, which we will take up in the following pages and the next chapter. In general, the correspondence reinforces the notion that the men enlisted in part from a sense of duty to family, community, and nation. Their enlistment reflected not just a household economy but a household sense of purpose. As the war dragged on, some of the initial enthusiasm wore off and letters more frequently expressed loneliness, fatigue, and the soldiers' sense of isolation. However, those same letters also provide valuable information about the kinds of routines and struggles that characterized daily life from the forestry camps to the trenches. As Mélanie Morin-Pelletier writes, although these family letters are an imperfect source, they offer privileged access to the thoughts and feelings of soldiers and their families.[47] Unfortunately, it is rare to have access to the letters written from home to the soldiers, so typically we get only one side of the equation.

SHOREHAM-BY-SEA AND THE END OF THE 165TH BATTALION

Whether homesick or excited or somewhere in between, the Acadian volunteers found themselves on their way to the military camp at Shoreham-by-Sea. We do not know much about the experience of the 165th Battalion at the Canadian camp, for few of the soldiers' letters say much about it. The men were among the last volunteers to arrive from Canada, and many of those already at the camp were convalescents who had already seen combat, like Camille DeGrâce. It is likely that many of these men did not wish to return to the trenches. The large numbers of sick and injured arriving daily from the front (usually from hospitals) dwarfed the small "drafts" of fit men being sent to France. In his account of a mutiny that broke out among the men of the 23rd Battalion (Reserve) in June 1917, Private A.Y. Jackson described low morale and overbearing military discipline: "the poor food and bullying by NCOs had been too much for us."[48] Drinking and venereal diseases were common scourges, and military leaders seem to have designed work to keep the men busy and exhausted. The typical six-and-a-half day training syllabus of that unit included early morning physical training and hours of drill, bayonet fighting, musketry (ranges), grenade throwing, and engineering (i.e., trench work), as well as lectures on topics such as map reading, anti-gas drills, and fieldcraft.[49] The austere conditions at the camp disappointed Padre Gaudet, who recorded that the soldiers suffered and became ill from living in tents in the cold, muddy conditions. Sickness was an ongoing concern, and upon arrival, the soldiers endured quarantine and medical exams. Gaudet took note of thirty-two cases of mumps and twelve of measles among the men of the 165th.[50]

The accounts sent home by the soldiers were less bleak, no doubt in part due to concerns about the military censors. However, many of the volunteers seemed genuinely enthusiastic. Jérôme Arsenault, who hailed from the same parish as the unit chaplain, had been one of the first Acadians to sign up for the 165th Battalion. Although he declared his age to be eighteen when he enlisted, the 1911 Census record suggests he was probably just fifteen, and perhaps seventeen by the time he reached Shoreham-by-Sea. His youthful energy is evident in a letter he wrote home on 12 April 1917. He explained that they were seeing many things that they would never have seen if they had stayed in New Brunswick and that after passing another medical exam he was ready for the trenches. In his words, "there is nothing like being a soldier," and he believed that "everyone must fight for their King and their country."[51]

Abel Belliveau, originally from Saint-Paul, New Brunswick, found that military life was relatively easy at Shoreham-by-Sea. He related to his family that "we do not train as much here as in Canada. After a month in this camp, I have not gone on a single route march. I assure you that I find this quite good."[52] Jean-Baptiste Nowlan belonged to the Canadian Army Medical Corps and arrived at Shoreham-by-Sea a couple of weeks after the 165th Battalion. Although born in New Brunswick, he had enlisted in Winnipeg, Manitoba. In a letter to his sister, Nowlan shared in the good spirits of the other Acadian soldiers. He described the picturesque landscapes of England and the verdant, fertile countryside that compared well with the "Garden of Eden" of his birthplace in Kent County. Nowlan noted that he was getting along very well despite a recent bout of the flu.[53] Edward "Eddie" Mazerolle, yet another native of Kent County, found that the area was nice but not as nice as Canada. He reassured his family that "we are not working too hard and we have lots to eat."[54] Ferdinand Malenfant sent a postcard depicting the nearby beach at Brighton.

These varying accounts of conditions at Shoreham-by-Sea demonstrate that, for the most part, the Acadian volunteers cast their situation in a positive light and were eager to continue to the front. Although some contingents of Canadian recruits ended up waiting a long time in England, events unfolded quickly for the men of the 165th Battalion.[55] At first, it seemed certain that they would join their new units at the front in a matter of weeks. There did not appear to be any hard feelings about the 165th being broken up. The soldiers must have understood that arriving at only half strength meant the end of the dream of an Acadian national unit fighting in the trenches. Indeed, nearly all of the units sent over in 1916 were similarly disbanded.[56]

They were eager to do their part. Less than a week after their arrival at Shoreham-by-Sea, LCol Daigle called a general assembly. In an unusual display of democracy in the ranks, the CO asked the soldiers to vote on joining the 10th Battalion (Reserve), which sent reinforcements to the 22rd Battalion (French-Canadian), or the 13th Battalion (Reserve), associated with the 26th Battalion (New Brunswick). The soldiers took note of this unusual consultation; indeed, several of them mentioned it in their letters and notebooks. Unfortunately, the military censors struck out the voting results reported by Eddie Mazerolle,

Figure 3.2 Postcard from Ferdinand Malenfant to his sister Anna

who had indicated that nearly everyone in "A" Company had voted the same way.[57] The chaplain reported that nearly two-thirds of the five hundred soldiers present voted to join the 22nd Battalion. However, he also noted that nearly the entire leadership preferred the 26th Battalion and tried to convince their subordinates to vote the same.[58] Ferdinand Malenfant must not have been excited by either option, because he applied for a transfer to the Army Service Corps the same day.[59] This rare insight into the differing opinions within the ranks indicates that the majority preferred to fight alongside other francophone soldiers rather than anglophone New Brunswickers. Language mattered more than region to the rank and file.

Despite the results of the vote, when the 165th Battalion broke up a few days later, most of its members ended up with the 13th Battalion.[60] The officers had at least temporarily gotten their way. LCol Daigle, Major Arthur Legere, and the other officers had long emphasized a distinct Acadian identity separate from that of other French-Canadians. As we saw in the previous chapter, the CO had been less than enthusiastic about a previous proposal to integrate the 165th into a French-Canadian brigade. These leaders wanted to stay with other units from the Maritime provinces. They preferred possible assimilation with an anglophone unit over integration with other

French-Canadians. Setting aside the nationalist politics, this may be yet another clue that there were already plenty of Acadians fighting with the 26th Battalion. Part of the hope may well have been to meet up with Acadians already at the front or heading that way from units such as the 105th and the 132nd Battalions, which had also recruited from Acadian counties.[61]

But when orders arrived just a few weeks later for the men to depart for France, the military authorities assigned them to neither the 22nd nor the 26th Battalion. They would not be going to the front at all, but rather to the Canadian Forestry Corps (CFC). The first two companies (A and B companies, comprising some three hundred men, mainly from New Brunswick) headed to France at the end of May 1917 along with Padre Gaudet. Abel Belliveau advised his parents that he had chosen to stay in England for the time being. His name had been on the list to go but "I prefer to wait longer and go over with the major of our company." Belliveau ended up sticking with this officer, leaving in mid-June, and rose to the rank of company sergeant major (CSM) of the 47th Company, CFC. These three companies, comprising more than four hundred Acadian volunteers, were assigned to the 5th District in the Jura region of France, near the Swiss border. A fourth company of Acadian volunteers, the 48th, also departed in June and was comprised mainly of the men of "C" Company (including most of the Nova Scotia recruits). However, this subunit was assigned to the 12th District, CFC, in the Bordeaux region and would be separated from the rest of their Acadian brethren for the rest of the war.[62]

Gaudet expressed his relief at the decision. In a letter that later appeared in *L'Évangéline*, he related that "we will not be exposed to bullets and shells, which should be a consolation to the mothers and family members of the soldiers of the 165th Battalion of Acadian French. Truly, Our Lady of the Assumption is good to her children. She has brought us safely across the ocean and she sends us to a region far from the theatre of war."[63] Other newspapers were a little slower to share the news. The *Saint John Globe* related the "rumour" that the men of the 165th Battalion would be "engaged in a construction corps," while *Le Moniteur acadien* published a short stub indicating that the Acadian national unit would be converted into a forestry unit under the command of Maj Legere.[64] As for LCol Daigle, he had been struck by an automobile while conducting business in London. His damaged leg would heal, but his companion had been killed in the accident. Canadian officials at Shoreham-by-Sea gave Daigle and several of the other officers in the unit the option to revert in rank to lieutenant or return home. Their lack of military experience had finally caught up with them. Daigle chose to return to Canada, although most of the junior officers elected to remain.[65]

It seems that the unit's transfer to the CFC, and its eventual disbanding, generated little public outrage. The stub article in *Le Moniteur acadien* only appeared on page 4 of the edition, and there was no follow-up. The editors continued to publish soldiers' letters home sent in by their families, but there was no additional appeal for funds or recruiting. Even the dismissal of the unit CO seemed to spark little discussion. The car accident may have provided an appropriate distraction to soften the blow. As 1917 stretched on, the federal election and the conscription debate became much more compelling themes for public discourse. Bishop LeBlanc and other Acadian political elites supported conscription. So did *Le Moniteur acadien*, whereas the other newspapers and most of the Acadian population opposed it. Andrew Theobald has provided a comprehensive study of the debate in New Brunswick, and Patrice Dutil and David Mackenzie offer a national perspective on the wartime election.[66] We will pick up the story of the former 165th volunteers working in the CFC in the next chapter. At this point, the disbanding of the unit offers an opportunity to review the group that had made it overseas before it was broken up.

PROFILE OF THE OVERSEAS CONTINGENT OF THE 165TH BATTALION

Throughout this book, we have developed and compared the socioeconomic profiles of different groups of Acadian volunteers within the 165th Battalion. In this section, we take a closer look at who made it overseas and compare these soldiers with other groups of Acadians and French-Canadians, including those in the 22nd and the 26th Battalions.

Of the 1,038 Acadian volunteers identified for the 165th Battalion, 540 (52 per cent) went overseas with the unit at the end of March 1917, and some 53 more served in Europe later. Thanks to the work of students at the Institut d'études acadiennes of the Université de Moncton, it is possible to compare the overseas contingent of the 165th Battalion with two other samples of Acadian soldiers in the CEF. As described in the introduction, the first sample concerns Acadian volunteers enlisting before the creation of the Acadian national unit (between September 1914 and December 1915), and the second concerns Acadians serving with the 26th Battalion (New Brunswick). The latter group included forty men who enlisted during the same early time frame, including sixteen recruited directly into this infantry unit before it left Canada in June 1915; the rest joined later through other regional battalions. The list included forty-three men transferred from the 105th Battalion (Prince Edward Island Highlanders). Smaller groups came in to the 26th Battalion from across the Maritime provinces, including five from the 106th Battalion (Nova Scotia Rifles), seven from the 132nd Battalion (North Shore), and four from the 140th Battalion (Saint John Tigers).[67]

The earliest contingent of Acadian volunteers was older, taller, and broader in the chest than those of the 165th Battalion. The men who made it to the front with the 26th Battalion were also broader in the chest, but they tended to be younger and a little shorter. Clearly, we should not put too much stock in physical measurements when evaluating the fitness of the volunteers. Doctors eliminated some on the basis of ailments and injuries, not size necessarily. Indeed, Nic Clarke's analysis of rejected volunteers across Canada finds that stature was not the primary factor.[68] One recent study pointed out that most of the CEF recruits were hardly supermen in terms of physique; the average recruit was 5 feet, 7 inches tall and weighed about 140 pounds.[69] As we saw in chapter 1, there was a great deal of public pressure to fill up the Acadian national unit. However, there were limits to this enthusiasm; about one-quarter of the 165th Battalion recruits were ultimately discharged as medically unfit. Clarke's study indicates that this was typical of units recruiting in 1916; 50,000 men were rejected for service nationally during that year alone. Ian Miller estimates that over the course of the war, fully one-third of Torontonians volunteering to serve were declared medically unfit – some 20,000 men.[70]

Earlier Acadian recruits may have been more physically robust, but the samples also show that more of them declared prior military service. In fact, more than half of the Acadians who arrived in the 26th Battalion were members of the Active Militia, and nearly two-thirds of the Acadian volunteers serving with the 26th Battalion declared prior service of some kind. A further one in four of the earliest Acadian volunteers came directly from regional militia battalions. This is in stark contrast to the results for the 165th Battalion, where just one in ten volunteers was a member of the Active Militia. Clearly, local militia service was common in some Acadian communities and deserving of further study.

Table 3.1
Comparative analysis of age, height, and girth of Acadian volunteers

	165th Bn overseas	1914–15 sample	26th Bn sample
Average age	22.26	23.04	20.81
Average height	5.54 feet	5.59 feet	5.49 feet
Average girth	34.90 inches	36.47 inches	36.11 inches

Table 3.2
Comparative analysis of previous military service of Acadian volunteers (%)

	165th Bn overseas	1914–15 sample	26th Bn sample
Active militia	10.0	25.0	58.7
Prior service (militia, CEF, other)	4.9	13.6	5.2
Total declaring military experience	14.9	38.6	63.9

In total, about one-third of CEF members declared they had military experience of one kind or another, about 3 per cent of them as former British regular soldiers.[71] Desmond Morton noted that military authorities had a marked preference for militia veterans in the early days of the war, but also observed that most of those veterans declined to enlist because "their patriotic duty to defend the nation" conflicted with "their traditional primary role as breadwinners for their families."[72] To form the overseas army, Militia Minister Sam Hughes chose to create a new, separate organization instead of relying on regional militia battalions or their commanders. However, scholars have shown that the militia contributed more men than has often been realized, especially in the early days. For example, Lee Windsor has demonstrated that the 3rd Regiment (New Brunswick) provided a significant number of gunners and officers for the first two overseas contingents of the CEF. Later in the war, most militia units focused on home defence.[73]

Curt Mainville's research on Saint John, New Brunswick, found that a majority of the CEF volunteers from that municipality and the surrounding countryside did have previous experience in Canada's Active Militia.[74] Similarly, Claude Léger's study of the 132nd Battalion revealed close links between that unit and the 73rd Regiment (Northumberland).[75] In our two samples of Acadians serving elsewhere, those from Prince Edward Island stand out: fifty-eight of the seventy-five men concerned declared previous militia service, most of them in the 82nd Regiment (Abegweit Light Infantry). Regional differences were important; the fact that the 165th Battalion had fewer volunteers with prior militia service could reflect that the local regiment in southern New Brunswick, the 74th (New Brunswick Rangers), operated out of Sussex and exclusively in English, drawing heavily from Saint John, Fredericton, and Albert Counties.

A review of the soldiers' military files reveals some exceptional cases. For example, Antoine Boudreau enlisted in May 1915 with the 55th Battalion (New Brunswick and Prince Edward Island). Boudreau hailed from the tiny community of Saint-Pierre, New Brunswick, and had previously served for several years with the US Army, including in Mexico and the Philippines. He died on 21 April 1917 from wounds sustained at Vimy Ridge. The apparently unrelated William Boudreau, of Campbellton, New Brunswick, also declared previous experience with the US Army when he enlisted with the 132nd Battalion (North Shore). He bore a tattoo of an American eagle on his right forearm. Despite a serious heart condition identified while training at Valcartier, Boudreau found himself promoted to sergeant. He transferred to the 26th Battalion in short order upon arrival in England. He was lucky enough to survive the war. As we have seen, the 165th Battalion was not without men with military experience. Joseph Doucet, born in Bathurst but working in Moncton as a deputy sheriff, transferred to the 26th after an initial stint with the CFC. Like the Boudreaus, he declared previous regular service with the US Army, and he was also a member of the Active Militia. He died at Amiens on 9 August 1918 after being struck by an artillery shell.

Few unit histories include a detailed sociodemographic analysis of their members. However, scholars have published studies about two front-line CEF units whose experiences were very similar to those of the Acadians in the First World War. Curt Mainville has compiled data for the entire original cohort of the 26th Battalion (New Brunswick), the nearly 1,500 volunteers who signed up in 1914–15 before deploying overseas. At the same time, Jean-Pierre Gagnon's classic study of the soldiers of the 22nd Battalion (Canadien-Français) offers several avenues of comparison. Most of the Acadians who fought in the trenches did so with one of these units. In addition, some general CEF statistics are available thanks to Morton. The results underscore some themes we have already encountered, such as the relative youth of the

Table 3.3
Comparison of key characteristics of CEF volunteers[1]

	165th Bn (A)	1914–15 (A)	26th Bn (A)	26th Bn originals	22nd Bn	CEF
Born in Canada	94%	100%	97%	72%	88%	47%
Age at enlistment	22.3 years	23.0 years	20.8 years	25.7 years	24.3 years	26.3 years
Less than twenty years	47%	46%	58%	20%	21%	10%
Married at enlistment	11%	13%	5%	7%	17%	20%
Prior military service	15%	39%	64%	49%	29%	35%
Agriculture	21%	13%	23%	8%	6%	22%
Labourer/ manufacturing	35%	43%	41%	68%	35%	25%

1 165th Battalion Database; Gagnon, *Le 22e bataillon (canadien-français)*, 315–64; Morton, *When Your Number's Up*, 277–9; (A) refers to the three groups of Acadian soldiers.

Acadian volunteers, the importance of prior military experience, especially for the early volunteers, and the high proportion of mobile, urban workers. Given the rich comparison possible, it is worthwhile to explore each of these themes in more detail.

Not surprisingly, a much higher proportion of French-Canadian soldiers had been born in Canada. In the case of both the Acadians and the members of the 22nd Battalion, most of the rest had been born in the United States. While military historians have tended to focus on the apparently sedentary nature of French-Canadian farming families compared to English-Canadian populations, Yves Frenette effectively summarizes that "migratory movements remained the primary factor configuring Francophone North America."[76] A separate study revealed that hardly any of the young people living in the small coastal community of Cocagne, New Brunswick, in 1871 were still living there fifty years later. While many of them undoubtedly chose to marry or work in nearby parishes or in the burgeoning industrial city of Moncton, some crossed the border into Maine and wound up permanently residing in the United States.[77] The francophone family networks that resulted from these temporary and permanent migrations proved surprisingly strong, reinforced with regular correspondence and occasional visits back and forth as well as by, increasingly, organizations like the Société mutuelle de l'Assomption. Indeed, a few of the Acadian recruits, including Maxime Pelletier and Joseph Belanger, seem to have always lived in Maine before crossing the border specifically to enlist with the 165th Battalion in March 1916. Smaller groups of volunteers originated in France or other French-speaking countries such as Belgium and Switzerland; several men came from Saint-Pierre and Miquelon.

We have long known that much of the CEF, particularly the initial contingents, was composed of recent British immigrants, many of them reservists who felt a duty to respond to the call to arms.[78] Atlantic Canadian units stood out for their more "Canadian" roots, in that there were fewer immigrants among these soldiers and their families were longer-established in the region.[79] Jean Martin called the 22nd Battalion in 1915 "the most incontestably Canadian unit" in the CEF and noted that the 26th Battalion (New Brunswick) was the only other CEF unit recruited before 1916 that included at least 70 per cent Canadian-born recruits.[80] Even there, nearly one-quarter of the volunteers were recent British immigrants, and several others came from Newfoundland and the British Caribbean. The United States was also well represented. Just as we saw with the French-Canadian migrations, broad anglophone networks were spread out across many regions, supported by relatively easy access to ports and railways. These results together suggest that we should not be too quick to label people by their declared residence at enlistment.[81] As we will see in the final chapter, many of the former soldiers continued to move around after returning to Canada.

With regard to age, the Acadian soldiers clearly tended to be younger than their counterparts across the CEF, but also those in the 22nd and the 26th Battalions. Even those first signing up were more than three years younger, on average, than the rest of the force. The 26th originals were closer to the CEF average, despite a certain number of Acadian volunteers, while the 22nd recruits tended to be younger. Similarly, in his study of the 19th Battalion, based in Toronto and Hamilton, David Campbell found that these infantry soldiers had an average age of twenty-five.[82] Chris Sharpe contends that marital status was a more important factor than language and ethnicity for explaining differences in enlistment rates between Quebec and the rest of Canada. Since French-Canadian men tended to marry earlier than their anglophone counterparts, there were fewer eligible single men, particularly from farming families, available for military service.[83]

Still, we need to account for why Acadian recruits tended to be even younger than those from Quebec. It may be that there were specific family strategies in play, as we saw in the first chapter and will develop in the next section when we conduct a more detailed analysis of the 1911 Canadian Census. It is also interesting to note that almost all of the original members of the 26th were single. They were even less likely to be married than the volunteers of the 165th Battalion, and much less likely than their counterparts in the CEF as a whole. Also, anglophone New Brunswickers seem to have employed specific family strategies around military service; a large proportion of the 26th Battalion recruits were single men working in factories and industrial trades; those at home working on family farms were much less likely to volunteer. In other words, there was quite a bit of continuity across anglophone and francophone communities in the Maritime provinces in terms of who was enlisting.

Of course, being married was not an "official" barrier to enlistment, and some families even accompanied the soldiers overseas. Militia Minister Hughes initially insisted that married recruits provide proof that they had their wives' permission to enlist. However, Morton found that just 379 men across the CEF were sent home because a wife or parent protested their enlistment.[84] The Borden government dropped the requirement in the summer of 1915, not only because more men were needed but also, probably, because that policy had not been widely observed and was difficult to enforce. The government may also have been concerned about breaking up or undermining families. Morton's study of the support provided to families during the First World War delves into numerous debates and policy changes intended to encourage enlistment through more generous financial support. Initially, the separation allowance (SA) was set as a monthly payment of $20 for a private's wife or a widowed mother. Borden increased this to $25 on the eve of the 1917 federal election, undoubtedly with an eye on the female relatives of soldiers, who would be voting for the first time. Inevitably, there were bureaucratic delays and questions about eligibility. In 1916, military authorities established that two years of cohabitation could be accepted as the equivalent of a marriage licence, and in 1917, the rules were changed again so that marriages observed after enlistment would be considered eligible. The approval of the commanding officer, certificates from local clergy, and other administrative requirements made for a long and frustrating process. Soldiers often waited several months for the first SA payment to come through, which caused additional hardship for those struggling to get by.[85]

Faced with mounting evidence of soldiers' wives and children living in penury, the government tried to compel soldiers to allocate more of their pay home; it also established the Canadian Patriotic Fund (CPF) to raise and distribute additional funds to those in need. Functioning as a kind of sprawling national aid society, the CPF ultimately issued allowances to about two-thirds of the relatives receiving SA, but only about one-third of the wives. Morton found that this was because many working-class families refused charity on principle or refused to allow the intrusive visits required by CPF members to ensure that those receiving the funds were spending them wisely and living up to their moral vision of a chaste and frugal life.[86] As with military service and masculinity, there was a moral and religious component to family support. Many observers looked down on women who worked after they were married, particularly after they had children. There could also be a racial component; for example, the wives and families of Indigenous soldiers from James Bay faced obstacles and additional public scrutiny in their appeals for support.[87] Ultimately, while some young families could get by with additional support from the CPF, others did not qualify or lost their benefits, and heads of household supporting larger families probably could not afford to join the CEF. Most significantly with regard to the volunteers of the 165th Battalion, those transferred to the CFC did not qualify for the additional support provided by the CPF.[88]

This discussion of the CPF provides additional insight into the age of the soldiers. The national executive set standard rates to support children of various ages, but once children turned sixteen, they were expected to make their own living and the support provided to their families was reduced.[89] Recall here that many of the recruits signing up in 1916 were teenagers. In fact, across the three Acadian groups studied here – the 165th Battalion volunteers, and the samples enlisting earlier or serving at some point with the 26th Battalion – around half were not yet twenty years old. The results are staggering when we consider that only one in ten CEF members was so young (and about one in five of those with the 22nd and 26th Battalions). This is the most significant way in which the sociodemographic profile of the Acadian recruits was unique. Military service was one option when Canadian families needed adolescents to contribute to household expenses or, at the very least, to look after themselves, but why did so many Acadian youths adopt this course? The appeal of a national unit and the urging of local elites may have been factors for those signing up for the 165th, but these do not explain the results for the Acadian soldiers serving elsewhere. We are back to the idea that there was a particular family or community strategy at play that integrated military service (and pay) into the household economy. The simplest answer is poverty, which could make military service, and the associated salary and allowances, appealing.

It is worth briefly emphasizing again the importance of prior military service: those already familiar with military training and culture appeared particularly likely to enlist. While about one-third of the CEF declared prior military service upon enlistment, more than seven hundred reservists, just shy of half the total, could be found in the initial contingent of the 26th Battalion. Even in Quebec, where most militia units languished prior to the war, men with previous military experience accounted for about 30 per cent of the volunteers.[90] Similarly, many of the 19th Battalion originals were members of militia regiments in southern Ontario.[91] There is a lot more work to be done on the contribution of the pre-war militia to the CEF, including the degree to which militia service, parades, and summer camps fit into the local culture and social hierarchy.[92]

Finally, the employment backgrounds declared by the volunteers varied considerably across the CEF. Desmond Morton writes that the occupational profile of the recruits changed considerably over the course of the war. Of those enlisting by 1 March 1916, only about 6 per cent were farmers or ranchers, and about two-thirds declared manufacturing or general labourer positions.[93] The figures for the 22nd and 26th Battalions, as well as the early Acadian volunteers, bear this out. Given the initial enthusiasm for enlistment, recruiters were more than happy to take the men already close by rather than engage in time-consuming and expensive visits to rural counties. We have already seen how they put little effort into recruiting in French or visiting Acadian counties in rural areas of the three Maritime provinces. In the case of the 22nd Battalion, Gagnon has shown that a majority of the recruits were truly of urban origin: they had been born and raised in Montreal and Quebec City. Regional centres like Rimouski, Rivière-du-Loup, Granby, and Shawinigan Falls provided proportionally even larger contingents, although smaller in terms of raw numbers. There is a clear parallel with the Acadian case: Moncton as well as smaller towns like Meteghan, Nova Scotia, and Caraquet,

New Brunswick, provided the lion's share of the recruits. Indeed, in the sample of early Acadian volunteers enlisting by the end of 1915, there was a higher proportion of men born and residing in the same urban areas.

However, the recruiting campaign of the 165th Battalion looked a little different, because the officers made an effort to tour the countryside across all three Maritime provinces and also because nearly all of the men (about four in five) had been born in rural parishes and about half had already moved at least once. At first glance, it seems that the Acadians were similar to their French-Canadian brethren in their urban and manufacturing backgrounds, but a closer look shows that while such men dominated early, it was actually those with rural roots who contributed most to the Acadian national unit in 1916. The Acadians who signed up for the 26th Battalion were similarly more mobile and rural in their backgrounds. Given that the rest of the 26th was predominantly urban – indeed, the proportion of urban-dwellers and manufacturing workers was highest with this group – the Acadian volunteers would have been different from the anglophone members of the unit with regard not only to their language and their relative youth but also to their occupational background and mobility.

This comparative analysis has netted a few important findings. For example, while the CEF was generally a young man's enterprise, the Acadian volunteers were significantly younger than their anglophone brethren and even than other French-Canadians. The results with regard to prior military service demonstrate that there was more Acadian participation in regional militia units than commonly realized. Undoubtedly, this previous service was also a factor in who was accepted for the CEF, particularly for front-line infantry units such as the 22nd and 26th Battalions. Urban, working-class men predominated among the recruits, while educated local notables formed the officer and NCO corps. However, Vance's hypothesis that just because people enrolled in cities did not mean they were city-dwellers proved accurate for many of the Acadian recruits.[94] Theobald observed that despite the concentration of recruiters in the cities, volunteers did emerge from rural areas of New Brunswick, and this included Acadians.[95] Furthermore, larger, taller Acadians with previous militia service were the first to be accepted into overseas service in 1914–15. As a consequence, the Acadian national unit drew from a more limited pool of available and willing men in 1916.

FAMILY IMPACT OF OVERSEAS SERVICE

The Acadian volunteers of the 165th Battalion came from a variety of family backgrounds. The nearly six hundred men who deployed overseas would be absent for about two years from the time the ss *Metagama* departed Halifax in March 1917 to demobilization in the spring of 1919.

Recruits declared their next of kin in their attestation papers and often prepared a will while in uniform. Unsurprisingly, given the relative youth of the soldiers, their next of kin was normally a parent (82 per cent), and most of the soldiers (74 per cent) were living in the same place as their next of kin when they enlisted. An analysis of the residence of the next of kin provides some interesting insights into family mobility. Up to this point, we have emphasized the large number of young, single men moving from countryside to towns in search of work who saw military service as an attractive option. However, just 68 of the 592 cases involved a parent next of kin living in the birthplace and a soldier who had moved away from home. In fact, in about twice as many cases (124) the parents had moved with the soldier to a new residence before the war. In other words, entire families often moved together in search of new opportunities. Phyllis LeBlanc notes the enduring strength of this "family emigration" model for those Acadians moving to the United States, although she also found many single women departing home.[96] Our own work looking at the women of Kent County reinforces this interpretation.[97] Only about one in four of the files indicate that the soldier or the next of kin had moved away from the rest of the family prior to enlistment.

Of course, married soldiers normally (although not always) declared their wife as their next of kin. Martha Hanna published a study of war wives in Manitoba that highlights how these women sought additional income and often moved during their husbands' absence in order to seek support from extended family networks or to team up with other women.[98] That support could take many forms, both economic and emotional. In their analysis of two exceptional series of letters, Mélanie Morin-Pelletier found eloquent descriptions of the "physical and emotional burdens carried by the spouses and mothers of deployed solders, as well as the impact their absence had on the daily life of those closest to them."[99]

Our initial analysis of the 61 married volunteers of the 165th Battalion who went overseas reveals particularly high mobility. Nearly half (43 per cent) of the wives moved at least once while their husbands were away, and one in five moved multiple times. Younger women from working-class backgrounds were more likely to move, and usually they relied on their own family rather than that of their husband.[100] Interestingly, married soldiers were just as likely as unmarried ones to declare a residence different from their next of kin, and about one in four were living separate from them at the time of enlistment. The ill-fated Jean-Baptiste Daigle, a fisherman from Petite Aldouane, New Brunswick, had moved to Moncton prior to enlistment, leaving his wife and children behind. His wife Salomé brought the family into the small town of Richibucto while he was gone and undoubtedly relied on the $15 of monthly assigned pay and the additional $20 of monthly separation allowance she received. After Daigle's death in a violent altercation with a French farmer, his widow received a total of $180 in pension and benefits from the army – less than six months' salary. To put this in perspective, Daigle's wife received about $650 in 2021 Canadian dollars each month, and compensation of about $3,500 after his death.

Some married couples lived even farther apart at the time of the husband's enlistment. For example, Alphé Muise was originally from Weymouth, Nova Scotia, and had left his wife Marie Ella and two small children there to work in Moncton. Valérie Albert Richard left his wife Blanche Liliane in Salisbury, Massachusetts, before the war. Originally from Memramcook, New Brunswick, Richard must have travelled to the United States for work. However, we find him before the war living with his mother in Moncton and working there as a carpenter. He must not have been married long to Blanche, since Richard was just twenty-one years old and there is no mention of children. Valérie received training as a signaller and was one of the few 165th Battalion volunteers to be sent directly to the front. Assigned to the 22nd Battalion in June 1917, he was killed in action just a month later. As with Jean-Baptiste Daigle, Richard's widow received $180 from the army.

Another exceptional case was that of Joseph Doucet, already mentioned as a rare Acadian volunteer with significant regular army experience. Joseph was working as a deputy sheriff in Moncton when he enlisted, but his wife, Mary Anne, remained in Bathurst. Significantly, he is not recorded in the 1911 Census because he was serving with the US Army abroad at the time. Mary Anne must have been accustomed to the long absences of her husband and knew the risks associated with military service. As Doucet was an officer and received considerably more pay, he sent $50 home each month, although he cancelled this assignment in November 1917 for "personal circumstances" about which we can only speculate. Tragically, Doucet died of wounds from artillery fire suffered while fighting with the 26th Battalion at Passchendaele in 1918. Mary Anne was listed as the beneficiary of his will, and she received $240 as a widow's gratuity and pension.

Although the impact of their absence was most obvious in the case of married soldiers, the records also reveal that military pay and allowances proved to be essential to the household economy for families of single soldiers. Pay documents are complex and difficult to read, but we conducted a detailed examination of a sample of 60 of the 592 men from the 165th Battalion who travelled to Europe. Virtually all of these men (56 of 60) assigned part of their regular pay to somebody at home. Although soldiers most frequently named their fathers as their next of kin, their mothers were just as likely to receive their assigned pay. In two of these latter cases, the women concerned were widows and also received a separation allowance. When joining the unit, soldiers were asked if they were the sole support of a widowed mother; if they were, they could obtain this additional benefit. Curiously, in those exceptional cases where a sibling received assigned pay, the soldiers were more likely to designate a sister, even if they had living older brothers. The designation of mothers and sisters as beneficiaries may be clues that Acadian women were directly involved in managing household finances. A case in point was Frédéric Doiron of Shediac, New Brunswick. His father, François, was still alive but elderly, so Frédéric sent the monthly payment of $20 to his sister, Élodie. This despite the fact that he had two well-employed older brothers still in his home town. Another interesting case is that of Édouard LeBlanc of Saint-Léonard, New Brunswick. He named his mother, Célaine, as his next of kin, but chose to send his assigned pay to his married sister. We learn from the records that his mother had since remarried and moved to Grand Falls.

There were clearly times when the departure of a husband or older son brought hardship to the family that depended on their presence, particularly when tragedy struck. A case in point was that of Frank Laroque of Bathurst, New Brunswick. His wife Agnes and their two small children moved to Saint John, probably to be with him while the 165th Battalion was in garrison there. They remained there afterwards, until she died suddenly in February 1918. The military record does not explain the circumstances of her death, but the children were left without a guardian, since Frank's parents remained in Bathurst. The assigned pay was taken over by the CPF office in Saint John, then by a temporary guardian, Miss Josephine Hachey. In the end, the children were sent to their grandparents, with Frank's father Israel receiving the final payments before demobilization. This is one family that we are unable to find in the 1921 census, which suggests further movement after the soldier's return.

Most soldiers sent $15 to $20 home, about half their monthly pay. Meanwhile, the army fed and sheltered them, provided clothes and equipment, and even added small allowances for canteens and fieldwork. In addition, a few lucky soldiers earned promotion or bonuses for specialized duties in the CFC camps (see the next chapter). Sergeants earned about 50 per cent more than privates, while officers earned three to four times as much depending on their rank. The men selected for the Royal Air Force also earned flight pay. The federal government recognized that the base pay of soldiers was a paltry amount – $1.10 per day, unchanged since the beginning of the war.[101] While it was unwilling to change this salary, it did institute new policies to provide additional financial support, including travel and clothing allowances for soldiers upon demobilization. It also established the War Service Gratuity (WSG).[102] The amount of the WSG varied with length and place of service as well as with rank but was set at a minimum of $70. According to Morton and Wright, the average CEF soldier earned $240, but most of the former 165th Battalion volunteers appear to have obtained up to $420. A few of the married officers earned the maximum of $600. This was a significant financial boost: the equivalent of about one year's salary for many returning soldiers.[103]

In their home communities, young men would have been expected to perform odd jobs or help with the family farm. Some men and women travelled to cities like Moncton or to the United States to earn wages in industrial jobs and regularly sent money home. Military service abroad fit into larger patterns of the household economy and family emigration, particularly for those living closer to the margins. Although the military salary was not generous by the standards of the day, the assigned pay and separation allowances provided important income to support younger siblings and aging parents, while the recruit's absence reduced the number of mouths to feed. What remains to be considered, and will be taken up in chapter 5, is the longer-term impact of military service and the soldiers' absence. Did the immediate financial benefit outweigh the impact on the life course – the ability to establish oneself in an occupation and start a family? Of course, some soldiers did not return at all. In addition, many veterans found that despite the WSG and other allowances, they still struggled to reintegrate into Canadian society. The next chapter describes their experiences overseas.

Figure 3.3 Alban Bourgeois and Marguerite LeBlanc of College Bridge, NB

4

Life in the Canadian Forestry Corps

May 1917–November 1918

After a brief assignment to the 13th Battalion (Reserve), military authorities transferred most of the former members of the 165th Battalion to the Canadian Forestry Corps (CFC). This chapter examines military life and conditions in the CFC camps, from the actual work to problems of discipline and relations with civilians. We also consider groups of recruits receiving promotions and technical pay as well as broader issues of health and safety. The daily routine orders (DROs) from the 5th District (Jura) serve as the primary source – they were a kind of unit "newspaper."[1] We supplement these with soldiers' letters and diaries.

Major Legere, the Deputy Commanding Officer, was appointed commander of the 39th Company, and both he and Lieutenant-Colonel Daigle successfully lobbied for this sub-unit to be known as the "Acadian" Company and to wear the 165th Battalion cap badge. Daigle also obtained permission to assign Captain Gaudet to the organization as its chaplain, arguing that "one of the conditions" of the creation of the 165th had been "the direction of a Chaplain of our race."[2]

Men from the 165th Battalion left with the 39th Company and arrived in France on 19 May 1917. Acadians also filled the ranks of the 40th Company, which arrived in France a week later, and then the 47th Company, which arrived on 23 June 1917. These three companies, constituted by 351 Acadian volunteers, joined the 5th District of the CFC, based in the Jura region of France near the Swiss border. As previously mentioned, at the end of June a fourth company of Acadians also arrived in France, where they formed the 48th Company of the 12th District, stationed south of Bordeaux.[3] In all, 88 per cent of the former 165th Battalion volunteers were assigned somewhere within the CFC. Only thirty-nine of the recruits directly joined other CEF units – fourteen went to the 22nd Battalion and several others in the 26th Battalion. This small sample reflects the mentality reported in the previous chapter, that most of the rank and file preferred to serve in another French-Canadian unit rather than in an anglophone Maritime battalion.

Military historians have generally given the CFC short shrift. In addition, there has been little public commemoration of the foresters, presumably because they did not suffer the horrors and heavy casualties of daily life at the front. They were a group apart and had a distinct experience of the war overseas, although technically they were still part of the CEF. Yet from a purely numerical perspective, the CFC is deserving of more attention. The Canadian Corps grew from two divisions of about 35,000 men in 1915 to about 100,000 men by October 1917; at its peak in 1918, the CFC numbered almost 25,000 soldiers and an additional 7,000 labourers. In other words, about one in five members of the CEF served in the CFC. Born from an initial request from London in May 1916 for 2,000 specialist woodsmen, the CFC came to employ forty-one companies in Great Britain and sixty in France.[4]

Cameron Bartlett writes that the foresters "laboured for two and a half years to produce enough timber to keep the soldiers serving at the front supplied with shelter, food and ammunition, and to support the vast logistical system that moved supplies and reinforcements across hundreds of miles of front lines." He notes the crucial role played by CFC companies in repairing railways and roads damaged by the Germans' spring offensive of 1918 and in constructing gun platforms and walkways during the gruelling battle at Passchendaele. The Allies consumed timber in astonishing quantities as they carried out the Hundred Days campaign.[5] In a rare mention of the CFC, the *Official History of the Canadian Army* recounts that the CFC provided about 70 per cent of the timber required by the Allied war effort.[6] The Director of Timber Operations in France, Brigadier General John Burton White, praised the men of the CFC after the Armistice of 11 November 1918. "By your skill and consistent hard work you have met every demand made on the Canadian Forestry Corps by the fighting forces, both British and French, for the numerous lumber products so necessary in this great war, and without which the victorious progress of our Armies would have been impossible."[7] Still, as is obvious from the numerous histories and public commemorations that followed, forestry was not considered a glorious or memorable contribution. That attitude was also clear during the war; as we saw in the previous chapter, members of the CFC did not qualify for the additional financial support provided by the Canadian Patriotic Fund.[8]

The Jura was certainly far from the front, and service in the CFC was far from the lofty ambitions expressed when the Acadian national unit was founded.[9] A letter from a sergeant in the CFC in England captures the disappointment: he noted to his parents in Moncton that they will "no doubt be surprised to learn that a part of the 165th is at our camp having been turned into a forestry company."[10] Acadian newspapers had little to say about the CFC, choosing to publish stories about other men serving at the front. *Le Moniteur acadien* printed a single stub article in June 1917 announcing that the 165th Battalion had been converted into a forestry unit.[11] For their part, the editors of *L'Évangéline* tried to spin the situation as a temporary "attachment" of the unit to the CFC.[12] In fairness, they continued to occasionally publish letters from former members of the 165th serving in the CFC, such as one from Fred Frigot of Caraquet, New Brunswick, which he wrote to his sister, Léotine. Frigot saw the good in the transfer, noting that he had a good chance of returning to Canada and that at the conclusion of the war he planned to go and see the trenches. He also described visiting the countryside, seeing German prisoners, and having his portrait done.[13] Many of the soldiers did not share Frigot's pragmatism. Victorien Lagacé of Belledune, New Brunswick, wrote to his parish priest that "it is not really here that our cause calls us and we are waiting to face the enemy and there fulfill our purpose as soldiers."[14] Louis C. Daigle of Richibucto, New Brunswick, simply invented a more martial environment in his letters home, always adding "soldier" after his name. For example, while comfortably stationed in the Jura, he wrote: "Dear parents, do not worry about me, here I am fulfilling my purpose, the work of a soldier; no matter how much the guns rumble, or the earth tremble under my feet, I always keep my composure, my Canadian blood."[15] Daigle was there to fight for Canada, even if the CEF was not to give him the opportunity.

Two recent publications call more attention to the experiences of the Acadian foresters during the First World War. David Devigne partnered with local archives and the Engineer Branch of the Canadian Armed Forces to produce a beautifully illustrated commemorative book about the work of the CFC in the Gascony-Bordeaux region; in it, he several times mentions the 48th Company and its Acadian origins.[16] As well, Jean-Louis Grosmaire has recently published a novel based on an imagined Acadian forester's experiences in the Jura. The importance of exchanging letters with loved ones is well represented in the story, as is the disappointment felt by many of the soldiers about the transfer to the CFC.[17] At the same time, Grosmaire captures the curiosity and some of the likely first impressions of the Acadians as they arrived in the Jura:

> The forest is spectacular here. The countryside is full of valleys, with small rivers, streams, and old villages. The people look like us. Their beautiful accent sings. They do not speak like us, but use many of the same words as us. A welcome change from the English we have been hearing lately. Here, it is good country, a little rough at first glance and one has to learn to love it.
> I feel right at home.[18]

It is to be hoped that public memory of the Acadian foresters will be enhanced by these initiatives; perhaps families holding on to letters, postcards, photographs, and other objects from that time might be encouraged to bring them forward. The absence of collective memory about this contribution to the war is perhaps best demonstrated by a political essay completed by Henri-Dominque Paratte, an Acadian studies expert in Nova Scotia. In it, he unironically compares the political and language rights of contemporary Acadians and residents of the Jura as different examples of minority cultures seeking greater recognition, making no mention of the direct historical contact between the two populations.[19]

Another reason why the CFC deserves attention is its unusual diversity. Indeed, it appears that military authorities viewed the CFC as a logical destination for those unlikely, in their view, to make good soldiers, including members of minority groups. Bartlett notes that this decision was undoubtedly influenced by "the racial theories of the day but was also a pragmatic solution to the CEF's crippling shortage of reinforcements."[20] For example, the Acadians assigned to the Jura worked alongside Russian prisoners – that is, former members of the Russian Expeditionary Force sent to the Western Front but suspected of Bolshevik sympathies – as well as the Afro-Canadian members of No. 2 Construction Battalion, groups from the Chinese Labour Corps, and various enemy aliens and conscientious objectors.[21]

The DROs indicate that the 39th Company (Acadian) worked very closely with attached Russian labourers in the fall of 1917. A transfer order in December of that year sent the Russians along with No. 2 Construction to another part of France (Alençon).[22] Still, we know that a significant number of Russians remained in the 5th District because instructions in January outline that their normal work schedule was to be eight hours a day – less than the standard shift of a forester – and in the spring, there are several mentions of them falling ill from influenza.[23] We also know that No. 2 Construction had returned to the Jura by May 1918. A tragic incident would highlight this diversity: a member of this unit named Charlie Some was murdered on 22 September 1918, apparently by a French colonial soldier from Algeria.[24]

Padre J.V. Gaudet commented on the presence of many Black soldiers at Mass in June 1917 and at the subsequent Dominion Day celebration.[25] Grosmaire has his protagonist Jean-Baptiste explain to his sweetheart, Angelaine, that there is a clear division of labour, with the Afro-Canadians focusing on roadwork and the Acadians on cutting trees.[26] The Acadian foresters must have been aware that they had been relegated to a secondary role in the CEF – indeed, to one shared by others deemed suspect. In a letter to his parish priest, Lieutenant Aimé Leger thought it necessary to add in parentheses that the men of the 165th Battalion were serving in loyal (*fidèles*) forestry companies. For his part, he was excited to have been selected for the Royal Flying Corps. Tragically, Leger died in a training accident on 11 September 1917, when his plane went down near Shoreham-by-Sea, not far from where his home unit had first arrived in England eighteen months earlier.[27] The available soldiers' letters do not make more mention of meeting and working with different groups, an indication that they were kept apart. Kirrily Freeman relates that the six hundred members of No. 2 Construction Battalion continued to experience racism and segregation in the CEF, part of a deliberate attempt to make them "invisible."[28]

WORKING IN THE CFC CAMPS

The CFC grew quickly from an initial 1,600 men recruited into the 224th Battalion (Forestry) in April 1916 to nearly 25,000 soldiers divided into 101 companies in France and Britain by early 1918. The largest contingent of 18 companies was in southwestern France.[29]

Each company comprised 6 officers and 164 other ranks (ORS) on paper, although many had an actual strength closer to 120. Recruiters tapped into new sources of volunteers for this specialized work – for example, experienced lumbermen from the Ottawa Valley, including French-Canadians who had been reluctant to sign up for combat duty. However, after three more forestry battalions from Ottawa and Montreal had departed in the fall of 1916, it became obvious that not enough skilled woodcutters were available to satisfy the demand. In November 1916 the army authorized new forestry units to draw from previous CEF volunteers deemed underage, overage, or medically unfit.[30] Major Stehelin, himself overage, was assigned command of a forestry battalion composed of other Acadians who did not meet the standards for combat.[31] The arrival of the 165th Battalion in England coincided with a strong push to find recruits for the CFC among CEF members in the spring of 1917. Throughout that year, convalescing troops from the front provided additional men, and the number of "attached" labour companies increased.

With few actual foresters among its ranks and a ballooning establishment, the CFC created a new depot at Sunningdale in March 1917 to organize and train its recruits in the basics of woodcutting.[32] The labour pool differed significantly from that of the CEF as a whole: the average age of the foresters was closer to forty (compared to twenty-six for the CEF overall), nearly all of them were Canadian-born, and they were much more likely to be French-Canadian or Indigenous.[33] Sunningdale is where the former members of the 165th Battalion transitioned to their new role overseas. While undoubtedly happy to encounter other francophones, the Acadian recruits, with an average age of just twenty-two, would have stood out from most of the group, who included injured soldiers who had already seen combat. That said, the CFC became a bit of a meeting point for Acadians from different backgrounds in the CEF. For example, Joseph Barrieau of Rogersville enlisted in one of the first forestry units, the 242nd Battalion, based out of Montreal. Writing home in March 1917 from Sunningdale, Barrieau described his pleasure at meeting other Acadians who had been serving with the 26th Battalion in the trenches, including a Doucet from Collette, just up the road from his home town. They both joined the 22nd Company, CFC, and were thus among the first foresters to arrive in the Jura. Thus, when the men of the 165th arrived in the region, they encountered other Acadians who had already been transferred there.[34]

The travel afforded new opportunities to observe the landscape. Most of the volunteers made simple remarks about the pleasant countryside and the ripe fields ready for harvest. Eddie Mazerolle thought the villages were beautiful, but not as nice as those of Canada.[35] Louis Daigle found London overwhelming, "the biggest and oldest city in the world."[36] Captain Jean Malenfant was less impressed, writing to his wife with a touch of homesickness in 1918 that "it is always the noise and comings and goings of a big city and after seeing it once or twice, it is no longer interesting."[37] His son Ferdinand was one of the few to jot down some details of the route from Sunningdale to the Jura. The 47th Company left the CFC depot for Southampton on 22 June and crossed the English Channel to Le Havre, where the younger Malenfant recorded that he attended confession. They departed on 27 June, travelling two days by train. While passing through Rouen, he saw "many interesting things," including "where Joan of Arc was born her monument and where she was burnt." Continuing through Paris, the young soldier remarked that "Versailles Castle is a nice thing to see" and that the Seine River was "nice something like the Thames." After a brief stop in Dijon, the 47th Company arrived at the 5th District headquarters, in Andelot. It seems that the men spent a few days waiting for their assignment. Malenfant noted that he stayed in a simple hut and visited local towns such as Chapois, as well as several churches. Regarding the local population, he wrote that he "had a great time trying to speak like the French people. They are very nice all you see here is women and old men everybody is at war. You see little boys working in fields with their mother they never complains [sic] they seem to be always happy." He also thought that the view of the Alps was "very nice."[38] Not everyone was impressed with the Jura. Félicien Landry of Lakeburn, New Brunswick, wrote to his parents that "each person has their own misery in this place. All that we see around us is huge mountains and lots of rain, it rains every day and the thunder is something terrible here."[39]

Working far from the front did not mean that the foresters had an easy time of it. Between May and October 1917 alone, the CFC provided "more than three-quarters of a million tons of lumber." Each forestry company could provide between 25,000 and 35,000 foot board measure (FBM) daily, or about eight tons of sawn material. Literally as it sounds, FBM refers to a volume of wood equal to one square foot (length, width) and one inch of height. Production could be ramped up when needed; the record output at the 5th District's main mill at La Joux was 160,494 FBM in 19 hours.[40] Fedorowich describes a typical day at a CFC camp in Devon, England:

> Gangs of axemen and sawyers, supervised by a bush officer or bush foreman (usually an NCO), would go out every morning, even in the most inclement weather, to harvest the forest ... Teamsters would haul the wood to the mill, several miles away ... Once at the mill, the logs would be unloaded, stacked, and readied for processing. Processed lumber would be hauled to the nearest railway station for shipment. It was logging on an industrial scale, the likes of which had not been witnessed in the UK.[41]

CFC production focused on sleepers for roads, railways, trenches, and fortifications, as well as planks for constructing dugouts, duckboards, and accommodation. Cook describes the vast amount of planking used to support the attack on Vimy Ridge. Without those planks, it would have been impossible to advance quickly over the ruined terrain.[42] Lee Windsor describes the concentration of heavy artillery (including New Brunswick units) in the prelude to that battle, as well as the significant demands for transportation, housing, and platforms.[43] Other CFC tasks included the production of pickets, posts, poles, and spars.[44] The foresters typically worked twelve-hour days, six days a week, regardless of weather conditions. Devigne's work on the CFC in the Bordeaux region uncovered several photographs of the men and the camps using local archives.[45]

For the companies assigned to the Jura, the mountainous terrain at over 2,000 feet of elevation was particularly challenging, and additional supplies were needed.[46] It took several weeks just to establish camp, prepare the roads for transporting the logs, and build a water pipeline to power the mill and supply the soldiers and their horses. The men had to build their camps from scratch, as well as plant and tend crops to reduce the CFC's burden on army supply lines and on the small civilian population.[47] To facilitate their work, besides the mills themselves they built light railway lines and other infrastructure, such as the hospital at Champagnole. Ferdinand Malenfant recorded that after their arrival at Andelot, he worked a week-long shift on railway construction, followed by a week in heavy rain constructing the 47th Company accommodations as well as the storage facilities they would need to begin operations at La Fresse.[48] Louis Daigle

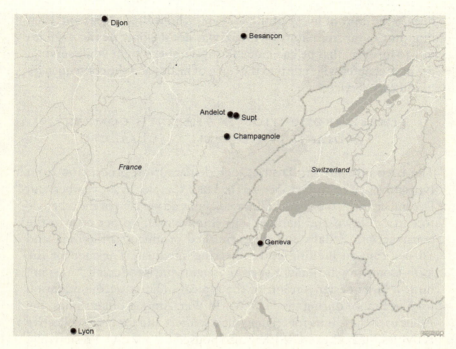

Figure 4.1 Map of the Jura region and key locations for 5th District

complained about the rain and the austere conditions. He described frenetic, exhausting days in which he barely had five minutes to himself to write.[49]

While those stationed south of Bordeaux could count on warmer weather, the Acadians in the Jura contended with freezing temperatures and deep snowdrifts between December and March. Padre Gaudet would have been accustomed to the difficult Canadian winters in New Brunswick, but even he complained sometimes about the conditions: "We have had a miserable week. It has been colder than all reason ... I will be obliged to buy some good firewood to warm myself in a Christian fashion, the wood from the sawmill is green and frozen, and I only have a tiny stove so when the great colds come, I am very uncomfortable. I have a terrible cold."[50] For his part, Fred Frigot thrived in the CFC, writing to his mother that she would not recognize him because he had gained twenty-three pounds and found the work relatively easy. In a perhaps not unrelated note, he thanked her for the frequent packages of candy and even canned lobster, noting that he was the envy of many of the soldiers, who waited weeks and even months to hear from home.[51] Frigot was not the only Acadian volunteer to mention that he had gained considerable weight while serving; the next chapter will return to the topic of health and the consequences of military service.

TIMBER PRODUCTION IN THE 39TH COMPANY (ACADIAN), 5TH DISTRICT (JURA), CFC

The DROs for the 5th District include details on production from November 1917 to October 1918. For example, in November and December 1917, the district allocated about 60 per cent of the schedule to cutting down and hauling logs (lumbering), 30 per cent to the construction of slabs and other finished products at the mill, and 10 per cent to making and collecting sawdust. The men of the 39th Company also had a special assignment: producing "Adrian" huts, a large design variant of the typical military accommodation used in France during the First World War. Among other things, the Allies used these huts for feeding their soldiers and for other collective activities, such as exercise (they also housed the YMCA). Presumably, the foresters cut the boards and crafted the wall and roof sections before loading them onto transport. At their intended destinations, the huts would be fully assembled. As of late November, the Acadians were spending more than half their working hours making Adrian huts; in December, only 15 per cent of their hours. In 1918, the huts were not mentioned at all.

Figure 4.2 indicates that output varied considerably, from a high of 416,858 FBM in the week ending 21 January 1918 to a low of 154,220 FBM in the week ending 19 March 1918. Various internal and external factors would have influenced the numbers. For example, the transition from assembling Adrian hut sections at the end of December seems to have led to a rise in timber production. The high numbers in January and February correspond with Allied preparations for an anticipated German offensive fuelled by the arrival of units from the Eastern Front. The Russians had signed a separate armistice with the Central Powers on 15 December 1917. The need to build defensive positions in depth, improved roads and railways for supply lines, and platforms for artillery guns and tanks had created a huge demand for timber. With the best and most accessible trees already harvested and the spring thaw turning the landscape to mud, the

Life in the Canadian Forestry Corps

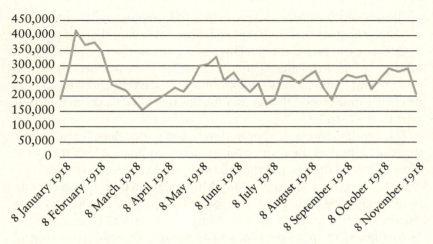

Figure 4.2 FBM produced by 39th Company, 5th District (Jura), CFC (DROs)

39th Company's output fell considerably by March. Periodic heavy rain continuing into the summer months also slowed down the work.

The DROs mention an outbreak of influenza in June, which perhaps further explains the falling production rates. Describing it as a district-wide "epidemic," the authorities ordered all blankets disinfected in order to limit the spread. This "first wave" of what would later be known as the Spanish flu, while "mild and result[ing] in relatively low mortality," caused a noticeable increase in hospitalizations both in Europe and in Canada due to "wartime conditions and patterns of contact." It was followed by a second wave, which proved more virulent for soldiers as well as civilians in the area. In September 1918, the 5th District HQ ordered monthly medical inspections in all CFC camps, noting that this second wave was "severe" and "highly infective." It also informed the men that those "with colds or feverishness should report sick early and not wait until seriously ill." And it took the unpopular step of cancelling all leave to places in France.[52] The subject of illness and hospitalization will be taken up later in this chapter.

The timber needs of the Hundred Days campaign in the fall of 1918 kept the CFC mills buzzing, albeit at a more modest pace than at the beginning of the year. Since the companies also farmed in order to provide some of their own food, it makes sense that there was less production during harvest time at the end of August and in early September. The 5th District HQ had ordered the planting of vegetables in all company locations and provided funds to purchase seed.[53] There is some indication that timber production was falling short of demand in October, not just in the 5th District but across the CFC, as the men anticipated an Armistice. The officers at La Joux worried about the "disturbing influence of such unfounded peace talk and wished it to be clearly understood that at no time has there been a greater need of relentless effort."[54]

The Acadian foresters appeared to be top performers. Their output was the highest in the district for the week ending 12 January 1918. They exceeded that output the following week; indeed, HQ noted this was "the largest production of any Mill to date in this District for one week's run." The 39th Company reported a total cut of 6,989,284 FBM for the month, an amount exceeding the previous best month of November 1917 by 26 per cent and apparently exceeding its assigned objective by 22 per cent. In fact, the 5th District frequently reported that the 39th Company had the highest production for the week (e.g., on 21 February, 14 March, 16 April, 23 July, and 14 August). However, this ceased to be the case in the fall of 1918. There was no apparent drop-off in production, so it might reflect the advances of other CFC companies in the Jura as well as the number of trees left in their assigned zone. The French authorities insisted that the Canadians conform to strict logging practices, which outlawed clear-cutting and preserved at least some of the older stands in order to facilitate recovery after the war.[55] Fedorowich found that CFC operations in Britain were less restrained.[56] Another factor influencing output may have been specific orders received from the Allies, as at the end of 1917, when Adrian huts were requested. For another example, we know that in the spring of 1918 the 5th District received special instructions to harvest 5,000 spruce trees for the construction of airframes.[57]

There is further evidence that the men were working smarter rather than harder as 1918 progressed. The men worked double shifts in January to achieve the higher FBM production, but the company reported nearly ten hours of lost time each week during the same period. In other words, nearly 15 per cent of the peak production time was being wasted as the mill sat idle. Fedorowich reminds us that throughout the CFC, "mechanical breakdowns in the mills were frequent, new plant was difficult to source, labour difficulties were commonplace, accidents and outbreaks of sickness interrupted production."[58] It seems likely that the pressure to produce in anticipation of the German spring offensive contributed to the double shifts.

Figure 4.3 39th Company Sawmill at La Joux

However, the CFC leadership soon realized that continuing to work the men on double shifts would lead to additional hardship and diminishing returns. For the rest of 1918, the men typically worked six shifts a week, or one shift a day, with their Sundays free. As the company adopted a more regular routine, the number of wasted hours dropped to negligible figures and, in some cases, to zero.

Some weeks, such as the one that included Dominion Day (1 July), featured planned holidays and celebrations to keep morale up and recognize the men's efforts. Dominion Day in 1917 fell just as most of the Acadians were settling down in the Jura. This was a particularly noteworthy holiday, for it was the 50th anniversary of Confederation, a fact commented upon by Padre Gaudet in his diary. He described the parade of vehicles bringing the Acadian foresters from the camps to the grounds prepared for the day. A large crowd of French civilians had gathered to watch the Canadians compete in footraces, wrestling matches, and various sporting events. Ferdinand Malenfant noted that despite periods of heavy rain, everyone appreciated the holiday and there were "great sports all over the country."[59]

The Dominion Day festivities expanded even further in 1918; the 47th Company achieved the highest score in the district with wins in several track events and the blindfolded section drill competition, but an American team seems to have come out on top overall. The

39th Company initially won the horseback wrestling competition, but were later disqualified (how does one cheat at horseback wrestling?). Other events in this "Grand Field Day" included baseball, football, tug of war, the centipede race (ten men running with a twenty-foot pole), and boxing (with three weight categories). The Commanding Officer of the 5th District communicated "his appreciation for the general good conduct maintained by all ranks in the whole District throughout the entire day" and offered "his thanks for the untiring efforts of all Committees and others who were responsible for making the day."[60] National pride and company bragging rights had been at stake, but more importantly, celebrations like this represented an opportunity to develop solidarity and contribute to camp life. The district also organized concerts, such as the one held at the local cinema in La Joux in February 1918, which included soldiers performing music and theatrical plays, as well as more boxing.[61]

5TH DISTRICT DIRECTIVES

The 5th District DROs include various directives from the military leadership. Some items simply passed on general instructions issued by higher headquarters, such as the one that prohibited any soldier from possessing a camera and taking photographs.[62] There were several entries related to the care of clothing and equipment. Weekly inspections of essential leather goods in short supply, such as larrigans (special footwear providing protection up to the knee), oilskins, and gloves, ensured that the soldiers kept them in a good state of repair. A board of survey – an official investigation presided over by a senior officer – was ordered to determine the condition and quantities of certain stores at the 39th Company.

Ill-fitting apparel appears to have been a theme; authorities condemned and promised disciplinary action against those soldiers who discarded their army-issued boots in favour of presumably better-made gear in England and also banned unauthorized alterations to uniforms, despite soldiers doing this to make them fit better, because this rendered otherwise serviceable garments "unfit for reissue." Those who sought profit by selling army clothing and equipment to the local population faced court martial. Another common theme was fire prevention. Companies had to maintain sentry pickets at their mills at all times, a duty presumably shared among the men. District headquarters worried about the increased risk of fire that came from

Figure 4.4 Foresters of 39th Company in 1917

heating stoves during the winter months and from dry spells during the summer. Some of the minimum requirements included thawing fire buckets each morning, emptying fuel tanks after work, and cleaning out pipes and pumps regularly. Smoking in mills was strictly forbidden, and a detailed instruction on the prevention of forest fires addressed the need to outfit vehicles and equipment with spark arresters and to ensure that adequate fire extinguishers and water buckets were stationed at central and high-risk locations, including the stables. These were not idle concerns; at least one company in the 5th District suffered a major fire at their sawmill.[63]

Safety concerns were also apparent in the directives related to motor transportation. Headquarters commented in January 1918 on the "large number of accidents which have lately occurred throughout the corps," blaming "incompetent drivers" and "an excessive rate of speed." Winter road conditions likely exacerbated the situation. The directive also highlighted the risk to the civilian population, reminding companies that the maximum speed while driving through towns and villages "must not exceed 6 miles per hour for motor cars and 5 miles per hour for lorries." Additional orders reminded soldiers not to travel through cultivated fields or allow their horses to damage crops by grazing. This must have been a problem reported by local civilians, because these orders were frequently repeated. Furthermore, after a fatal bicycle accident in which a civilian ran into a tractor left on a forest path at night, the staff ordered soldiers to ensure that lights be placed on all vehicles left stationary outside the camp. These directives reflected the dangers of conducting industrial forestry in close proximity to villages and the occasional carelessness of the soldiers. CFC leadership also worried about the social interactions between their members and civilians, directing that the latter could not ride on CFC vehicles or horses without the written permission of the local Commanding Officer. The headquarters later received complaints specifically about women riding in motor cars with the soldiers, a practice that "must cease immediately."[64]

We can infer that the local authorities made complaints about CFC members' bad behaviour from the declaration of certain places and even entire villages "out of bounds." The cinema at La Joux, which previously hosted concerts and other social events for the district, was closed to all foresters in September 1918 because of "non-compliance with orders to keep it clean and orderly."[65] Areas were sometimes declared out of bounds as a health and safety precaution. For example, the village of Arc-sous-Montenot and the nearby US military camp were closed to visitors in May 1918 due to the presence of diphtheria, and the nearby community of Villers-sur-Chalamont suffered an influenza outbreak in October 1918. However, the majority of the restrictions followed incidents at cafés, shops, and nearby homes and, in several cases, explicitly mentioned complaints from local mayors. For example, the "Maison Chevreuil" in La Joux (near the 5th District headquarters), the Hotel de la Gare at Levier, and the premises of the Widow Goguilly near the 70th Company mess were all closed to CFC members after unnamed issues. Individual claims submitted by French civilians indicate that some soldiers racked up considerable debts, especially for alcohol.[66] The staff sometimes issued blanket statements covering an entire community – for example, all hotels and cafés in the community of Vers-en-Montagne were declared out of bounds in November 1917. The entire town of Frasne was closed to CFC members at the request of the mayor in April 1918. Military authorities also sought to limit travel to larger cities – for example, soldiers were forbidden to visit Besançon and Dole, and officers required signed permits if they wished to do so.

Of course, the men wanted to have the opportunity to go on leave, and to travel while on leave. The DROs provide insight into how this worked. Thus, in December 1917 and January 1918, the DROs specifically named those who had been allocated block leave of fourteen days. Those named included twenty Acadian foresters as well as Padre Gaudet. Privates James Bourgeois and Alfred Gallant of the 40th Company obtained the highly sought-after privilege of going to Paris during the Christmas holidays. This may have involved a lottery, as it does not seem to have been related to good conduct: Gallant had several disciplinary infractions and was ultimately sent home early, officially for being underage but probably because of his repeated offences. Most of the other foresters opted to spend their fourteen days in Britain. Groups of men from the same company travelled together by train to authorized waypoints. The number of leaves authorized varied, from a high of fifteen for each company at the end of January 1918 to just one by August of the same year.[67] Serious disciplinary infractions could result in longer waiting periods for block leave; for example, the DROs indicated in August 1918 that anybody found guilty of drunkenness would have three months added before their next eligibility.[68]

Companies could also recommend overnight passes to give deserving soldiers a break from the camps. Typically, these men would spend the night in a local hotel or tavern, if nothing else gaining respite from army food. District leaders noted that they would approve only two passes per company each week and that only soldiers "of good conduct should be recommended." Clearly, military authorities were using eligibility for leave as a tool for strengthening discipline. The company leadership held significant influence regarding who would receive leave in the local area and abroad. They continued to worry about the behaviour of soldiers while they were gone – in particular, about the impression their deportment would make on the local population. Thus, the DROs specified that all soldiers must cut their hair and take a bath the day before departure on block leave and that they must carry at least one change of clothes. There were also frequent reminders that those who contracted a venereal disease must declare it to district medical officers and accept treatment.[69]

Given that each company had a war establishment of 162 men,[70] there was never enough leave for everyone. An overnight pass once a year and perhaps one period of block leave every two years was probably the best that most of the Acadian foresters could hope for. That explains why an evening or Sunday excursion to a nearby café or restaurant became such an important part of the soldiers' routine.

Figure 4.5 39th Company foresters with local civilians

Fedorowich describes the lumbermen's search for solace and companionship in local communities and through organized events such as concerts, church parades, and sports. Compared to British and French soldiers, the Canadians received considerable pay, and local businesses – official or otherwise – were happy to take their money.[71]

Ferdinand Malenfant was lucky: being a bandsman, he sometimes ate at the officers' mess at La Joux after performing there. He also noted several occasions when he took meals in the tiny village of Le Larderet, within walking distance of his camp with the 47th Company, either alone or with his friend and fellow musician "Fricot" Léo Leger. Le Larderet had a population of just over one hundred; nevertheless, besides a church, it had at least two cafés (Le Beau and Chateau) that were open to soldiers. This did not assuage Malenfant's loneliness. He wrote frequently to his wife, sometimes multiple times weekly, and, like most Canadian soldiers, he complained that he did not receive enough news from home. In his private notebook, he often mentioned looking over past letters and postcards and how he was thinking about "wife and baby who I love so much." He wrote poignantly in July 1917 about how far away they were: "I wish my taught [sic] could only reach their little hearts and there's [sic] reach mine How Happy we would be but we are waiting for the day when all Thoughts will be reunion together for ever."[72]

Few of the Acadian correspondences published back home contained much humour. However, Ferdinand Malenfant noted several accidents involving his friend Fricot, who was renowned as both a musician and a comedian. Making light of situations was a way to relieve stress and, one suspects, to express relief that more serious harm had not been done. For example, Fricot fell and strained his ankle while they were crossing the ice to their favourite café, which seems to have led to some levity as they tried to get back to camp. Ferdinand also noted a more serious incident: "Frico had a narrow escape he got tangle with a Bum shell and it went off and he tore a piece of his shirt to dress up the wound Very lucky." He does not explain where this happened, but presumably it was while he was working in the forest. There is no record of Léo Leger being admitted to hospital, so he must indeed have been lucky.[73]

Some of the foresters enjoyed even greater buying power in their search for distractions because they received incentive pay for specialized work as cooks, sawyers, and millwrights. These were prized positions. Private Léon Joseph Boudreau is a case in point. Like many of the Acadian volunteers, he sent home more than half of his regular monthly pay of $33. However, unlike most of his colleagues, he had experience working as a lumberjack near his home in Pointe-Verte, Gloucester County, New Brunswick. Having been selected as a log setter in July 1917, he drew an additional $1.75 per diem, more than doubling his base salary of $1.10. Each company could appoint two log setters, who worked in the mill to process the timber.[74] Boudreau must have excelled at this task, for he would be selected to work in the district workshop as a sawyer in February 1918, for which he earned the princely sum of $3.00 a day in additional salary. Perhaps on account of his highly valued skills, and despite a few brush-ins with summary justice, Boudreau obtained block leave twice, first to England and then, after the war, to Brussels.

Disciplinary infractions could result in the loss of specialized pay. This happened to Private James Lagacé of the 39th Company, another woodsman from northern New Brunswick. After several months drawing technical pay of $2.25 daily as a saw filer, he lost this position in September 1918 after being assigned 28 days of field punishment no. 1 for being absent without leave for just one hour. The loss of pay and privilege probably stung worse than the embarrassment of being tied to a tree for a few hours each day. Similarly, Private Roy of the

47th Company, an older man and an experienced carpenter, lost his lucrative position as a mill engineer after being admitted to hospital with a case of venereal orchitis (inflammation of the testicles). Not everyone lost their position after charges or a bout of VD. Soldiers often complained about the arbitrariness of military justice, but they had little recourse.

The DROs make frequent mention of discipline and controls related to soldiers questioning orders. For example, a December 1917 directive emphasized "prompt, immediate and unhesitating obedience to lawful orders." Soldiers who wished to make a complaint "must do so through the proper channel," that is, through the chain of command. They could not even write home about their grievances. Military censors reviewed each letter home, and the 5th District foresters were reminded that it was "forbidden to write criticisms of superiors or operations, statements that would bring the Army into disrepute, false statements regarding any individual, or to the organization that would bring discredit."[75] Tim Cook has written about the "inherent frustration at the sometimes stupid and senseless demands from above." We can imagine that the endless inspections, medical examinations, picket duties, and control measures sometimes angered the Acadian foresters. Each company would have had its share of "anti-heroes," colourful personalities who were savvy to the ways of the army and who knew how to take occasional liberties – for, example, by feigning illness to escape duty.[76] The jokes and legends that grew around such men would have helped alleviate the boredom and banality of life in the CFC.

Private Boudreau, the experienced woodsman mentioned earlier who enjoyed promotions and multiple occasions for block leave despite his disciplinary problems, may have been one such soldier. A close look at his military file reveals an impressive array of infractions, including malingering, disobeying an order from an NCO, and frequent absences without leave in the 18 months between September 1917 and February 1919. Each infraction brought a sentence of field punishment no. 2 as well as a brief forfeiture of pay. The other company soldiers witnessed his frequent penance, growing his legend. He certainly could afford to miss a few days' pay. Perhaps most revealingly, Boudreau's absences typically involved sneaking out overnight to a nearby village, where other soldiers may have observed him or heard about various escapades. In the next section, we examine disciplinary problems more closely.

DISCIPLINE IN THE ACADIAN CFC COMPANIES

There is little mention of disciplinary problems in the historiography devoted to the CEF. The military authorities tended to minimize cases of assault, sexual violence, theft, and other crimes against the civilian population, as well as ignore cases of unduly harsh treatment of enemy prisoners, including summary executions.[77] What has been written tends to focus on courts martial, because of the detailed legal records available in the archives. Scholars have been particularly interested in the 25 Canadians sentenced to execution by firing squad. That number included seven French-Canadians, five of whom were members of the 22nd Battalion.[78] These twenty-five Canadians were included in a list of more than three hundred executed members of the British Expeditionary Force who received posthumous pardons in 2006.[79]

Given the seemingly high number of French-Canadians, there has been some debate over whether they were less disciplined than their anglophone counterparts in the CEF. Patrick Bouvier tackled the question head-on in his study of CEF deserters facing courts martial overseas. Bouvier identified 148 soldiers charged with desertion who bore a name of French origin, professed the Roman Catholic faith, and lived in Canada before the war (that is, they were not recent French immigrants). While the majority came from Quebec, the group included eight soldiers from New Brunswick, as well as French-Canadians from Ontario and the West. Not surprisingly, he found that most of the men fit the general profile of French-Canadian volunteers that we have already discussed; they tended to be younger, single men with experience working in cities like Montreal as general labourers and tradespeople.

Ultimately, military judges found only 61 of the 148 soldiers guilty of desertion. These men faced substantial penalties, including imprisonment, loss of rank, and significant fines. They sentenced most of the others to minor punishments for the less serious crime of absence without leave. Bouvier explains that the principal difference between the two offences was the soldier's perceived intention. Authorities saw desertion as an attempt to flee military service permanently, whereas absence without leave covered a variety of circumstances from overstaying a leave pass to missing assigned duties.[80] Still, even a conviction for absence without leave could carry a penalty of up to two years' imprisonment. Teresa Iacobelli writes that the military chain of command used considerable discretion when exercising military justice in order to match the punishment to the gravity of the offence. This included considering the individual circumstances of the case and whether collective discipline needed reinforcing. Maximum penalties were reserved for repeat and serious offenders, and commanding officers frequently consulted with subordinate leaders to determine the appropriate sentence.[81] Christopher Pugsley, though, suggests that the Canadians had a reputation for harsh discipline, citing the "draconian methods" of field punishment that so impressed Australian and New Zealand officers. These were "hard men facing hard times," and "if soldiers did not conform, they were broken as an example to the rest."[82]

Bouvier asserts that his findings convincingly demonstrate that discipline was not as much of a problem as "persistent rumours at the time" suggested.[83] While aware that anti-francophone bias existed in some circles, Maxime Dagenais disagrees with Bouvier's conclusion. His detailed study of the summary justice practised at the unit level, in which he compared the results for the 22nd Battalion with those of the other units in the 5th Infantry Brigade, 2nd Canadian Division, found that French-Canadian soldiers did indeed have higher rates of service infractions. While the 22nd Battalion reported 2,457 minor infractions and 233 court-martial convictions between October 1915 and November 1918, the 25th Battalion (Nova Scotia) reported just 920 minor infractions and 109 courts martial. Similarly, the 24th Battalion (Victoria Rifles) reported 911 and 119 cases respectively during the same period.[84] Dagenais contends that circumstances at the time partly explain his findings. While the CO, LCol Tremblay, had earned the respect of the men, his extended absence due to illness as well as the high casualty rate at the Somme – half the battalion was lost – contributed to the situation.[85] It also seems likely that the additional pressure on the 22nd Battalion as the only front-line French-Canadian unit played a role in the number of recorded service offences, in that the unit's leaders were anxious to demonstrate their effectiveness to their often critical anglophone superiors.

What was summary justice? Prior to the 1950 National Defence Act, Canada had no legislation governing the legal administration of its military. The British Army Act established summary justice for minor offences, which could be presided over by unit COs. The idea behind summary justice, still present in the Canadian Armed Forces today, was that prompt and transparent procedures at the unit level would be quicker to find the truth and would do more to promote collective discipline.[86] Lengthy court martials presided over by military judges took up valuable time and created distractions and stress for everyone involved. In addition, judges at courts martial had much greater powers of punishment. For the CEF overseas, better to deal with minor transgressions quickly and move on. Marc-André Hemond explains:

> The investigation usually took place in the morning and was required to be conducted in the presence of the accused. During the investigation, which consisted of the interrogation of witnesses, the accused had the right to cross-examine any witnesses and demand that they be sworn. Following the hearing of accusations, the commanding officer could dismiss the charge if he found that no military offence had been committed. However, if he found otherwise, the accused then had the right to make a statement and call witnesses in his defence, as well as present other applicable evidence. Following this, the commanding officer could decide to dismiss the charge, deal with the charge summarily, or present the charge and findings to a court martial.[87]

Key here was the public nature of summary justice – other members of the unit could observe. The headquarters also published the findings in DROs for all to see.

The most common punishments "awarded" to soldiers found guilty of summary offences included field punishment and forfeiture of pay. Those promoted to acting rank might lose their position, as might those enjoying technical pay for more specialized work within the unit. Sometimes the men were simply "admonished" for their conduct, meaning a formal record but no other apparent penalty. Field punishment no. 1 (FP1) "kept the convicted in irons, attached to an object for two hours per day, for no more than three out of four consecutive days and no more than twenty-one days total." This often involved a prominent tree or fence post, and the soldiers commonly referred to the practice ironically as "crucifixion." Where being attached to an object proved impractical, field punishment no. 2 (FP2) still involved being tied up or chained, but the soldier remained mobile.[88] Given the frequent movement from the camp to different sections of woods, among the trees, and back and forth to the company mill, it is little surprise that FP2 was much more common in the CFC. Sometimes, COs determined that the charges were serious enough to be referred to a court martial. This was a rare occurrence in the CFC camps; in the case of the Acadian companies, it referred to the "field punishment compound" at Rouen. There, in addition to the casual humiliation and discomfort of daily periods of bondage, offenders faced imprisonment and hard labour.

With regard to the 165th Battalion, military personnel records do allude to disciplinary cases arising before the unit left Canada. Of the 593 Acadian volunteers who made it overseas, only 26 faced consequences for violating military justice before they left. Most of these cases involved a single absence without leave, and the only punishment appears to have been forfeiture of pay for the period concerned. Unit leaders chose not to punish such absences too harshly so long as the soldiers returned and resumed their service. A few soldiers did get into more serious trouble. Nine faced detention of varying lengths; in most of these cases, though, the records do not mention the specific charges and the period of imprisonment was only one to seven days. Detention occurred at a designated site at Camp Valcartier or at the barracks in Saint John. Given that just 4 per cent of the volunteers heading overseas faced some form of summary justice before departure, this hardly suggests an undisciplined unit. We might assume that deserters and others later deemed unfit for service had greater issues with summary justice. However, there are few indications of this. Just 14 of 443 volunteers (3 per cent) who did not go overseas had a disciplinary problem recorded in their file (other than desertion, in the case of the deserters). The most troubling case involved one of the anglophone volunteers, Edward Chase, who clearly did not fit in either with the Acadian battalion or with the military in general. Initially detained after being discovered drinking in the barracks, Chase would go on to face several sentences of imprisonment, first by military and later by civilian authorities, on account of his frequent absences and disobedience. The charges against him included resisting arrest and escaping from detention. He ultimately spent three years in and out of jail between 1916 and 1919.

Ovila Richer, who appeared earlier in this book because he was significantly over age at fifty-three years old when he enlisted with the 165th Battalion, was one of the men in the CFC referred to court martial and who ended up in the prison compound at Rouen. In fact, Richer, a Quebecer, had a particularly difficult military career. He enlisted three different times in Canada, first in 1915 with the unhappy 41st Battalion based in Quebec City, then in 1916 with the 69th Battalion, a

French-Canadian unit raised in Montreal that also spent time in Saint John. He was one of the last recruits for the 165th Battalion, signing up in December 1916 while the unit was in winter quarters. He had no apparent Acadian ancestry, so this choice probably reflected his inability to re-enlist at home because of his previous desertions. His medical issues became apparent almost immediately, as he spent two weeks in the military hospital at Saint John for "adenitis" – inflammation of his lymph nodes and other glands. Somehow, Richer passed the final medical examination in March 1917 and went overseas.

Having been posted to the 39th Company, CFC, Richer missed the boat in Southampton and found passage to Le Havre, France, on another military transport two weeks later. Upon arrival, the Army Provost sent him to the Canadian General Base Depot (CGBD) at Étaples. This large camp served multiple functions; it was a training base, a treatment facility, and a detention centre. The latter was clearly the destination for Richer, but he managed to sneak out into the nearby town. Discovered, he forfeited three days' pay for being out of camp without permission. After a week with the CGBD, Richer travelled to the 5th District Headquarters in the Jura and promptly received an additional sentence of seven days of FP2 for missing his company ship. Just two weeks later, he was in front of his CO again, this time facing a charge of conduct to the prejudice of good order and discipline after he had misappropriated military stores "to his own use." The file does not specify the exact nature of his crime, but he received ten more days of FP2. A month later, by this time identified as a serial offender, he spent fourteen more days in FP2 and forfeited a day's pay for being absent without leave overnight, and an additional ten days FP2 after he was found drunk in the camp during his sentence. Headquarters decided to transfer Richer to the 47th Company, perhaps hoping that he would improve with a fresh start.

This was not to be. While most soldiers charged with absence without leave had missed a few hours or perhaps a day, Richer disappeared for nearly a week, from 28 August to 3 September 1917. It is unclear whether he returned on his own accord or if he was apprehended, but he had not gone far and seems to have been drinking excessively. Soon afterwards, he spent several weeks in hospital with nephritis (kidney failure). When he attempted to leave camp again before facing justice, his CO assigned him twenty-eight days of FP1. This more severe punishment did nothing to prevent an obvious downward spiral of drinking and violent behaviour. He broke out again, and this time, on

12 October 1917, he assaulted a French woman in the village of Vers-la-Montagne. Additional charges of drunkenness in nearby communities were recorded in November. Finally, a court martial sentenced Richer to sixty days of FP1, detention, and hard labour at the Rouen compound. However, the military judge agreed to commute his sentence and remove the hard labour, probably because of his continuing poor health. In and out of hospital at Rouen, then in Paris, and finally in England, Richer was sent home and ultimately discharged as medically unfit in July 1918.

Richer's case, while not typical, does reflect common disciplinary challenges in the CEF in general as well as in the CFC camps, such as absence without leave and drunkenness. The three predominantly Acadian companies of the 5th District reported a total of 122 infractions during the twelve months between November 1917 and October 1918; absence without leave (40 per cent) and drunkenness (23 per cent) accounted for nearly two-thirds of these charges. The rest mainly involved disobedience, negligence, and getting into fights.

In his study of the 5th Infantry Brigade, Dagenais also found that absence without leave was the most common matter dealt with via summary justice. During a similar period between October 1917 and November 1918, the 22nd Battalion reported 461 absences, 71 charges of drunkenness, and 155 other minor infractions. Meanwhile, the 26th Battalion (New Brunswick) reported 228 absences, 28 charges of drunkenness, and 129 minor infractions between January and October 1918.[89]

Absence without leave was an even greater problem in infantry units, while drunkenness was less common. This undoubtedly reflected life at the front, where soldiers would have been more motivated to miss work due to the danger but probably had less opportunity to drink to excess.[90] There may also have been more willingness to turn a blind eye at the front. Cook argues that the military authorities accepted drinking in part because soldiers insisted on comforts like alcohol, tobacco, cards, and other pastimes. This put army leadership and veterans' groups in opposition with temperance groups lobbying for prohibition at home.[91] In the CFC camps, much of the drinking addressed through summary justice involved incidents in neighbouring villages.

It is also interesting to note the number of charges in relation to the total strength of the units concerned. The 22nd Battalion, with around 1,100 soldiers, reported 687 infractions during a twelve-month period,

Life in the Canadian Forestry Corps

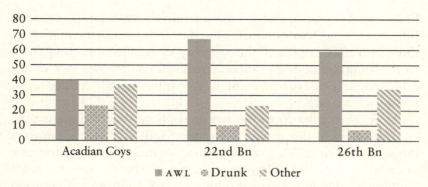

Figure 4.6 Nature of charges (%) in Acadian CFC Coys, 22nd Bn, 26th Bn CEF

while the 26th Battalion, with just over 1,000 soldiers, reported 385 infractions during a ten-month period. Meanwhile, the three Acadian CFC companies, with approximately 420 men, reported relatively fewer – a total of 122 infractions incurred by just 83 offenders.

A more detailed review of the personnel files of the 593 former members of the 165th Battalion who made it overseas reveals that 191 faced at least one charge during their military service from the time of enlistment through to demobilization. If approximately one-third of the soldiers appear in the disciplinary record, two-thirds did not. What about unreported cases? It is certainly easy to imagine that colluding soldiers helped one another occasionally escape the camp for a meal and a drink or, perhaps, for female companionship. However, the degree of detail in the personnel files and the DROs suggests that leadership was thorough; even being late for roll call, refusing to take a bath, or throwing away a ration could result in charges. In most cases, the humiliation of field punishment or the sting of lost wages seems to have set soldiers back on the straight and narrow path. Indeed, 102 of the 191 offenders faced a single charge, and 12 of these arose while the 165th Battalion was still in Canada. Thirty-nine others who fell into trouble twice perhaps needed a reminder of the rules or were caught up in a bad situation outside of their control. This leaves just 50 of 593 men who faced multiple charges (at least three different incidents). The winner of the dubious honour of highest number of summary convictions was Private C. LeBlanc, an underage fisherman originally from the Magdalen Islands, although he had moved to Barachois, New Brunswick, before enlisting. His record is particularly noteworthy because all of his infractions occurred in

France with the CFC, that is, over a relatively short period between June 1917 and October 1918. In addition to being absent without leave, LeBlanc exasperated the company leadership by refusing to do work, being drunk and insolent, creating a disturbance in a village café, and, in the days leading up to Christmas 1917, "committing a nuisance" in camp.

Figure 4.7 breaks down the 388 convictions recorded among the 191 offenders of this group of former 165th Battalion volunteers throughout their military service. When we include the training time in Canada, which adds thirty-seven charges, the proportion of absence without leave rises somewhat, although still far from the numbers reported by the infantry at the front. Iacobelli notes that forestry units recruiting in Canada experienced high rates of desertion because of competition from civilian production heightened by the burgeoning demand for wood caused by the war.[92] For their part, the Acadian volunteers overseas, consistent with the information recorded in the DROs described in the previous figure, had fewer cases of absence without leave but faced more charges of drunkenness and other minor infractions related to disobedience, poor conduct, negligence, and violent disturbances. Sometimes convictions mentioned multiple issues, for example, disobedience and insolence towards an NCO or superior officer, so those cases are categorized according to the first and principal charge.

Charges such as disobedience and conduct prejudicial to good order and discipline covered a wide range of offences. As we have seen, military authorities issued directives on everything from how to maintain equipment to how soldiers should be dressed when preceding on leave. Some convictions may appear frivolous, such as those involving soldiers who refused to take a bath when ordered to do so; however, they speak to larger issues around health and safety. In chapter 2, we learned that military inspectors found some of the Acadian volunteers left behind in Saint John in a deplorable state, with vermin-infested clothing. The CFC leadership worked hard to ensure cleanliness in order to avoid illness and infection. Extra uniforms and blankets were in short supply, so adequate laundry services were essential. Soldiers faced field punishment for being "found in a filthy condition."

Another more unusual case involved Private W. Copeland, an experienced woodsman from northern New Brunswick. The OC of the 47th Company appointed him acting corporal, although he would lose that position after being absent without leave in January 1918.

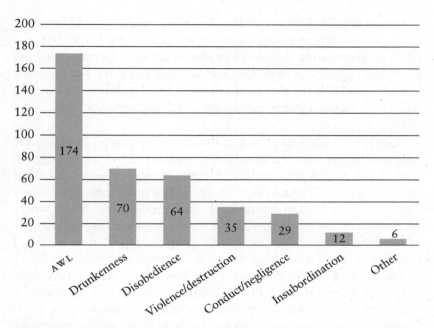

Figure 4.7 Summary charges among the 165th volunteers who went overseas

Arrested for being drunk and resisting arrest in December 1918, Copeland was also discovered to be "improperly in possession of 1000 frames." The content of the film is unrecorded, but it must have been concerning because he faced trial by court martial in Rouen and received the sentence of two years' imprisonment with hard labour. In May 1919 the military judge commuted Copeland's sentence to detention and allowed him to return to Canada. Most of the cases involving conduct and disobedience related to negligence, such as sleeping on the job or refusing to complete assigned work. At least one charge concerned causing damage to mill machinery, although the light sentence of five days' FP2 suggests that the case concerned an accident rather than deliberate sabotage.

Regarding drunkenness, as mentioned earlier, the conclusion is not necessarily that the Acadian foresters drank more than other soldiers, although they may have had more opportunity. Rather, the issue was that their drinking occurred mostly in nearby villages among the civilian population. The charges often contained details that the soldier was drunk and created a public disturbance or was drunk in a public place, indicating that it was the damage to the reputation of the

Canadian army, not the act of drinking itself, that merited punishment. Even in cases where alcohol was not specifically mentioned, it was likely an aggravating factor. For example, Edouard Comeau received a sentence of fourteen days' FP2 and forfeited two days' pay for being absent without leave throughout the night of 5 July 1917, during which he created a public disturbance and damaged property in the village of Chapois.

Faye Wilson discusses the role that drinking played in masculine military culture. Many middle-class Canadians as well as government leaders like Militia Minister Sam Hughes promoted temperance and tried to limit soldiers' access to alcohol. Overseas, some CEF leaders understood the need to create supervised canteens and messes where soldiers could consume alcohol safely, thereby reducing the number of incidents in local villages.[93] Judging by the repeated mentions of problems in the DROs, the primary access to drink for CFC soldiers continued to be through local cafés, hotels, and restaurants. One outstanding claim from a French civilian involved rum procured by the company leaders for their soldiers during Thanksgiving supper.[94] Canteen accounts from the 5th District also show regular purchases of beer and cigarettes as well as loans issued to soldiers.[95] Concerts and sports days organized by the army leadership and the Red Cross could help; Abel Belliveau described going to concerts on successive days because there was nothing else to do.[96] The foresters sought escape from the daily drudgery of the camps, and Kent Fedorowich explains that the higher "buying power" of the Canadian woodsmen as a result of their better salaries and generous technical pay led to competition with soldiers from other countries – particularly the British and Americans – as well as with one another, for drink and women.[97] Indeed, Félicien Landry wrote to his parents in June 1917 that he had no need for money, although he would appreciate good cigarettes because they were hard to find.[98]

The small communities of the Jura established a multitude of places to profit from the presence of the CFC, but their capacity to do so was still limited, and the district headquarters found it difficult to ensure a reasonable rotation of hundreds of thirsty and bored soldiers. Cameron Bartlett writes that the foresters maintained generally positive relations with the local people but adds that "inevitably, there was also a dark side to some of the Canadian soldiers' interactions with the locals; soldiers were often accused of stealing from nearby homes."[99] The Acadians' ability to speak French certainly intrigued the locals and helped them connect. Claude Léger consulted a local history report written in Champagnole in 1988 that drew a distinction between the Canadian foresters generally, known to be hard men who enjoyed their liquor, and the Acadians, who were devout Catholics, spoke French with an antiquated accent, and felt at home with the local population.[100] Ferdinand Malenfant regularly mentioned visiting cafés and restaurants.[101] Fred Frigot described reading French newspapers, which helped him stay current on what was happening in the war, and even visiting new friends in their homes to discuss the situation. He told his sister that they wanted to know whether he would return to France after the war. In a subsequent letter to his mother, he described the importance of the bonds among soldiers and how he and the other men from Caraquet, even though they were in different CFC companies, got together regularly to socialize and share news.[102] William Foret, in a letter home to his parish priest, similarly remarked on the importance of the group from Shediac sticking together and supporting one another. He added that he found the area very agreeable and that he was well aware that it was a different story beyond the horizon (by which he meant closer to the front).[103]

This did not mean that the soldiers always got along in camp. Several "disturbances" in the accommodation huts and the mess suggest that arguments and even brawls were regular occurrences. Not surprisingly, the official record downplays these incidents, and the soldiers did not write home about them. In his private notebook, Ferdinand Malenfant described the "Battle of the Bath House" as a two-day ordeal involving firearms in which he "nearly got wounded." He laconically referred to it as "some fight" and noted that Emile LeBlanc and someone named "Cooper" were among the antagonists. This intriguingly suggests conflict between francophone and anglophone foresters.[104] We might also wonder how Sergeant Blais suffered so many cuts to his fingers and face in August 1918, and how Private Pelletier ended up with a gunshot wound to his left leg shortly after Christmas.[105]

The DROs and the information on disciplinary matters in soldiers' personnel files support the notion that the majority of the Acadian foresters got along just fine with the local population, but there were certainly some disturbances as well as incidents of theft and damage to property. In one serious case, Private J. Richard of the 47th Company stole 2,000 francs from a local resident on Christmas Eve 1918. He was remanded to the military prison at Rouen, where a court martial held on 5 February 1919 found him guilty of theft as well as conduct to the prejudice of good order and discipline. He was awarded two years' imprisonment with hard labour. More minor disturbances led to summary convictions, and often the soldier concerned was required to make restitution. For example, Private J. Lelievre of the 47th Company suffered five days of FP2 and was also ordered to repair a fence he had broken in August 1917. Private P. Lavoie of the 40th Company had multiple incidents of creating disturbances in Andelot shortly after his arrival in June 1917 and again at a hotel in Champagnole in September of the same year. These disturbances included at least some violence, as in both cases he resisted arrest and was convicted of striking a military policeman. Those policemen certainly had a thankless job; the DROs frequently mentioned resisting arrest or breaking free from escort among the charges made against the more serious offenders. Another case, involving Private C. Gaudet of the 40th Company, reveals that CFC leadership went so far as to assign sentries (pickets) in nearby villages in order to head off incidents. Gaudet struck one of his fellow soldiers assigned to this duty in the village of Pontarlier in August 1918. The post-Armistice revelry led to additional concerns and security.[106]

The worst recorded incident involving violence between Acadian foresters and French civilians was the death of Jean-Baptiste Daigle. One of the older, married volunteers, Daigle fit the description of an "anti-hero." A fisherman from Petite-Aldouane, not far from Richibucto, New Brunswick, Daigle had moved to Moncton before the war in search of work, leaving his wife at home. Having been assigned to the 40th Company, he faced summary justice on three separate occasions for drunk and disorderly conduct. The first time, shortly after he arrived in the Jura, he was simply found drunk on a public road. The second offence, which also involved being out in public, included the charge of creating a disturbance and bore the more considerable penalty of ten days' FP2. The third incident involved drunkenness and disobedience. Given that he had been charged three times for drunkenness within four months of arriving, it is surprising that the CFC leadership raised him to the rank of lance corporal in October 1917. Unfortunately, Daigle continued to drink to excess, and he died in an altercation with a French farmer, Mathieu Edmond, in the hamlet of Montmarlon, on 5 June 1918. As previously mentioned, his widow, Salomé, received some compensation. In the 1921 Canadian Census, she is recorded as a widowed head of household with three children and as having moved to the farming community of Saint-Charles. This was one case in which military service had a clear and lasting impact on the family back home.

Daigle's military personnel file includes witness statements from the court of inquiry ordered into the matter. These records reveal more about what happened and touch on interactions between CFC soldiers more generally and the local population. The village mayor, Léon Girod, as well as his daughter, stated that Daigle and several other soldiers had been drinking at the café they had established in their home. They reported no issues and that when asked, the soldiers left without complaint around 9:30 p.m. Girod went on to relate that Edmond woke him at 10:45 p.m. looking for his gun, which the mayor had previously borrowed, and that he needed help because some Canadians were breaking his windows. In his own statement, Edmond reported being woken by the sound of glass breaking and that when he went outside to investigate he found two soldiers throwing rocks at his house. A confrontation ensued, and blows were exchanged. Unable to drive off the soldiers by force, Edmond went searching for his shotgun. He claimed that he did not initially intend to load it but decided to do so after hearing more glass breaking and his wife shouting. He hurried back to confront the soldiers:

> There, I met one of the Canadians who, when I passed by, hit me on the right side of the face. I fell, and the gun slipped from my hands. I got up to my feet as quickly as possible, got hold of my gun, and just as I was getting up, I saw the other Canadian coming behind me. I pressed the trigger without aiming, at the same time receiving a blow on the head. The shot once fired, as I was always receiving blows on the head, given by one who I recognized the next day as the Soldier Richard, Patrick, I tried to go towards the Maire's house, always calling for help. I must have fell twice. The second time, the Canadian fell across my body in such a way that it was possible for me to squeeze his head with my arm and turn him underneath. I then could disengage myself, got up, and on getting up gave the soldier a blow over the head with the butt of the gun.

While the military record simply noted that Daigle died instantly from the gunshot wound to the left temple, Edmond's testimony described a protracted brawl in which at least three Acadian foresters were present (he mentions Private Goguen as well). Besides emphasizing the numerical superiority of his assailants, Edmond declared that he had been responding to his wife's cries for help and had simply been trying to protect her.

From the statements of the soldiers involved, we learn that four Acadians had travelled together to Montmarlon that evening. Their statements only add confusion to the sequence of events. Private Richard, who grappled with Edmond and suffered a head injury from the butt of his shotgun, claimed that after the party had left the café, Daigle suggested turning back to the village to meet some friends. Either because it was dark or because they were drunk, Daigle and Richard did not find the right house, and Richard decided to head back to camp on his own. Since the village of Montmarlon had only a handful of dwellings, this suggests how drunk they must have been. Richard came across Private Goguen on the road but "not knowing him pushed him aside and I immediately went and sat on a big log by the side of the road where I remained five or six minutes, got up and started walking on the road in the direction of the camp." Shortly after that, he heard a gunshot and decided to investigate. According to Richard, at this point Edmond approached him and threatened to shoot him. The soldier defended himself and then ran away, passing in front of Daigle, "who was lying on the side of the road." Richard, not realizing that Daigle was dead, cut across the fields in order to return to camp. Tellingly, he did not report the matter. Private Goguen confirmed that Daigle and Richard had decided to turn back and related that he left Private LeBlanc walking towards the camp because he wanted to see where they were going. He described coming across Private Richard "standing on the road, and when I came up to him, he hit me in the face with his fist. I still have a black eye from the blow. I called out to him, but he took no notice, so I left him there and turned back to come to camp." Goguen added that he heard the sound of breaking glass and then the gunshot and so went back to investigate. By then, the mayor and several other civilians had arrived, and they took him to the café, where, Goguen claimed, Edmond pointed the shotgun at him and threatened him.

The court of inquiry documents are revealing in several ways. First, the fact that the mayor and other villagers, including Edmond himself, collaborated in the investigation with detailed statements, suggests that maintaining cordial relations with the CFC was an important consideration and that there was some level of trust in the company officers. At the same time, the inhabitants had taken care to hold Private Goguen overnight at the café and had asked him some questions of their own. All of the testimonials claim that the mayor and Edmond previously knew none of the soldiers, even though the village was just three miles from the 40th Company camp, there was only one café, and the soldiers knew the road and also how to cut across the fields when returning to camp. Edmond stated that he recognized Private Richard the next morning because he had been fighting with him, although the dark and the frenzied description of the scuffle might cast doubt on this assertion. Indeed, Daigle seemed to know other locals and wanted to visit one of them. Also, why did the soldiers throw rocks at Edmond's house after they were unable to find this other home? What instigated their attack on Edmond in the first place? Why did Private Richard assault Private Goguen on the road? It was obvious that Daigle had been shot and at least wounded, so why did Private Richard not report the incident or seek help from his comrades at the camp? It is very likely that there is more to the story here than is being told and that both the soldiers and the civilians involved sought to downplay the events.

The officers who comprised the court of inquiry were not entirely certain what to make of the case and the conflicting testimonials, so they left out the details they did not like. For unknown reasons, the president of the board absented himself and did not sign the report. The two lieutenants involved – quite junior members to be conducting such an important investigation – made a point of insisting that the soldiers were not drunk, even though the men had admitted to consuming 2 to 2.5 litres of white wine each in a short period. The officers attributed this conclusion to the fact that the soldiers left the café quietly when asked. While indirectly acknowledging that the soldiers had instigated the incident, they judged that the destruction of a few windows "did not warrant the introduction of a firearm" and dismissed the suggestion that Edmond's wife was in any danger, since the farmer had left her in the house when he went to get the gun. While the officers had difficulty figuring out which of the other soldiers had been present and what role they had played in the tragic encounter, they contended that "it looks very strongly as though aim was taken by the accused and that L/Cpl Daigle was foully murdered."

The partisanship is obvious in these conclusions: there is no explanation for the soldiers throwing rocks at the farmhouse, nor is there consideration of the fact that Edmond was outnumbered at least two to one and faced attack in his own home at the hands of trained soldiers. Private Richard had clearly been struck and admitted to brawling with Edmond. The ridiculous statement about the soldiers not being drunk ignores the obvious evidence in the soldiers' own statements about stumbling around in the dark, hitting each other as well as Edmond, and failing to report what had happened when they got back to camp. Not everyone accepted the report; Padre Gaudet wrote that Major Legere accused him of "seditious discourse" because of his questions about the circumstances surrounding the incident.[107] Fortunately for Edmond, it would not be the 40th Company court of inquiry that determined his fate. Instead, even though a civilian, Edmond faced a court martial for his lethal attack on a soldier. A correspondence dated January 1919 confirmed that the regional commander at Besançon found him innocent and sent him home following a trial held on 17 December 1918.[108]

In general, the disciplinary records reveal that some of the Acadian volunteers struggled to accustom themselves to the routine in the CFC camps and to get along with one another. One in five of the original volunteers simply left while the 165th Battalion was training in Canada, but desertion overseas was a much more serious and complicated matter. How would they return home? Instead, disgruntled, bored, or unhappy soldiers turned to drink, got into fights with their comrades, or neglected their duties. Although about one-third of those who deployed overseas faced summary justice at least once during their military service, most of them shaped up quickly and avoided further incident. Less than 10 per cent of the men appeared to be serial offenders so as to prompt harsher punishment, including courts martial or discharge by military authorities. As we have seen, the CFC camps were busy, expectations for production were high, and available reserves were limited, so the unit's officers had reasons to keep the men working. At the same time, if they allowed too much laxity in the camps, with soldiers freely moving back and forth to village cafés, restaurants, and hotels, incidents harming production timetables and leading to fraught relations with civilian authorities could arise. The death of Jean-Baptiste Daigle was an exceptional and tragic incident emblematic of a masculine military culture fuelled by alcohol, as well as the considerable efforts on the part of army leadership and civilian communities to curtail it.

GOOD CONDUCT BADGES, PROMOTIONS, AND APPOINTMENTS

The majority of the soldiers were never charged with anything, and a significant number of them were recognized for good conduct and leadership through badges, promotions, leave, and incentive pay. The DROs record 98 Good Conduct Badges (GCBs) for the twelve months between November 1917 and October 1918, the same period for which they document 122 summary infractions for 93 offenders. In other words, it was just as likely that soldiers would be recorded for good conduct as for bad. As the DROs explained, anyone completing "a period of two years during which he is clear of any entry in the Regimental Conduct Book" was eligible. Nearly one-third of the soldiers in the 47th Company (forty-three of them) earned a GCB. Only five of the 98 Acadian foresters later lost their chevron owing to disciplinary problems, a further indication that these reliable performers formed a distinct subgroup within the company. We might also wonder whether some of these badges went unrecorded. When we look at the complete personnel records for the 593 former members of the 165th Battalion who made it overseas, we find that 191 faced at least one disciplinary charge, 110 received a good conduct badge, and 292 others were not recorded as receiving either. The prominent display of the GCB on the sleeve of the uniform was a visible marker of exemplary service.

The GCB did not carry any financial incentive, so those motivated largely by economic goals would have been more interested in gaining an appointment with technical pay while at the CFC camp. The DROs are not as helpful on this front, recording just a handful of these appointments sporadically during the period consulted. However, an examination of the complete personnel files allows us to identify thirty-one Acadian volunteers selected for various jobs, including saw filers (those who maintained the saws), sawyers, edgermen (responsible for the final condition of the planks created in the mill), log setters (who ensured that the mill machinery was properly set up), and millwrights.[109] The list included five cooks, a clerk, and a tailor – jobs not necessarily related to lumbering. Interestingly, only six of these tradesmen also earned a GCB. Previous experience explains some of the appointments. Louis Cormier, a lumberman who had lost an eye in 1912, could still see well enough to serve as an edgerman. Four of the six saw filers reported a job in carpentry before enlistment and so were undoubtedly selected due to their familiarity with the tools. On the other hand, one of the declared woodcutters, Isidore Jean, of Saint-Jean-de-Dieu, Quebec, was still a teenager when the 47th Company appointed him as their engineer. How much experience did he really bring to the CFC? Just seven of the thirty-one men concerned had declared lumbering or carpentry as their primary occupation.

There are indications that at least some of the other men had worked as seasonal forestry workers. For example, the military doctor reported that Philip Levesque, another French-Canadian from Quebec, although working in Edmundston, New Brunswick, when he enlisted, had multiple axe cuts on his legs. Many of the volunteers from Madawaska and Restigouche Counties in New Brunswick, as well as some from the Baie Sainte-Marie in Nova Scotia, where the Stehelin family owned a large mill employing many Acadians, likely brought previously acquired lumbering skills to the CFC. The 1911 Canadian Census provides further clues, at least for those old enough to be working at that time. Thus, James Lagacé of Gloucester County, New Brunswick, worked at a lumber mill with his father before the war. Joseph LeBlanc of Chéticamp, on Cape Breton, had worked as a miner, which might explain why the 40th Company entrusted him with some of the mill's heavy machinery. He would later be sent for advanced training in metallurgy at a school in Abbéville. Still, unlike the men recruited in Canada specifically for forestry duties, the men of the 165th Battalion had been recruited and trained for the infantry. At least some of those trained infantrymen later selected for specialized positions in the CFC must simply have shown an aptitude for those positions during the forestry training organized at Sunningdale in England. Given that their average age was two years older (just over 24 years) than that of the Acadian volunteers as a whole, general life experience and maturity may also have played a role.

Continuing in this vein, we might expect that older men would be preferred for NCO positions in the CFC camps. The military *appointed* soldiers to acting rank, usually on a temporary basis to address a specific need or absence, but *promoted* them to substantive rank, which was a more permanent decision. Often, after a certain amount of time at an acting rank, the military "confirmed" the individual in that position, that is, they made it permanent.[110] Substantive rank always included the commensurate pay, whereas acting rank could be with or without the increase. Most of the thirty-nine cases mentioned in the 5th District DROs concerned acting appointments, although five individuals were confirmed in the substantive rank of sergeant. In the military personnel records, we found 186 men granted appointments and promotions among the 593 Acadian volunteers of the 165th Battalion who went overseas. We eliminated the fifty-five cases occurring before the unit left Canada or during the initial days at Shoreham-by-Sea, as these men reverted to the rank of private upon transfer to their new unit in France and were not selected for promotion again. This left us with 131 cases, 60 of which were on an acting basis, that provide insight into what CFC military leadership was looking for to create an effective NCO corps.

To review the basic hierarchy, soldiers could be promoted to lance corporal (LCpl), corporal (Cpl), sergeant (Sgt), and warrant officer (WO). Andrew Brown writes that NCOs have been the backbone of every modern Western army. It is their responsibility to "safeguard tactical expertise, corporate memory, and general efficiency. These practised soldiers draw on their years of experience to maintain discipline among the rank and file, to serve as experts in the employment and maintenance of weaponry, to act as instructors, and, as tactical leaders in the field, to execute battle plans by leading the junior ranks in combat."[111] In his study of the Hundred Days campaign, Lee Windsor emphasizes that an important factor in the CEF's success was that it was able to replace fallen leaders, including NCOs, using a "merit-based system that identified, cultivated, and redistributed men who stood out among their peers because they demonstrated the qualities that make good leaders."[112] Of course, the circumstances of NCO selection and replacement were different in the CFC camps than at the front.

Starting with the top, four Acadians achieved the rank of WO as well as appointment to the senior position of company sergeant major (CSM). This was the highest NCO position in each CFC Company; the individual worked closely with the Officer Commanding (OC) to ensure company production and was also responsible for discipline and camp routine. For example, the CSM typically laid charges and recommended GCBs. Surprisingly, younger men sometimes rose to this high position in the CFC. For example, Joseph Pitre, originally from Maine but living with his family in Rogersville, New Brunswick, before the war, was just eighteen when he enlisted and not yet twenty-one when he was promoted to WO in February 1919. Pitre had first been selected as a Sgt in the 165th Battalion, reverted to the rank of private upon transfer to the 39th Company, and, after a stint as engineer, then sawyer, began rising up the ranks again, beginning in October 1918. Maxime "Eddy" Daigle of Edmundston, New Brunswick, was part of a farming family long resident in the Madawaska. There was nothing obvious that set him apart from his comrades. He started in the 40th Company, then transferred to the 47th Company, where he quickly rose from Sgt to WO in November 1917. He was just twenty-two years old when appointed CSM. Abel Belliveau, around the same age as Daigle, was an experienced carpenter from Moncton and one of the more prolific letter writers, which suggests a certain level of education. He was another volunteer selected for NCO rank in Canada, and then again in France. In chapter 3, we cited his description of the special quarters and privileges he enjoyed as part of the NCO corps while aboard the SS *Metagama*. Éric Léger of Richibucto was first appointed acting CSM of the 39th Company in September 1917; he was confirmed in that position in November of the same year. He also had a farming background, but he was clearly well-educated, for he worked as a bank clerk before the war and one of his siblings was a teacher. Like his three colleagues in the 5th District, he was relatively young – just twenty years old when he enlisted. None of these men declared previous military experience; in fact, the only obvious difference between them and the other volunteers is that they were tall. The average height of this cohort of Acadian volunteers was five feet, six inches (see chapter 3). Belliveau stood five feet, eight inches, and Éric Léger was five feet, ten inches. These four men seemed to be in excellent physical condition, judging by their chest measurement in relation to their height. Perhaps traditional stereotypes associating physical stature with military leadership factored into their selection.[113] It is also likely not a coincidence that three of the four CSMs were from southeastern New Brunswick, like the majority of the volunteers.

The six men temporarily appointed to the position of acting CSM without the matching substantive promotion to WO were a more diverse group, one that included men from the Madawaska as well as from Cape Breton. Thus, they were more representative of the broader Acadian community. Three of these men were older, established professionals, and four had some previous military experience. Laurie Comeau, another younger NCO, may have been headed for promotion to WO before his sudden death from tuberculosis in October 1917. Abel Belliveau, still just a Sgt at that time, advised his parents of this

Table 4.1
Acadians appointed to the position of acting CSM in 5th District, CFC

Name	Declared age	Declared occupation	Height	Military experience	Declared residence
Harry Boudreau	30	Insurance agent	5 ft, 4 in	No	Richmond, NS
Joseph Charest	44	Postmaster	5 ft, 5 in	No	Madawaska, NB
Laurie Comeau	19	Waiter	5 ft, 7 in	104th Bn	Amherst, NS
Arthur LeBlanc	34	Electrician	5 ft, 8 in	4th Bn	Moncton, NB
Thomas LeBlanc	21	Schoolteacher	5 ft, 9 in	Normal school	Chéticamp, NS
Louis Michaud	20	Labourer	5 ft, 6 in	Yes	Madawaska, NB

loss, a sign that the NCO corps were close and worked together. Judging by the tone of the letter, in which Belliveau describes his desire to return home and asks for his parents' prayers, he was certainly affected by Comeau's death.[114]

These temporary appointments did not always end well. Arthur LeBlanc appeared destined for advancement and had already been selected as acting regimental sergeant major for the 165th Battalion by LCol Daigle in May 1916, perhaps because of his previous training as one of the first CEF Acadian volunteers in 1914. He was soon appointed acting CSM for the 39th Company, but just two months later he lost the position due to a summary charge for conduct to the prejudice of good order and discipline. That the CFC leadership took this case particularly seriously because of the member's rank is attested to by the additional details noted in the file. LeBlanc was found guilty of belittling "the prestige of his superior officers by making derogatory remarks as to their ability" in the presence of other NCOs and the men. He was given another chance at the rank of Cpl in November 1917 but again reverted to the rank of private in January 1918 after being convicted of a charge of absence without leave. Meanwhile, Thomas LeBlanc temporarily lost his position for "highly improper conduct," namely, for suggesting that soldiers should be allowed to pay cash for an early return to Canada. Clearly, CFC officers wanted to ensure that their NCOs, whom they relied upon to enforce discipline and order, set a good example. Some did not enjoy the task. Joseph Charest reverted to the rank of Sgt at his own request after three months serving as acting CSM for the 47th Company. His civilian experience as a postmaster prepared him well for the duties of an orderly room sergeant, looking after the men's pay and administration.

Some of the acting CSMs were older men whom the younger volunteers may have looked up to, but it seems that for substantive promotion, the officers preferred to evaluate those among the younger foresters who showed the most leadership potential, taking education and physical presence into consideration. They may have thought that selecting among the larger group would foster trust and respect, which were preconditions for the position. Company commanders almost certainly would have consulted with their sergeants and other NCOs to determine who was likely to have the most sway. While the CSM assisted the company leadership with larger questions and concerns, this larger NCO group ensured the completion of day-to-day tasks as well as the health and safety of the men. These leaders worked most closely with the rest of the group.

A more detailed study of the forty-two sergeants and acting sergeants appointed in the three Acadian companies of the CFC's 5th District suggests a more predictable focus on older men, particularly those with previous military experience or skilled trades and education. Although not taller than their subordinates, these NCOs tended to be broader in the chest, another indication of their relative physical maturity and life experience. In fact, their average age of twenty-six at enlistment was fully four years higher than that of the overseas contingent of Acadian volunteers as a whole. Twelve of the sergeants were at least thirty, and two men, Frederick Barrieau of Adamsville and Joseph Gaudet of Rogersville, were well into their forties at the time of appointment. An exceptional case was that of Fred Cormier, who was just fifteen when he enlisted with the 145th Battalion. He later transferred to the Acadian national unit. This was a case of technical expertise. He was selected for the signals detachment and later sent to the 23rd Battalion (Reserve) in England. His age probably explains why he was not sent to the front before the end of the war. Back in the CFC camps, we find that fourteen of these NCOs, fully one-third, had previous military service, a rare commodity among the former 165th Battalion volunteers. In addition, the occupational background of these NCOs was completely different: the majority of them were tradesmen, sales clerks, or skilled labourers.

Appointments and promotions while the 165th Battalion was still in Canada had tended to favour those from southeastern New Brunswick. Virtually all of the officers came from prominent families

Table 4.2
Declared occupation at enrolment (%) 165th Battalion volunteers

Sector	Overseas contingent	Sergeants
Agriculture	22	12
Education	3	10
Fishing/sea	9	2
Labourer	36	12
Mining	3	0
Professional/official	2	2
Clerical/sales	6	20
Trades/transportation	17	41
Forestry/woods	2	0

in that region, and there was a strong Moncton contingent across the ranks. It is not surprising that these officers tended to choose men they knew to serve as NCOs. However, CFC officers did not show the same favouritism; men from northern New Brunswick and especially Nova Scotia, regions with strong natural resource industries, including forestry, were overrepresented among the sergeants.

The sixty-six junior NCOs, the corporals and lance corporals, were more broadly representative of the overseas contingent of Acadian volunteers. They were only slightly older on average than the rest of the men and of similar physical stature. They also came from across the Acadian regions of the Maritime provinces; the only area that stood out for the relatively high number of men selected for promotion was Gloucester County in northern New Brunswick. Few of the corporals and lance corporals had previous military experience, and only a handful declared their principal occupation as forestry, but artisans and sales clerks again stood out. Education, including basic math skills, as well as skilled trades were clear factors in the choice of NCOs. According to the 1911 Canadian Census, over 90 per cent of them could read and write and almost two-thirds were bilingual – a clear help in the CFC camps. There may also have been a preference for those with more varied life experience. More than half of the sergeants and nearly half of the junior NCOs were not living in their birthplace at the time of enlistment, suggesting a link between mobility and maturity.

A final way in which Acadian foresters might be recognized and rewarded by the CFC leadership was through plum assignments and training opportunities. For example, Alcide Amirault of West

Figure 4.8 A group of sergeants from 39th Company in the Jura

Pubnico, Nova Scotia, completed a six-week cooking course at a culinary school in Rouen, and Joseph LeBlanc of Chéticamp was selected for a two-month training course at the Abbéville School of Farriery. Several Acadians pursued spots with the RFC. At least three Acadian pilots died during flight training or while on missions: Aimé Legere of Cocagne and Albert Melanson of Bathurst, New Brunswick, as well as Rémi Pertus of D'Escousse, Nova Scotia. With the Hundred

Days campaign of 1918 and the continuing demand for leaders and men at the front, at least some of the Acadian foresters recognized for their potential would have the opportunity to contribute directly to the fighting.

DISEASE, INJURIES, AND HOSPITALIZATION IN THE CFC CAMPS

The Acadian foresters were largely insulated from the dangers of combat, but they still suffered from serious diseases and injuries during their time in France. The DROs recorded 205 hospital admissions during the twelve months between November 1917 and October 1918. Unsurprisingly, influenza led the way in terms of serious illnesses, with more than seventy cases. In his study of the 48th Company in the Bordeaux region, David Devigne identified forty cases among the Acadian foresters requiring hospitalization during an outbreak in September 1918, and several subsequent deaths.[115]

Regarding the 5th District in the Jura, an influenza outbreak is obvious from the thirty-five hospital admissions in June 1918, although nobody died. As mentioned earlier, this was part of the epidemic's first wave, which had relatively low mortality. The second and more deadly wave, which became a worldwide epidemic that killed more than fifty million people, erupted in the fall of 1918, but there were only a handful of cases recorded among the Acadian companies of the 5th District.[116] Perhaps the health measures adopted by the CFC and discussed earlier, such as increased laundry services, additional blankets, and quarantine measures, proved effective. The sparse population and limited traffic in and out of the Jura undoubtedly helped. Among the eleven non-combat deaths reported for this group, three were from pneumonia, one from tuberculosis, and another from heart disease. Among the other illnesses reported, many were communal infections such as conjunctivitis and tonsillitis, but others related to individual afflictions such as ulcers and abscesses. A number of cases simply indicated "NYD," an acronym for "not yet diagnosed."

Venereal diseases were a persistent problem in all of the Allied armies and particularly with the CEF. While the French army encouraged the use of condoms and made them available to all soldiers, the British and Dominion leaders were reluctant to regulate what they saw as an issue of immorality. Frequent inspections and social shaming drove sexual activity underground and discouraged reporting,

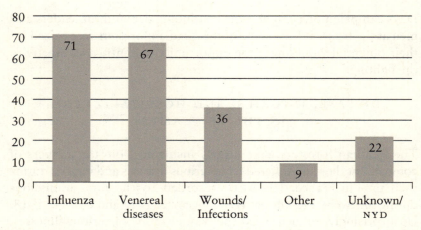

Figure 4.9 Hospital Admissions recorded in 5th District DROs, November 1917–October 1918

which only accelerated the spread. In an article studying the moral education film *Whatsoever a Man Soweth*, Brent Brenyo discusses how venereal disease was considered an issue of racial health linked to broader concerns about the purity of the Anglo-Saxon "race." Contemporaries believed that a combination of medical and moral prophylaxis was needed to dissuade soldiers from engaging in sex outside of marriage. Canadian Prime Minister Robert Borden was so concerned about venereal disease and its effects that he addressed the matter at the Imperial War Conference of 1917.[117]

Military authorities often preferred to blame the women involved, or simply ignored the problem.[118] Padre Gaudet wrote to his uncle, another Catholic priest, describing a sermon he delivered to the foresters about *The Devil's Daughter*, a painting recently unveiled at the Royal Art Gallery of London, which depicted a seductive woman adorned with skulls. He roundly condemned the women who had brought death to 2,000 Canadian soldiers and incapacitated 250,000 men across the British Expeditionary Force, suggesting that these diseases had greatly prolonged the war.[119] Soldiers had little confidence in the medical system. Those requiring treatment faced dubious, painful remedies such as cauterizing sores with carbolic and salicylic acid; applying mercury, which had adverse side effects; and conducting painful "washes" composed of silver nitrate and potassium permanganate inserted through the urethra.[120] Soldiers also suffered pay stoppages and could be stripped of their GCB or even lose promotions and appointments with technical pay because of venereal disease. This certainly did nothing to encourage reporting; the CFC leadership issued frequent reminders of the directives against concealing infection and that soldiers must subject themselves to blood exams when ordered or face a court martial. However, there is no evidence that the 5th District officers pursued such charges.[121]

The infectious nature of VD is obvious from the DRO records of hospital admissions. Gonorrhea was the most reported illness, with forty-four cases (about two-thirds of the total). Twenty-one of these cases occurred during the two months between the end of February and April 1918. Most of the incidents of chancroid, open sores on the genitalia caused by a bacterial infection occurred, in a two-week period in June. Syphilis was much less common, and all five cases occurred in late summer. If left untreated, both gonorrhea and syphilis could lead to serious complications, including infertility and, in the case of syphilis, "the breakdown of various systems in the body, finally ending in psychosis and death."[122]

The seasonal trends for reported sexually transmitted infections (STIs) followed times of increased contact with civilian populations, for example, during planting and harvest times. They also confirmed broader patterns of STI transmission; most of the common bacterial infections, including gonorrhea and syphilis, followed three-month cycles with peaks in spring and fall.[123] Doctors treated two particularly unlucky soldiers for both gonorrhea and syphilis. These STIs had dormancy stages, so treatments might appear initially effective only to flare up again later; several of the DRO admissions refer to a "relapse" or to "chronic" conditions. Gonorrhea, in particular, appeared persistent for some soldiers, who had to be hospitalized on multiple occasions over several months.

VD was a serious issue, but it did not affect everyone and its prevalence should not be overstated. Of the 351 Acadian volunteers in the 39th, 40th, and 47th Companies, just 55 (15 per cent) reported at least one case of venereal disease. This was quite consistent with the estimated rate for the CEF as a whole.[124] However, these numbers also reveal that sexual activity was routine among the soldiers and the local population. Given the relative youth of many of the volunteers, their first sexual experiences may very well have been with prostitutes or even with one another, part of a larger military masculine culture. There does not appear to be a comprehensive study in the historiography of same-sex relationships among members of the CEF. However, some work on the British Expeditionary Force and the German army has explored this issue in other national contexts.[125] Returning to the CFC, several hospital admissions recorded in the DROs involved soldiers on leave in Paris and London, a further sign of commercialized sexual relations.

In general, the foresters of the 39th, 40th, and 47th Companies seemed relatively fortunate in suffering few deaths related to illness and injury. One notable exception was Félicien Roy, originally from Saint-Antoine, New Brunswick, who fell from a train and fractured his skull while bringing timber from the 40th Company camp to the mill at La Joux. He died in hospital the next day. Padre Gaudet presided over the funeral. Roy was buried at the cemetery in Champagnole. Comeau, Daigle, and the other deceased mentioned earlier can be found in a small gravesite behind the parish church at Supt.

As seen at the end of the previous chapter, although most of the Acadian volunteers in the 165th Battalion served in the CFC, a few transferred directly to infantry and other CEF units, while others moved to the front line from the CFC during the final months of the war. These men saw their share of death. In addition, we know that thousands of Acadians during the First World War enlisted somewhere other than the 165th Battalion, often in Maritime anglophone units such as the 26th (New Brunswick) and 25th (Nova Scotia) Battalions. The rest of this chapter offers a brief look at the wider experiences of Acadian volunteers in the CEF.

ACADIANS ACROSS THE CEF

Mourad Djebabla has suggested that we can help change the narrative about the supposedly lacklustre French-Canadian participation in the First World War by "bringing out of the shadows" some of the individual experiences of those who did voluntarily enlist.[126] Geoff Keelan points out that Quebec volunteers are often forgotten in public memory.[127]

Some of the Acadian foresters and former members of the 165th Battalion certainly had interesting personal stories. We might look to those picked up in a final draft to support the Hundred Days campaign in 1918, which brought eight hundred foresters back to the fighting units of the CEF. This latter group included Fred Martin of Amherst, Nova Scotia, who transferred to the 26th Battalion in May of that year. Martin was a seemingly unlikely choice; the transfer

Figure 4.10 Photograph of funeral parade for Pte Félicien Roy

coincided with his seventeenth birthday, and, while still in Canada, he had spent time in a military hospital with epileptic seizures. Joseph Doucet of Bathurst, New Brunswick, was a more obvious choice for the infantry due to his previous experience with the US Army and as a sheriff. He would be less fortunate than Martin, dying from wounds suffered in August 1918. In fact, we have identified that at least five of the twenty-seven Acadian foresters who transferred to the front died there. For example, Felix Labrie of Paquetville, New Brunswick, died from machine-gun fire while serving with the 22nd Battalion in an attack near Chérisy. Pascal LeBlanc of Newcastle, New Brunswick, was killed by concussion from an artillery shell while advancing with the 38th Battalion on the Drocourt–Quéant line. This high mortality rate – nearly 20 per cent in less than a month of fighting in November 1918 – reflects the intensity of combat operations during this final stage of the war as well as the relative inexperience of the Acadian volunteers.

Nicholson calculated a general CEF mortality rate of nearly 10 per cent, mostly as a result of combat.[128] For the Acadian volunteers of the 165th Battalion, there were 11 non-combat deaths, mostly from diseases like tuberculosis and pneumonia, and several combat-related

Figure 4.11 Author's photograph of CEF gravesite at Supt, 2019

deaths, among the 593 men who made it overseas. The samples of Acadians enlisting earlier in the war or serving with the 26th Battalion offer a stark contrast. Almost one in four of those fighting with New Brunswick's front-line unit were killed in action or died of their wounds.

Table 4.3
Mortality rates of Acadian volunteers overseas and CEF (%)

	165th Bn overseas	1914–15 sample	26th Bn sample	CEF
Died	2.8	18.1	25.8	9.3
KIA or DOW	1.3	18.1	23.5	8.4
Illness/accident	1.5	0.0	2.3	1.2

In their letters, many of the soldiers expressed their desire to do their part for Canada. As mentioned, some of the men of the 165th Battalion did not hide their disappointment at being relegated to the CFC. Presumably, they had wanted to kill Germans, although few soldiers were explicit about the violence inherent in their patriotic duty. A rare exception was Antoine Arsenault, of Rogersville, New Brunswick, who wrote to his parents: "Do you remember when I told you that I would be happy if I could kill a German? It has happened, but I am not yet content, I want to kill many more." The rest of the letter is more typical; he writes about family news and his desire to return to Canada. We could not locate his military file, so we do not know where he served, but the newspaper editors specified that he had enlisted at the age of fifteen in September 1916. Was this teenager really a hardened killer or simply trying to impress the home front?

More information is available for two Acadian soldiers whose series of letters (mostly unpublished) are held at the CEAAC. We have already met Joseph Ulric LeBlanc of Cap-Pelé, New Brunswick, who was among the first Acadians to enlist, joining the 5th Division Drive Train as part of the Canadian Army Service Corps (CASC) on 25 November 1914. Joseph Edward "Eddie" Devarennes of Sackville, New Brunswick, signed up in January 1916 but chose the rival 145th Battalion based in Moncton instead of the Acadian national unit. Ulric served as a driver throughout the war, moving between England and France. Eddie became a signaller and, after some training in reserve battalions in England, was attached to the 38th Battalion in July 1917, where he served for the rest of the war.

Ulric explained to his parents that many of his letters were written in English because the censors could not understand French. In a subsequent letter in French to a friend, he cut short his description of the battlefield at the Somme "because of the fear of military censorship," and advised that he would keep the rest of the details for when he returned to Canada.[129] As for Eddie, all of his letters were in English, and his preference for working in that language, although he was clearly bilingual, may account for his decision not to join the 165th Battalion. As a transport driver, Ulric was rarely in combat himself, although he experienced his share of close calls from long-range artillery fire and air raids. After three years overseas as part of the Second Contingent, Ulric opined: "You cannot imagine the good it does to a man to get away from the line for a rest." He later advised his parents: "I see now that farming is the best thing for me at least what I prefer best and I've roamed around the old world enough."[130] Ulric was dreaming of a more idyllic life; he did not actually take up farming.

More typically, the letters home focused on requests for cigarettes and favourite treats that were hard to get in the army. Eddie noted that "a box from home tastes better than anything else, for the simple reason that you know that somebody thinks enough of you to go through a lot of trouble and a certain amount of expence [sic] to send them on." Once in France, he advised that future packages be sent in a tin box, because the last delivery had been crumpled. In addition to practical items like a toothbrush and razors, Eddie asked for pound cake or fruit cake to avoid the mess of frosting, and recommended canned goods like lobster and jars of peanut butter. He was quick to add that "no matter what you send or how it comes it is greatly enjoyed."[131] Above all, the soldiers wanted news about family members. They regularly complained about not receiving enough letters and clearly craved reminders of home, wanting to stay connected with what was happening. Ulric somewhat pointedly asked a friend to pass on his regards to their compatriots back home "even if they never write."[132] Writing was a lifeline for Eddy; even at the height of the Passchendaele campaign, he indicated to his sister that "I write every single week without fail," and he maintained regular correspondence with other family members, including his brothers in other CEF units.[133] Loneliness became more evident as service extended into multiple years away. While waiting for demobilization in Germany, Ulric related that "all I'm longing for now is my return to see all the family once again."[134]

Another way that CEF soldiers dealt with fear, uncertainty, and loneliness was through faith and prayer. In their letters home, Acadian soldiers frequently reassured their parents that they attended Mass and went to confession, and asked for prayers to be said for them. Some even wrote to their home parish priests, and others expressed gratitude for gifts of rosaries, bibles, and prayer books. Of course, not everyone took religion as seriously. Ulric reminded his parents that just "because I don't go to confession often that don't mean that I'm going to the bad."[135] He was nevertheless inspired by a statue of the Madonna in a French cathedral that was miraculously undamaged by a German artillery bombardment.[136] Albert Devarennes, Eddie's brother, described finding his faith at the front line, where he served as a machine gunner with the 2nd Battalion (Canadian Mounted Rifles), in "an awful hole and did not think I would get out alive a couple of times." This was clearly a turning point for Albert, who wrote that "I now believe in prayers and masses go to confession everytime I get a chance always say my act of contrition every night for we carry our lives in our hands if ever I was good I am certainly changed now for better if ever I get back I will know how to be a man."[137] Eddie made few references to religion, but in an impromptu poem closing one letter he wrote: "But with God's help, and our dear ones prayers, we'll return home once more."[138] Faith alone was not always enough to withstand the horrors of combat. After just two weeks on the line with the 22nd Battalion, Padre Gaudet quickly submitted his resignation. He did not go into detail, but wrote to his uncle that "I have seen the front, heard the machine gun and felt its breath of death." The terrible destruction had overwhelmed him.

Some Acadian soldiers demonstrated remarkable faith and perspective throughout their ordeal. Jean D. Doucet of Grand Étang, Cape Breton, enlisted in the 85th Battalion (Nova Scotia Highlanders) in the fall of 1915. He described his experience of combat as a "dream" difficult to describe, one that he had not expected to survive. This is understandable: his unit, held in reserve during much of the fighting at Vimy Ridge, launched a bayonet charge that took the final Canadian objective, Hill 145, at the cost of fifty-six dead and almost three hundred wounded. With the letter he wrote home to assure his mother that he made confession and taken communion as part of Easter Mass, the censors sadly passed on that Jean had been killed in action shortly thereafter (in June 1917).

Ulric's description of the Somme battlefield in 1916, published in *Le Moniteur acadien*, praised the courage of the Canadian soldiers while communicating the terror of combat:

> From the top of a hill, I bore witness to the prowess of our brave soldiers, during the memorable seizing of Thiepval ... A black and blue smoke choked the scene, terrible explosions were heard

without surcease; the earth seemed to vomit fire from its entrails. From where we stood, we felt the ground tremble beneath our feet as the murderous guns entered the action.[139]

Much of his account focused on the destruction he witnessed: the village of Albert lay in ruins, and at the cemetery of La Boisselle, the cadavers and tombstones had been thrown about from the force of the enemy bombardment. Ulric sought unsuccessfully to join the Royal Flying Corps, and after late 1917 he made frequent mention of applying for leave to return to Canada because of his long service overseas. Later in 1918 he seemed more content with his lot; by then he was working with the horses in a blacksmith shop – "I can make and nail a shoe on a horse now without trouble. You would laugh to see me under a horse as black as the ace of spade[s]."[140]

The soldiers' letters reveal that military service was often a family affair. Ulric's younger brother Lionel joined as an officer in the 165th Battalion. Ulric commented ruefully that "he won't suffer all the hardships that we privates have to suffer"; he clearly resented the fact that his brother received significantly higher pay.[141] Both he and Eddie Devarennes were spared the worst of the fighting on account of their roles as a driver and a signaller respectively, but other family members were not so lucky. Eddie was one of five brothers overseas. Meddie, Fred, and Arthur Devarennes enlisted with the 55th Battalion (New Brunswick and Prince Edward Island) in 1915. This was one of many units eventually broken up to provide reinforcements to the front. Meddie was underage at the time; after an extended stay in England, he returned to Canada, before re-enlisting with the 26th Battalion in 1918. Fred served with the Royal Canadian Regiment (RCR) and suffered shrapnel wounds to his left thigh and hand as well as a bout of diphtheria. Arthur was killed in action with the 26th on 24 September 1918. Albert and Eddie signed up together in 1916; Albert was married and had three small children when he enlisted. He was transferred to the 2nd Battalion (Canadian Mounted Rifles), and letters from him that have been preserved describe his harrowing experiences at Passchendaele. In a long letter he wrote to his father at a YMCA after coming out of the line, he described being caught in an open area with no cover against artillery fire and seeing "all around us poor fellows laying all over the ground no heads some no legs ... it was Hell to look at you people down there don't imagine what man can stand it is hard to believe but man and much can stand an awful lot."[142]

Albert tried to explain to his sister the matter-of-fact way that soldiers approached death, noting that "when we hear of a fellow getting killed it is on our mind [only] for half an hour see so much of it."[143]

The pragmatic fatalism of veteran soldiers was in sharp contrast to the patriotic idealism of Acadians just arriving overseas. That idealism was not the sole preserve of the soldiers of the 165th Battalion, as attested by the correspondences published in Acadian newspapers. André Arsenault wrote home from England, where he had just finished his training and was waiting to go to France. His letter names several other Acadians from his home town of Egmont Bay, Prince Edward Island, and how each week more men got the call from the reserve battalions. André explained to his mother: "Perhaps you do know how great it is for a young man in his prime to go and fight for God and homeland and to give his life if God deems it necessary to combat evil."[144] More experienced men like Albert Devarennes sometimes wrote of their hope to be lucky enough to "go to Blighty" – a common reference to being sent to hospital in England after suffering a minor wound.[145] Under no illusions about the glory of combat, René Goguen described Vimy Ridge as something "terrible" during which he killed two Germans and suffered a chest and lung injury from a bomb blast. Writing from an English hospital after the battle, he told his sister about the Somme offensive; in three weeks of attacks, most of the men of his battalion had been injured or killed, including all the officers. René considered himself extremely fortunate to still be alive. In language shorn of the youthful idealism seen in new arrivals, he thanked his family for their prayers and hoped for a quick recovery so that he could return to do his part in defeating the Germans.

The published letters shed further light on the often extensive family contributions to the war. Edmond Barriault of Rogersville, New Brunswick, signed up with the 242nd Battalion (Forestry) in Montreal, was assigned to the CFC in France, and was one of the foresters called to the front towards the end of 1918. His brother Arthur, a brakeman, enlisted with the railway troops. Edmond described meeting another Barriault from Rogersville while in France, this one serving in the US Army. This cousin had travelled to New Bedford, Massachusetts, before the war, but remembered meeting Edmond's family during a summer visit to his home town.[146] Speaking of Americans, Édouard LeBlanc enlisted in the 237th Battalion, a New Brunswick–based unit composed of men recruited from the United States. Of course, this was another indicator of the frequent migrations between the Maritime provinces and the New England states – his attestation paper indicates he was originally from Shediac. His brother André served with the 165th Battalion and the 47th Company of the CFC in France. Édouard served with the RCR and wrote a letter home from an English hospital after suffering injuries from a German gas attack.[147] The battlefield could also lead to new friendships; Adolphe Robichaud told his mother he had begun corresponding with a woman in Saint John because he had found her photograph and address in the pocket of her brother, a comrade who died at Vimy Ridge. That he had taken the time to write to her about her brother's passing and how he had been buried with honour with the other Canadians killed that day inspired this woman to write back, sending him a gift of cake and cigarettes.[148]

Further analysis of the Acadian soldiers' correspondence provides important indications of how they thought about military service. While most CEF soldiers were in favour of conscription, hoping perhaps for much-needed reinforcements, Ulric was clear that he had voted against the measure, telling his parents that Canada should conscript "the wealth of the country first," because soldiers' wages had fallen so far behind what they could earn back home.[149] For his part, Eddie thought that conscription would help the war effort but worried about the quality of the potential recruits. He thought that those who had not yet enlisted would likely be "frightened to death." On being informed that the Conscription Act had passed, he asked his sister to keep him informed about who was called up, commenting that "they have just as much a right to come over as we over here at present."[150] Major Legere picked up on these themes, expressing the soldiers' "satisfaction" that conscription would compel other Canadians to do their part.[151]

Notions of fairness and justice coexisted with ideals of masculine duty and courage. Indeed, the letters offer a rich source for a gender analysis of early twentieth-century Canadian and Acadian culture.[152] The soldiers wrote differently to fathers, mothers, brothers, and sisters. Many assumed that their mothers did not understand their call to serve. Some soldiers alluded to relationships with English and French women. For example, Eddie told his sister about "Kitty," who was "like an ordinary Canadian, but talks a little bit different." He explained that "she certainly is good company and I enjoy going with her" but that she was also "hard on the money." He concluded this section of the letter with "Nuff-Ced [sic] on that subject, you know I can't tell you all about our love affairs – (ha ha)."[153] In a later letter,

Eddie mentioned "a new one I've been writing to for three months ... a peach of a good looker." He then cautioned his sister not to share this news with anyone in Sackville: "Of course am only writing to get acquainted with English girls."[154]

Meanwhile, Ulric maintained correspondence with his fiancée Marcelline back in Canada, occasionally commenting on what was happening around him. He could not resist gossiping about relationships and marriages back home. While serving in Germany after the Armistice, he shared that "the soldiers out here are not allowed on the streets with the German girls." He added: "If I didn't have a good one in Canada myself probably I'd get arrested too because I feel like if I could jump over a house."[155] Much of the war historiography around gender focuses on war brides or prostitutes and venereal disease; a more detailed analysis of soldiers' letters could provide a more nuanced view of sexuality and the kinds of relationships soldiers desired and pursued. As Amy Shaw explains, "Canadian literature on the First World War has underplayed the personal, emotional side of the war." The historical narrative could be expanded to include the women who had their own experiences of the conflict and their own reasons for engaging with soldiers from home and abroad, whether physically or just through correspondence.[156]

Acadians served across the CEF in multiple combat and support roles. Many of the soldiers studied here had family members and friends already serving overseas. The letters reveal the ways in which the Acadians, particularly those from the same community, kept in touch. In training depots, hospitals, churches, and leave centres, Acadians were excited at chance encounters with compatriots who spoke their language, practised the same faith, or shared family roots. The study of the 165th Battalion sheds light on only one part of a larger network of French-speaking Canadian minority groups immersed in units across the CEF.

CONCLUSION

Although many of the Acadian volunteers were disappointed that they had been transferred to the CFC, they experienced much less death and injury than other CEF soldiers and could enjoy the benefits of serving together in more or less defined Acadian sub-units. Because they spoke French, they were able to connect more easily with local communities, thus facilitating CFC production. We know a fair amount about the organization of the work, the considerable timber production, and the setup of the camps. Due to the paucity of sources, we can only imperfectly reconstruct the social life of the foresters both within their units and with the French inhabitants. However, it seems clear that the Acadians regularly visited nearby communities after hours and on Sundays and that local entrepreneurs opened cafés and restaurants to serve them. Many soldiers turned to alcohol and, in some cases, female companionship to help manage the stress and boredom of life in the CFC camps. This became self-destructive behaviour for some, but most were responsible about these pursuits, while others avoided them entirely. Organized sports, concerts, charity fundraising, holidays, and Sunday Mass provided alternative outlets. It was difficult to obtain periods of leave, but many soldiers travelled to Paris or London at least once, using authorized transport routes and hotels. While discipline was clearly a problem for some, most soldiers stayed under the radar of their officers and NCOs and avoided trouble. Many earned good conduct badges or promotions and special appointments because of their good behaviour and leadership qualities. Those few who displayed consistent problems with violence and drunkenness faced greater penalties and an early return to Canada. The experiences of the 165th Battalion volunteers in the CFC camps only partly reflected the larger Acadian contribution to the CEF. The final chapter looks more broadly at the impact of military service on the soldiers and their families, and, in particular, on the sometimes difficult return to Canada and civilian life.

5

Demobilization and the Post-War Transition

The Armistice initiated a long process of demobilization and reintegration for CEF soldiers. Returning them to Canada was a huge logistical undertaking, complicated by the intensifying global influenza epidemic and the limited transportation infrastructure. Various federal and military initiatives attempted to assist the veterans in their transition back to civilian life. At the same time, there were ongoing demands on the military, including the expedition to fight the Bolsheviks in Siberia and the administration of the Imperial War Graves Commission. At the heart of this chapter will be a detailed analysis of the 165th Battalion soldiers' return home. With the help of the 1921 Canadian census, we will examine their residence, family situation, health, and employment. Alan Bowker reminds us that Canadians experienced 1919 "as a cascade of events tumbling over each other in a world turned upside down" by war, a pandemic, and inflation. Much had changed since 1914, so reintegration meant not only going back but also coming to terms with a new and uncertain world.[1] In their examination of the relationship between military service and life outcomes in the United States, MacLean and Elder write that "the effect of service lies in its larger social context, the forces that impel people to serve in the military, the political factors that shape the military experience, and the opportunities afforded to service members during and after their tours of duty."[2] In the case of the 165th Battalion volunteers, their circumstances as a minority group with limited economic opportunities in the Maritime provinces shaped their post-war experience. As it turns out, many of the former soldiers seem to have succeeded in reintegrating with the help of social networks.

FROM THE ARMISTICE TO DEMOBILIZATION

As we saw in the last chapter, "peace talk" was rampant by the beginning of October 1918. Several company mills were already closing down by the end of that month. After the Armistice, the CFC leadership confirmed that no additional logging would be carried out, and the foresters set themselves to "clearing up the bush" and planting new trees. The sites would be inspected before they were handed back to the French authorities.[3] Meanwhile, companies circulated demobilization surveys among the soldiers, who were asked to identify their preferred place of disembarkation in Canada. Inevitably, with more time on their hands and the understandable desire to celebrate the end of the war, some of the soldiers got into trouble. New regulations stipulated that those going on leave would move in parties accompanied by officers or NCOs. Across the CFC, DROs reminded the men:

> Whilst the modification of working hours has been made possible owing to the recent developments in the Military situation, all ranks will understand that in no way is the need for strict Military Discipline and good behaviour lessened. It is due to all to ensure that no untoward act occurs which may in any way reflect on the service and detract from the splendid reputation which the Canadian Expeditionary Force has gained from our French Allies.

Further good news included an increase in the monthly separation allowance from $25 to $30 and the creation of a War Service Gratuity (WSG) for all with overseas service, including CFC members, payable on discharge.[4]

Demobilization was a major undertaking that involved transporting soldiers from where they were serving to English ports, sailing them across the Atlantic, then getting them from their return ports in Canada to their final destinations. There was only so much rail and shipping capacity, and there were ferocious debates about who should have precedence. The initial guiding principle was to go by order of enlistment, which meant that the men of the first and second contingents such as Ulric LeBlanc should have gone home first. However, Ulric did not make it back to the port of Saint John until late May 1919, perhaps because in practice, those serving in the infantry and married men with families received greater consideration. Upon arrival in England from France, it took about a month just to process and regroup the soldiers for their journeys home, as well as additional time in one of twenty-two dispersal areas established in Canada. The requirements included medical exams, release interviews, and financial arrangements for any outstanding pay and allowances.[5]

Ultimately, military authorities decided to keep the units of the Canadian Corps together for purposes of discipline and to allow triumphant homecomings in their places of origin. Soldiers of the CFC and other support arms, however, were processed through Kinmel Camp in Wales and organized into drafts based on age, marital status, and period and place of enlistment.[6] Nicholson noted that two-thirds of the overseas force "reached home within five months, and before a year had passed repatriation was virtually completed."[7] Some Acadian foresters would have been present during the Kinmel Camp riots of 4–5 May 1919, during which five CEF members died and dozens more were injured.[8] In a study of the 19th Battalion, chiefly composed of men from Toronto and Hamilton, David Campbell describes the men's dissatisfaction at having to wait first in occupied Germany, then in Belgium, and finally at Camp Witley in England. The unit leadership organized concerts, sports, education classes, and short periods of leave to try to keep the men occupied, while looking the other way at minor lapses of behaviour and deportment.[9]

The Acadian foresters would not have been high on the priority list for demobilization. Of the 593 volunteers from the 165th Battalion who served overseas, 25 had already been sent home due to being underage or medically unfit, or for disciplinary reasons, and 15 others had died. The military personnel records indicate the date and place of demobilization for all but 16 of the remainder, thus providing us with information for 536 men. Only a handful had made it home to Canada by the end of February 1919. Some of them had served in the infantry, but most had not. In fact, several of those who made the transition to the front were also among the last soldiers to be repatriated. Several large groups of Acadian foresters travelled together during the month of March, on ships such as the SS *Scotian* and the SS *Belgic*, which docked at Saint John and Halifax respectively. By the end of March 1919 – the five-month period identified by Nicholson – about two-thirds of the CEF and almost three-fifths of the Acadian foresters were home. However, the results also demonstrate the chaos and arbitrary nature of the process. Married men were supposed to go home first, but of the 65 volunteers married before enlistment, only 41 (63 per cent) had received their discharge by the end of March.

Regarding the seventy-seven Acadians who received their discharge later than May 1919, most faced extenuating circumstances that explained the delay. For example, several imprisoned soldiers were among those who had to wait longer in England. A few others were in hospital with complications from influenza or some form of disability. This number also included a few Acadians who had elected to receive their discharge in London. Leance Comeau of Saulnierville, Nova Scotia, and Ephrem Gallant of Shediac, New Brunswick, both underage teenagers when they enlisted, got married in England in early 1919. However, Ephrem was back at home with his parents and working at a sawmill in 1921, while Leance crossed the border to Maine in the same year. Did their wives die or did the relationships not work out?

In the 1921 Canadian census, we found four other Acadians who had married French women while part of the CFC and who had brought them home. Ernest Daigle and Catherine Felicia were particularly well-travelled after the war. Daigle, originally from Saint-Charles, New Brunswick, met Felicia while assigned to 48th Company, near Bordeaux. They got married in January 1919, chose to demobilize in Quebec City in May of that year, and then proceeded overland to New Brunswick, presumably for a quick visit home, before moving to Malden, Massachusetts, in July 1920. Perhaps because they were unable to find work, the couple headed back to Bordeaux in 1921 before eventually returning to Canada via Halifax in 1930.

Some of the others who were late in demobilizing had accepted further employment with the army. For example, three Acadians worked for the Imperial War Graves Commission (IWGC), founded in 1917. Louis Robicheau, Eddie Romain, and Placide Boucher were all from Nova Scotia and only returned home in August 1919. Robicheau received a Meritorious Service Medal for his contribution to the IWGC, whose monumental task was to register and bury the dead on the Western Front. A distinctly imperial project, the IWGC aimed to bury side by side the soldiers and officers of Great Britain and all of its Dominions.[10] The Acadians' bilingual abilities must have been helpful for this work in the French countryside.

An unusual service record merits particular mention. John Anthony Melanson was born in Salem, Massachusetts, but moved back to Richibucto with his family while still a child. He enlisted in the 165th Battalion but was one of those mysteriously absent when the unit sailed from Halifax. He later enlisted with the 62nd Battalion in British Columbia, which suggests he had fled west on the railway after his desertion. Too late to join the bulk of the 62nd overseas, Melanson ended up as part of the 260th Battalion, a diverse unit composed of recruits from across the country assigned to the Canadian Siberian Expeditionary Force (CSEF). Melanson must have spoken English fluently, because he did not end up assigned to the 259th Battalion, the other unit of the CSEF, which included many French-Canadian conscripts from Quebec. Melanson departed from Victoria on 26 December 1918 for Vladivostok on the ss *Protileus*, arriving on 15 January 1919. The CSEF's mission in Siberia was to protect the counter-revolutionaries' lines of communication from the Bolshevik Army. The force of 4,192 men suffered from poor discipline and morale from the start; indeed, the conscripts of the 259th Battalion mutinied while the force was preparing to sail from Victoria. The divisions within the force were clear: men from Ontario moved quickly to physically repress the rebellion of those from Quebec.[11] After the arduous journey to Russia and months living in austere conditions, the two battalions returned to Canada in April 1919.[12] Melanson arrived in Saint John, New Brunswick, on 16 May 1919; we were unable to find him in the 1921 census. For Melanson at least, additional military service did not prove particularly glorious.

HOME AT LAST

Canadian communities often went to great lengths to welcome their victorious soldiers home. Nathan Smith describes the parades, receptions, and services offered to the returned men in Toronto. The enthusiasm of the family reunions often overwhelmed the official ceremonies that municipal leaders had planned and forced a rethinking of parade routes and gathering places. Smith emphasizes the important role played by veterans who had already returned home in organizing and publicizing these events.[13] Similar efforts were made in the Maritime provinces for the fighting units; for example, the 26th Battalion marched triumphantly in the streets of Saint John on 17 May 1919 and enjoyed a highly enthusiastic reception.

The return festivities for the mixed drafts of support soldiers, including the CFC members, were not as exuberant. When the ss *Celtic* arrived on 19 March 1919, "the men were in great spirits" and the "trainshed was densely filled with relatives and friends of the khaki boys"; however, the newspaper also reported that during the short parade route to the discharge centre "the street crowd was in a very cold mood. The men were cheered only at Mill Street crossing and by the girls in the doorway of M.R.A. Ltd. Small flags on sticks were the only bunting seen; these, too, at M.R.A.'s doorway, in spite of notification in morning papers."[14] Major Legere was one of the party and was greeted by several friends. The reception committee distributed cigarettes and chocolates, but there was no sign of the extravagant meals provided for some CEF units. The ceremony for those returning on the ss *Aquitania* in June 1919 was even more subdued; they were simply met by city representatives and given breakfast.[15] The fact that these stories about returning soldiers were buried in the back pages of the newspapers suggests that enthusiasm had been tempered and that interest had faded. Sometimes the homecoming literally went off the rails. Private J.A. LeBlanc was one of 250 men returning on the ss *Olympic*; he sprained his back when three cars of the train left the tracks between Truro and Moncton.[16]

In general, the return of the Acadian soldiers was a muted affair. *L'Évangéline* did publish lists prepared by some parish *curés* of those who had served, with special care to note those who died overseas. A reminder of the Church's role in promoting enlistment in the first place, these lists provide further indications that the 165th Battalion was just a small part of the Acadian contribution. For example, the parish of Inverness on Cape Breton provided fifteen men to the war effort, eight of whom served in other units, including the 25th Battalion (Nova Scotia) and the Royal Canadian Regiment. The parish of Glace Bay identified twelve men, only one of whom had served in the 165th Battalion. Three of these men died overseas; two more were seriously injured.[17] Still, there was little comment about or coverage of the returned men. As Claude Léger noted, "after the war, the soldiers and officers of the 165th returned home and most of them took up the anonymous lives they had lived beforehand, like the vast majority of CEF members."[18]

Victorin Lagacé was remembered not for his "battlefield bravery, although he had wanted to go to the trenches," but for his close call with "that terrible sickness named Spanish flu," which he contracted during demobilization. After a short hospital stay in Halifax, he returned to his parents at Pointe-Verte, New Brunswick. The newspaper noted the touching scene of the reunited family attending Mass together and thanking the Sacred Heart for his safe return. Significantly, the journalist ended the story by noting that Lagacé would need some time to recuperate at home.[19] Clearly, the expectation was that the returned men would resume their productive role in the civilian workforce and begin contributing to their households again.

We can also imagine, as Jean-Louis Grosmaire suggests in his fictional account of a returned member of the 165th Battalion, that the Acadian foresters were well aware that family and friends had fought and died at the front while they worked in relative safety in the forests of Bordeaux and the Jura. As one of many examples, James LaFrance arrived home in February after serving in the CFC, but his two brothers were still with the occupation force in Germany.[20] This may have discouraged the Acadian foresters from trumpeting their service in France and in some cases may have led to survivor guilt. Yet we can imagine small family celebrations across the region.[21] For example, CSM Abel Belliveau was welcomed home in Moncton at a house party organized by his brother that included music, refreshments, and games.[22]

HOSPITALIZATIONS AND HEALTH AMONG THE ACADIANS

As soldiers like Lagacé experienced, the demobilization process was complicated by the influenza pandemic, which spurred the CFC leadership to adopt strict protocols to try and limit the spread of the disease, including the temporary cancellation of leave. The 5th (Jura) and 12th (Bordeaux) Districts both directed that companies were to avoid other camps as well as neighbouring villages. CFC-wide statements included detailed instructions:

> The type of influenza prevalent in France at present is a severe one. It is highly infective and is conveyed from a sick man to a healthy one by microbes carried through sneezing, coughing and spitting. In crowded places like Cinemas, Theatres, etc. the danger of catching the disease is great and those places should be avoided. As chills and colds often start influenza, warm clothing should be worn and wet clothing should be changed. Men suffering from colds or feverishness should report sick early and not wait until seriously ill as such delay may mean danger.[23]

While they perhaps mistook symptoms like chills for causes, the military authorities nevertheless had a good understanding of how the disease was spread and took reasonable measures to protect the men. At the same time, this must have been a great challenge, especially at the large camps in Witley and Kinmel Park, where tens of thousands of soldiers were packed together. CEF doctors reported around 65,000 cases of influenza across the CEF during its time overseas. Most of the men recovered within a few weeks, but some had to be sent home and roughly 2,000 (about 3 per cent) died.[24] In the case of the former 165th Battalion volunteers overseas, we found 77 individuals hospitalized at least once for influenza. That was about 13 per cent of the total group of 593, and one in five of the 387 soldiers with at least one recorded hospital stay.

As seen in the previous chapter, five of the twenty-seven Acadian foresters transferred to the front in 1918 died there. A review of the military personnel records of all 593 former 165th Battalion volunteers overseas finds that nineteen of the fifty-nine men serving at some point in the trenches experienced combat injuries, such as gunshot and shrapnel wounds, that required hospitalization. Sometimes the injuries were severe and involved long periods of recovery. For example, Edward Pothier of Wedgeport, Nova Scotia, joined the 22nd Battalion as a signaller and suffered gunshot wounds to the left arm and back at Arras in September 1918. He was repatriated to Canada and received care in Halifax until December. In 1921, he was listed as a patient at the Nova Scotia Sanitorium in Kentville (a long-term care hospital). Pothier declared his occupation as streetcar conductor but also indicated that he had been out of work for twenty-four months, presumably since his return. Ambroise Langlois of Antigonish, Nova Scotia, also joined the 22nd Battalion and suffered a serious shrapnel wound in August 1918. The extensive injuries to his groin, left side, and chest resulted in extended hospital stays overseas and in Quebec until at least April 1919. In 1921, Langlois was at home with his parents, working odd jobs for a minimal wage while his father pursued fishing at D'Escousse, Nova Scotia. Ambroise must have recovered somewhat, for he travelled to Yarmouth and took a ship to Boston in 1922. However, there is a note in his file that he remained unemployed in 1942, the date at which he was registered for the American draft for the Second World War. Edward was just nineteen when he enlisted for the 165th Battalion, and Ambroise was twenty-three. Their injuries clearly had a profound impact on the rest of their lives.

It is not always so easy to see the consequences of combat injuries. Auguste McLaughlin had a particularly miserable time overseas. Another Acadian picked up as a signaller for the 22nd Battalion – evidently a dangerous job – he suffered several gunshot wounds as part of the defensive effort against the German spring offensive in April 1918 (the Battle of the Lys). His file indicates extensive injuries, including wounds to both legs and to his left shoulder and side. After several months of rehabilitation, he was assigned with other convalescing soldiers to the 10th Battalion (Reserve) in England; a few weeks later, in October 1918, he required treatment for a severe case of influenza. McLaughlin was repatriated on the *Empress of Britain* in January 1919. The Army determined that he had no disability and thus no entitlement to a pension. Before the war he had been living with his brother Charles in Saulnierville, Nova Scotia. Soon after returning there, Auguste decided to leave, eventually crossing the international border at Vanceboro, Maine, heading to join his father, who was living in Massachusetts. We lose track of him after this in both the Canadian and American censuses, which suggests that he did not settle anywhere permanently. Why did Auguste leave? Was he unable to work and thus a burden for his brother's family? Did he require medical follow-up that was unavailable in Saulnierville? Unfortunately, even with longitudinal analysis, one cannot always know the full story.

As other scholars have shown, providing pensions for injured soldiers was a controversial issue. Desmond Morton and Glenn Wright relate that 77,000 veterans were collecting a disability pension in 1933. The Canadian government did not want to repeat the supposed "pension evil" of massive debt created in the United States after the Civil War, but it also sought to avoid being accused of reducing veterans to mendicancy. The problem originated well before the Armistice; the Military Hospital Commission established in 1915 aimed to provide medical services to men who returned home after suffering combat injuries, including amputations and blindness. Not surprisingly, there was considerable public support for looking after these obviously deserving cases. But as the number of returned men increased, the newly created Department of Soldiers' Civil Re-establishment (DSCR) made a consistent effort to restrict support and eligibility. As of 1914, a totally disabled private was entitled to an annual pension of $264, a sum far below even the basic daily wage of a Canadian unskilled labourer (about $360 per year in 1914) and clearly not enough to survive on. Officers could count on considerably more; a lieutenant in a similar situation could hope for $480, while a lieutenant-colonel would receive $1,200.[25]

In the fall of 1917, the maximum disability pension was increased to $600, with additional sums for the dependents of married men. At the same time, however, the authorities encouraged veterans to work by keeping the pension below typical wages. The former soldiers were expected to be grateful and get back on their own feet.[26] Medical exams sought to declare men fit who had suffered multiple wounds (like Auguste McLaughlin), and relatively few men qualified for the full amount even when they were found to have long-term injuries. There is little evidence that the former 165th Battalion volunteers qualified for pensions. Joseph Doucet of Halifax, Nova Scotia, was a rare exception; we find him in 1921 out of work and trying to support four children on a military pension of $400.

In addition, doctors tried to identify those who had pre-existing conditions not attributable to military service. For example, up to 20 per cent of the CEF men arriving in England in 1916 never left the camps, having been found medically unfit.[27] The military authorities had tried to do better by 1917; chapter 2 discussed the large contingent of 165th Battalion volunteers who were deemed unfit before leaving Canada. Of the 593 men proceeding overseas, just sixteen appear to have been held back in reserve units and holding camps in England. Admittedly, the CFC had lower physical standards and more relaxed restrictions on age. One of the men held back was George Muise of Yarmouth, Nova Scotia, who was diagnosed with a heart condition and, after a hospital stay in England, was sent home. Surprisingly, he was collecting an army pension in 1921. Even as authorities sought to limit the number of veterans who qualified for financial support, the gendered expectations of male breadwinners to show strength and resilience translated into many partly disabled men declining to ask for assistance in the first place.[28] Others joined organizations like the Great War Veterans' Association (GWVA), which advocated on the returned men's behalf for better pensions as well as bonuses and gratuities. Still, there are few indications that Acadian volunteers sought to organize themselves in this way; most fit the general description of CEF returned men "quietly" resuming old and new jobs in their home communities.[29]

Serious mental health conditions could carry lifelong consequences for returned men. Mental illnesses remained poorly understood and little discussed in Canadian society, which meant that people were ill-prepared to support veterans afflicted by them. The chief specialist for "shell-shock" cases – what we would call today operational stress injuries – contended that these men "had consciously willed themselves into their state to escape their military responsibilities. To grant them pensions was to reward them."[30] Mark Humphries demonstrates that mental illness was closely tied to notions of masculinity, which is why the former carried considerable social stigma. A 1922 British War Office Committee of Inquiry into Shell Shock reported that nearly all of the "breakdowns" that had occurred in the BEF – including among soldiers in the Canadian Corps – were not deserving of recognition and were simply "emotional cases." These men had become hysterical – to use a feminized term associated with mental illness – or they were malingerers trying to avoid combat.[31] By November 1919, there were more than 1,400 returned soldiers under care for "nervous" or mental illness across Canada. Some doctors claimed that many cases originated in underlying conditions that had been undiagnosed during enlistment.[32] This was the case for Claude LeBlanc, who had suffered from epilepsy since childhood and found that his symptoms worsened while he was serving with the CFC. Initially hospitalized after a seizure at La Joux in June 1918, he was evacuated first to the general military hospital at Rouen, and then to England, before finally taking ship for Canada in October. The newspaper attributed his early homecoming to "a severe attack of Spanish flu," but he remained under treatment in a military hospital in Fredericton until at least December.[33]

Private H. Cormier was another 165th Battalion volunteer with an underlying mental illness aggravated by military service. His repeated minor disciplinary infractions while serving in the CFC, including malingering, neglect of duty, and absence without leave, were likely related to what military doctors later diagnosed as dementia praecox, an old term for schizophrenia. Shortly after his return in March 1919, Cormier was admitted to the military hospital in Fredericton. Telling doctors that he was "worried about himself," Cormier related hearing voices every night while trying to sleep and feeling like everybody was laughing at him because he had contracted gonorrhea during his military service. "Guilt, shame and fear" were certainly the most common tactics employed by military and medical authorities to discourage illicit sex; some argued that venereal disease was a form of societal betrayal and even "race suicide."[34] Increasing rates of VD among CEF soldiers during the demobilization process raised concerns about protecting the civil population at home.[35]

Significantly, Cormier was on his own after living with his sister before the war followed by the collective experience of army life. His parents lived in New Bedford, Massachusetts, and Cormier had elected not to return to his sister (to whom he had sent his assigned pay) but rather to board and try to find work in Moncton. Not quite eighteen when he enlisted, and with a less than glowing military record, Cormier had limited prospects. After nearly two weeks at the hospital, and then ongoing outpatient care, Cormier seems to have figured things out, for by 1921 he had secured employment as a ferryman with the Canadian National Railway (CNR) and accommodation with extended family living in Moncton. There was some effort to follow up with him, as a note in his military file reported as late as 1923 that he was still boarding in the city. Cormier was not the only returned man from the 165th Battalion needing care; we found P. Richard at the New Brunswick Provincial Hospital for the Insane in 1921. We might wonder whether some of the other men who perennially seemed to be in trouble overseas were in fact suffering from some kind of mental illness that prevented them from adapting well to military life.

Disciplinary problems were not always an indicator; another young Acadian forester in 48th Company with no other signs of problems in his file attempted suicide with a razor blade in September 1918. The medical report noted that this action had been triggered by the receipt of news that his sister back home in Canada had died; however, the doctor believed that the man was insane and not responsible for his actions. The medical report cited hallucinations, severe depression, and the need for custodial care because of an ongoing threat of self-harm. This forester spent nearly 18 months in military hospitals, first in Rouen, then in England, and then after repatriation in May 1919. He was released from full-time care in Halifax at the end of January 1920. In the 1921 Canadian Census we find him at home on Cape Breton, unemployed and with his family.

Another unusual case involved a volunteer from Beresford, New Brunswick. A member of 47th Company, CFC, he was treated for a gunshot wound to his left foot in August 1918. This required transfer to the hospital at Rouen. The member then disappeared for a couple of days. Was this injury self-inflicted or a result of violence in the camp? A simple accident while cleaning a firearm? Mark Humphries notes that self-inflicted injuries were an expression of defiance of military authority. Although the number of Canadian soldiers "who maimed themselves was always small [they] posed a significant problem for those who purported to hold a monopoly on power at the front."[36] Whatever the case, this soldier seemed reluctant to return to his unit. He was later hospitalized with a serious case of pneumonia and was sent home in March 1919. He was still living with his parents and siblings in 1921, employed as a farm worker. In cases like these, the decision to remain in the family home may have reflected a need for care and support rather than a purely economic decision.

Historians have tried to learn more about the mental injuries caused by combat. The CEF volunteers, including those ultimately rejected, would constitute an interesting potential group to study for broader insights into mental illness more generally in early twentieth-century Canada. Of course, there is also much more research to do on the experiences of the returned men. As Nathan Smith notes, most "did not say much about combat or their experiences to reporters," and it can be hard to get at the emotional and psychological consequences of military service for the soldiers and their families.[37] There are nevertheless some clues and individual cases that point to larger themes. For example, an Acadian soldier originally from Tracadie, New Brunswick, returned home after the war and chose to live alone in a small cabin outside of town he built for himself. Clearly in some kind of psychological distress and unable to care for himself, his parents checked in on him and brought him food on a daily basis over several months. According to a short article in *L'Évangéline* published on 24 January 1922, his mother found the door barred and drops of blood at the entrance. She went back to get her partner, and together they forced the door, only to find that their son had been dead for some time. The grisly discovery made the news, but there was no further comment on the circumstances leading to his death.[38]

There was also occasional coverage of practical difficulties experienced by veterans. For example, a 1923 article made reference to a speech by Jean George Robichaud, the Member of Parliament for Gloucester County, New Brunswick, in the House of Commons, about the plight of war widows and disabled soldiers. He complained that pensions were being denied to deserving people because they received no help in filling out the application forms and because government officials sent to investigate their claims falsely represented the income of the families concerned. These problems had a common root: the forms were only available in English, and the officials sent to his county could not speak French even though the majority of the population was francophone.[39]

Complications from influenza and other diseases also affected some of the returned Acadian volunteers. Most hospitalizations were due to contagious diseases: influenza, but also pneumonia, tuberculosis, and a variety of liver, kidney, and urinary tract conditions. Morton and Wright found for the CEF as a whole that there were three times as many hospital admissions for illness as for combat injuries. But to what extent should we attribute these illnesses and their complications to military service? The influenza pandemic affected civilians as much as soldiers, and other illnesses like tuberculosis had been a scourge on Canadian society even before the war. One area where there clearly was some correlation with life in the army was venereal disease. Across the CEF, the next most common illness requiring hospitalization after influenza (65,000 cases) was gonorrhea (48,000 cases), followed by syphilis (18,000 cases). The next most common non-venereal illness was pneumonia, with 8,000 recorded admissions. However, pneumonia proved the deadliest of the commonly reported diseases; nearly one-quarter of the cases were fatal.[40] In fact, five Acadian recruits died of pneumonia while the 165th Battalion was still training in Canada. Community transmission of diseases, including pneumonia, would have been exacerbated by the corralling together of so many volunteers from all over the Maritime provinces. In the CFC camps, highly infectious diseases, including scabies and tonsilitis, also made the rounds among men living in close proximity to one another.

As seen in the previous chapter, VD was a significant issue for the 350 Acadians in the 39th, 40th, and 47th Companies of the CFC; it accounted for about 15 per cent of the men hospitalized at least once during their time in the camps. When we look at the entirety of their military service as reflected in their personnel files (for example, those hospitalized while still training in Canada), the proportion rises to 19 per cent. When we look only at the 593 men of the former 165th Battalion who went overseas, the proportion rises again to 21 per cent, somewhat higher than Cassel's CEF average of 16 per cent. In total, 125 of the 387 men hospitalized at some point during their overseas service (32 per cent) and 180 of the total number of 662 recorded hospital admissions (27 per cent) were due to VD. Ulric LeBlanc wrote to his parents that he was well aware of these diseases:

> But with a sweetheart in Canada a soldier that's got a conscience and brains will not go and do thing that he [sic] should'nt do as

far as connection are concerned. I might be talking a little like kiddish but every word I say I mean it. Soldiers especially think they can do almost anything as far as sex matters are concern but this little chap never was caught in the hunny [sic] traps yet. And I hope and pray that it will never happen but my time comes and that will be in marriage life.[41]

Ulric referenced the importance of his friends, including two Acadian comrades, in helping him stay out of trouble.

Beyond the potential health impact of VD, the social stigma attached to it, and the danger it posed to others, had other consequences for those afflicted. Of the five soldiers hospitalized in the Jura due to syphilis, three could not be found in the censuses after the war. A fourth, a soldier from Adamsville, who had been living in the Moncton area prior to enlistment, contracted gonorrhea while the 165th Battalion was in Saint John, then syphilis in the 47th Company, CFC. After demobilization he left New Brunswick, and we find him in Maine staying at a boarding house and working at a paper mill. The fifth did go home to Cape Breton and was still single in 1921. This admittedly small sample suggests that VD and its complications could affect returned men's ability to reintegrate and find a marriage partner.

POST-WAR TRANSITION

The former members of the 165th Battalion did not come home in one large group but rather in several smaller contingents. For example, fifty-five Acadian soldiers returned to Saint John on the *Empress of Britain* on 25 February 1919, and an additional seventy-three arrived with the ss *Cassandra* on 9 March 1919. Thanks to a number of sources, especially the 1921 Canadian Census (and the 1920 US Census), we were able to locate many of these men after their demobilization. We have detailed census data for 628 of the 1,038 recruits (61 per cent), and limited information for another 117 who crossed the border around that time. Regarding those who went overseas, of the 578 soldiers who returned home, we found 383 in the censuses (66 per cent) and an additional 60 travelling to the United States. In short, we have some information for about three-quarters of the 165th Battalion volunteers and detailed records including residence, employment, and family situation for about two-thirds.

Residence and Household

When comparing the situation of the soldiers before and after the war, the most obvious difference is their marital status. Nearly half the men were married by 1921, most of them in the short period between demobilization and the census. Some of them may have been like Joseph Ulric LeBlanc, who left a fiancée behind when he enlisted and quickly got married when he returned.[42] Others may have had to make up for lost time and find a partner. The results point to a clear trend for the volunteers to establish themselves as heads of their own households. Included in the 1921 results for nuclear families are 38 households of newlyweds still awaiting the birth of their first child.

While the ideal of an independent married couple with children remained strong, there is plenty of evidence for multigenerational homes. About one in four of the Acadian families here had at least one extended relative, and households with more than one married couple increased in prominence after the war. Grandparents, uncles, aunts, and siblings could all contribute income, assist with childcare, and work around the house. We might assume that larger household groups tended to be associated with farming, but the proportion of extended and multi-couple households was roughly the same for the group as a whole as it was for those declaring agriculture as their principal occupation (33 and 35 per cent respectively).

Those working in urban settings could also benefit from extended family support. James Bourgeois, originally from Adamsville, New Brunswick, lived with three siblings in Gardner, Massachusetts, in 1920. They all declared manufacturing jobs. The head of household was his sister Annie's husband, Joseph Boucher. Others moving to urban settings in search of work took up temporary lodging. In fact, more than twice as many of the former soldiers were boarding than before the war. David Cormier worked at a sugar refinery and rented accommodation from an anglophone family in Saint John. There were two other lodgers listed in the household. Boarding situations varied considerably, from single lodgers living with farming families to veritable worker communities near mills or in large cities. To give an example of the latter, Alfred Belliveau, originally from Moncton, was in Chicago in 1920, living with twenty other people from across the United States and Europe. There was even a recent immigrant from Sweden. Belliveau was a salesman, but the group included a nurse, a mason, a cook, and a window-maker.

Figure 5.1 Honeymoon photograph of J. Ulric LeBlanc and Marcelline Blanchard

The results so far suggest that there was no dominant trend of reintegration to civil society. About one-third of the men married quickly and established households of their own, but just as many continued their search for employment in various living conditions, leveraging extended family networks and rental accommodation across the Maritime provinces and the American Northeast. An additional group, nearly 40 per cent of the former volunteers, were still living at home in 1921. Did they simply need a bit more time to launch their own careers and families, or was this an indication of illness, injury, or poverty? For the youngest volunteers, especially those only sixteen or seventeen when they enlisted, returning home was probably not a sign of a particular need and simply a logical choice. The data bears this out: the average census-corrected age of those living in the parental home in 1921 was twenty-four, compared to nearly twenty-seven for those declared heads of household in the census. Most of the underage soldiers returned home after demobilization. There were certainly exceptions. Cyriaque Dionne of Edmundston, New Brunswick, was one of three brothers living together and looking after their widowed mother. All three were in their thirties and unmarried, certainly an exceptional situation in Acadie at that time. Dionne had

Table 5.1
Household comparison 1911 and 1921 (%)

	1911	1921
Married	10	46
Parental home	81	39
Head of household	9	42
Nuclear family	65	59
Extended family	26	24
Multi-couple family	4	9
Boarding/lodging	7	16
Domestic servant	2	6

a good job as a commercial agent, so his living situation was not due to a lack of funds. Vital Martin of Saint-Basile, Quebec, was part of another unusual family – five unmarried siblings in their twenties and thirties lived at the family farm with their parents. While the others were working on the farm, Vital earned a modest salary in a lumber workshop, leveraging his experience in the CFC.

The household information also indicates that more of the soldiers had domestic servants after the war, a clear sign of greater affluence. Indeed, several of them had been domestic servants themselves before enlisting.

Employment and Earnings

In a recent article about French-Canadian soldiers after the First World War (in Quebec), Carl Bouchard and Michael Huberman contend that military service contributed to higher wages and better jobs:

> We attribute this result to the gains in human (individual) and social (group) capital during the war. In fact, in accomplishing new tasks during the war, the civilians who became soldiers acquired informal experience and new skills. The majority of Francophone soldiers served in Anglophone regiments, and so could improve their English, a considerable asset on the job market after the war, especially in the urban environment. Finally, the men benefited from a gain in social capital by the creation of a larger network due to their interactions with men and women beyond their circles and who had different life experiences.[43]

These conclusions contrast with the historiographical consensus, which tends to emphasize the difficulties that veterans faced, including high rates of unemployment. For example, Jonathan Scotland suggests that veterans "were left worse off because of their military service," citing poor employment prospects beginning in 1920, as well as a 1935 federal report that claimed that at least 38,000 of the roughly 189,000 CEF veterans not eligible for some sort of assistance were unemployed.[44] Desmond Morton and Glenn Wright characterize the soldiers' economic plight and search for support as the "second battle." Against Bouchard and Huberman, they argue that most of the former soldiers had acquired few marketable skills as a result of their service and that they often brought home problems such as illness and addiction to alcohol that rendered them less likely to succeed in the civilian economy. In sum, "war service had robbed ex-servicemen of training, experience, seniority, and energy, the only qualities employers valued in their own struggle to survive."[45] Organizations like the GWVA lobbied for better access to pensions, cash bonuses, and training programs. Morton summarizes the situation of the returned men with the statement that they "would have to make their own way in a world that had little time for their stories and even less for their problems."[46]

There were, in fact, considerable albeit insufficient efforts to assist veterans. The Soldier Settlement Bill (SSB) of May 1917 made land available in the Canadian West for those interested in farming, and pensions for those who could demonstrate a combat-related disability were among the most generous in the British Empire. The WSG provided hundreds of dollars to those who had served overseas, and preferential hiring programs for the public service and other sectors, including the railways, aimed to help former soldiers find jobs.[47] In his official history of the CEF, G.W.L. Nicholson writes that by the end of 1919, "a total of 91,521 pensions had been granted, amounting to some $22,500,000 annually. At the same time, 8,000 soldiers were receiving medical treatment, while more than 23,000 were enrolled for vocational training. In such manner did a grateful country attempt in some measure to repay its debt to those who had served and survived."[48] Jeffrey Keshen describes the significant government investments in a media campaign to reassure Canadians that injured veterans and their families were being looked after – indeed, more generously than in other Allied nations.[49]

In reality, many of these programs were bureaucratic, difficult to access, and subject to constant review. Eligibility criteria for pensions were extremely restrictive. The SSB failed spectacularly due to the poor quality of the land, the collapse of the market for agricultural produce, and the ill-preparedness of many of the veterans involved. Preferential hiring programs only worked for those who had the necessary skills. One noticeable success was the transportation sector – many CEF veterans had learned mechanical, driving, or construction skills while overseas.[50] Joseph Ulric LeBlanc had failed to find an auto sector job in Boston before the war, but his time as a driver for the Canadian Army Service Corps translated into a well-paid position in Shediac in 1921. As described below, some of the 165th Battalion volunteers were later hired by the CNR, or they leveraged their CFC experience for forestry jobs.

For Acadian veterans and their families, the language barrier created further obstacles to accessing pensions. Just three of the former 165th Battalion volunteers declared receiving a military pension in the 1921 census. As declared, this issue was raised in the House of Commons by the MP for Gloucester County in 1923. The widowed mother of an Acadian soldier who had died overseas had not filled out the paperwork correctly, so her case had not even been considered. This MP asked that all veterans' families be sent a summary of the available benefits as well as the application forms so that they would understand the process. He further insisted that the officials that reviewed the applications be fluent in French. The editors reporting the story added a note of frustration: "We are wondering why our deputies have to keep insisting on this point. Does the government really not know that in New Brunswick there are 120,000 Acadiens who all, without exception, understand French better than English? If they do not know, then it is time for them to learn it once and for all."[51] The creators of the 165th Battalion had hoped that Acadian military service would provide greater recognition and acceptance of their minority community. The failure to administer pensions in French suggests that little headway had been made.

Mark Humphries writes that even the act of pension-seeking carried a stigma for many veterans, especially those unable to work due to trauma and mental illness. Emotional trauma that prevented readjustment to civilian life was evidence of an individual flaw or deviant behaviour, since "real men did not break down, nor did they allow their emotions to interfere with their manly duty as breadwinners and providers."[52] Desmond Morton similarly notes that mental illness and injury were "little understood and less discussed" and often dismissed as cowardice or hysteria. In practical terms, the government was simply not prepared for the large number of people needing long-term care.[53] Tim Cook notes that "it was easier to put up stone monoliths to the fallen than to deal with the anguish of the living."[54] Morton and Wright add that even those without debilitating injuries often suffered from "restlessness" and experienced disillusionment when reintegrating into civilian life after their transformative experiences overseas. Government agencies and families often did not know how to help them.[55]

Did the situation of the 165th Battalion volunteers more closely resemble the portrait of poverty and disillusionment emphasized by the traditional historiography or the image of improved job prospects suggested by some more recent studies? There is evidence for both interpretations. One approach is to focus on salaries. Table 5.2 provides one of the strongest indications that economic motivations played a significant role in decisions to enlist in the 165th Battalion. The annual salary declared by the volunteers was much lower than that of the French-Canadian volunteers in Quebec and also that of the general population of wage-earners in the city of Saint John, New Brunswick. At the same time, the apparent increase in salary after the war for the Acadian volunteers is much higher – they were earning more than double what they had in 1911. Meanwhile, Bouchard and Huberman's group saw only a 20 per cent increase in revenue. When compared with a control group in their study, the soldiers made more but actually saw less of an increase between 1911 and 1921, suggesting that, particularly in the case of volunteers (their sample included many conscripts), there were more idealists leaving good jobs behind. In fact, when comparing the results for the Quebec-based soldiers against those for people living in the province and especially in Quebec City, French-Canadian soldiers did not benefit from the same wage increases.

The large jump in salary levels among the former 165th Battalion volunteers is partly explained by life course. Many of the youngest recruits declared no income at all in 1911, and those who did disproportionately held part-time, seasonal, or entry-level positions. Improved job prospects and wages would have been typical for anyone moving from adolescence to adulthood. At the very least, we can say that military service does not appear to have negatively influenced the economic potential of these young men, as it did for veterans in Quebec. One way to try to account for life course is to

Table 5.2
Average declared annual salaries ($) in 1911 and 1921[1]

Group	1911	1921	Increase
165th Bn volunteers	350	749	114%
165th Bn volunteer households	690	1,406	104%
Bouchard-Huberman soldier sample	535	642	20%
Average salary in province of Quebec	646	851	32%
Average salary in city of Quebec	584	1,036	77%
Average salary in city of Saint John	520	971	87%

1 Bouchard and Huberman, "Les anciens combattants canadiens-français," 561; Statistics Canada, "Total number of wage earners and average yearly earnings, census years 1911 and 1921, in cities of 30,000 population and over," *Canada Year Book, 1927/28*.

compare the soldiers' wages with those of the larger household. Their parents, siblings, and other relatives were also making considerably more money in 1921. Given the large number of Acadian soldiers from southeastern New Brunswick, this might have been part of a broader economic improvement due to an expanding manufacturing sector and the importance of the CNR as a regional employer. Indeed, LeBlanc has shown that the demographic success of the Acadian population in the Moncton region was directly related to better job opportunities.[56]

A more detailed occupational analysis sheds additional light on what was going on. While a focus on wages emphasizes those living in urban settings, the results underscore that a significant minority of the volunteers came from farming communities. Official statistics indicate that the New Brunswick population was still 72 per cent rural in 1911 and 68 per cent rural in 1921. Nova Scotia had more city-dwellers; 62 per cent of the population declared a rural residence in 1911 and just 57 per cent in 1921.[57] As seen in chapter 3, people living in the countryside were underrepresented in the 165th Battalion, but the picture changes when we consider who was *born* there. A modest uptick among the former Acadian volunteers declaring their principal occupation as farming in 1921 indicates that some were quite happy to return to the land. Arthur Bourque of Cocagne, New Brunswick, is a case in point. Just eighteen years old when he enlisted, Bourque had already left the family farm to work as a woodcutter by 1916. However, he seems to have had his fill of forestry, because after serving in the 39th Company, CFC, he returned home and worked with his father. Even Ulric LeBlanc, whose father was a medical doctor, had a brief

Table 5.3
Declared occupation of 165th Battalion volunteers at enlistment and in 1921

Sector	Enlistment	1921
Agriculture	21.5	24.3
Student	2.7	0.3
Fishing/sea	8.6	6.4
Labourer	37.0	25.7
Mining	2.2	2.0
Professional/official	2.3	2.5
Clerical/sales	4.2	5.8
Trades	17.6	14.5
Forestry	2.9	7.8
Railroad	1.1	4.7

moment while overseas when he dreamed of becoming a farmer as part of an idealized view of returning home to a more settled life.[58] Still, we should not overstate the trend. While nearly half the household heads in soldiers' families in 1911 and 1921 were principally farmers, just one-quarter of the former recruits pursued this in the latter year. For many former soldiers, their departure from home was definitive.

The most noticeable occupational change relates to general labourers. We saw that mobile young men holding such positions were the main source of recruits in 1916. In 1921, many of these individuals were now working in more specialized positions in forestry, railways, and sales. Jobs with the CNR were particularly sought after. Of the forty top declared wage-earners among the former 165th Battalion volunteers, fourteen were employed by the railway as clerks, ferrymen, and engineers. Alban LeBlanc had already moved from the family farm in Kent County to Moncton before the war, finding work as a grocery clerk. After the war, the twenty-two-year-old continued to board in the city, but now he was working as a ferryman with an annual salary of $2,000, nearly three times the average of his peers. Other top earners included machinists, miners, and public servants. Bruno Albert was working as a carpenter in his hometown of Caraquet, New Brunswick, in 1911, making an annual salary of $200. After the war, he moved to Shippagan and obtained a job as a fisheries officer with the government, earning $1,500. Albert was one of the few married volunteers, and his 1921 census information confirms his absence: he had two children before enlistment; then there was a noticeable gap until the newest baby, who was just twenty days old at the time of reporting. His military career was unremarkable, although he did receive a good conduct badge while with the 47th Company, CFC. Albert kept his head down and did a good job, suffering only a brief hospital stay with bronchitis in the winter of 1917. Perhaps his veteran status and improved bilingualism played a role in his selection for the lucrative public service position.

While the railway and the public service offered high wages and benefits, the forestry service was also a viable option for the former foresters. This was an example of new professional skills learned in uniform; just two of the forty-eight men declaring forestry as their principal occupation in 1921 had worked in this sector before the war. As seen in chapter 1, this does not preclude brief seasonal stints in lumber camps, which would not have been recorded in the census. Some of these men fit the profile of young men looking for work away from home, but others were new household heads trying to establish themselves. Wilfrid Laroque of Gloucester County left a large fishing family behind when he enlisted; after the war he was living in a large forestry camp of eighty-six people in Lincoln, New Hampshire. Unfortunately, the American census does not record annual wages, but between the census record and the documentation from his border crossing, we know that Larocque had been selected by the Parkes-Young forestry company, who paid for his passage through Vermont and signed him to a six-month contract as a sled leader. Larocque had served as an acting lance corporal with the 47th Company, CFC, during the war. Another former CFC lance corporal, Adelard "Dollar" Lebrun, found an excellent position in a sawmill near his home town of Saint-Hilaire, in Madawaska County. The annual salary of $1,000 would have been more than enough to support his new wife and infant son.

In their study of French-Canadian veterans in Quebec, Bouchard and Huberman found considerable professional mobility in the group, with 31 per cent declaring a different principal occupation from the time of enlistment to the 1921 census.[59] Once again, the Acadian volunteers of the 165th Battalion stood out, with fully two-thirds working in a completely different occupational category after the war. Some of these, including the one hundred former soldiers who declared a farming occupation in 1921, fit the profile of a younger son who had moved away in search of wages and adventure and eventually returned home to take up the family mantle. Others had clearly been inspired by their military experience to try new things. Opportunities were not equal: there were some farmers, fishermen, and general labourers who returned to the same limited prospects. However, those entering the railway, forestry, and service sectors were largely new hires. Military service proved a breakthrough for many previously marginalized Acadians.

Not everyone's circumstances improved. Thirty-five of the returned men declared no occupation at all, several declared no income, and many more were temporarily out of work due to layoffs or medical conditions. Bouchard and Huberman found that the unemployment rate in Montreal rose quickly to above 10 per cent by November 1920. They also cite the presence of large numbers of women in the workplace, a presence that, despite official policy to privilege veteran hires, remained relatively stable throughout the 1920s.[60] A closer look at the 1921 census returns for the former 165th Battalion soldiers reveals that 186 of the 622 declaring an occupation (about 30 per cent) were out of work at the time of recording. About half of those, ninety men, had been out of work for at least three months, and a few declared that they had been unemployed for as long as a year. The post-war transition could be particularly difficult for those battling physical or mental injuries; fifty-three of those out of work (just over one in four) declared that it was due to a medical condition.

Some workers were more likely to be unemployed in 1921, including general labourers (64 of 162 men), miners (7 of 12 men), and those working in forestry (26 of 48). Proportionally fewer of those working in agriculture (12 of 151) or the trades (27 of 85) declared that they were unemployed. The seasonal nature of resource industry work could be to blame for these high levels of unemployment, given that the census was recorded in the spring. Unemployment rates were lower among those who had left the region for the United States or western Canada. Those boarding or lodging were also less likely to be out of work, probably because they could not afford such rental accommodation without an income. Within New Brunswick, those in the Moncton area were considerably less likely to be unemployed than those in the rural parts of Kent and Gloucester Counties. As with the average salary increases, unemployment was as much a household as a veterans' concern; heads of household were just as likely to be out of work. In general, then, the former members of the Acadian national unit appear to have shared in the larger regional economic downturn, which contributed to urbanization and out-migration.

Before leaving the question of economic prospects, it is important to point out that this detailed snapshot of the veterans in 1921 tells only part of the story, namely the immediate reintegration during the first two years after demobilization. The Great Depression was coming, and in the Maritime provinces, the economic downturn started rather sooner, in the 1920s. Lara Campbell has shown how "the rapid organization of veterans into a number of groups after the First World War, and their consolidation into the Royal Canadian Legion in 1925, marks them as a vocal, articulate, and politically aware constituency that developed during the post-war discontent."[61] There is little evidence that the former Acadian foresters participated strongly in this movement. Most of them had not fought in the trenches, and they remained a minority group responding imperfectly to the "code of Britishness" raised by veterans' advocacy groups. Additional research into local legion branches in the Maritime provinces might shed new light on the participation or exclusion of Acadians from these groups. It would also be interesting to examine whether former 165th Battalion members ended up in the revamped militia units beginning in 1920. Lee Windsor found that First World War veterans were crucial to this transition among New Brunswick artillery units.[62] Now that the 1931 Canadian Census has been released for study, there will be another key source for studying the longer-term results of the post-war transition.

Campbell notes that while it is easy to study what veterans' groups published and lobbied for, we still know relatively little about their individual experiences during the 1930s.[63] In their innovative study of Second World War veterans in Australia, a group of scholars found a widespread belief that military service negatively influenced civilian employment, income, and chances of homeownership, but little evidence that this was actually so.[64] In short, there is still much to do to confirm or nuance the positive and negative economic consequences of First World War military service. Some of the 165th Battalion volunteers clearly benefited from professional experiences with the CFC and preferential hiring practices such as with the CNR. Others fit the profile of veterans struggling to reintegrate with civil society and being disproportionately affected by the economic downturn. As we saw with household information, there were distinct paths and groups, with some successfully establishing themselves quickly as married heads of household starting to have children of their own, and others returning to the parental home, and a third group continuing to be highly mobile. In fact, the results for geographic mobility after the war indicate that the number of these men on the move was rising.

Geographic Mobility

Our database provides several reference points for the life course of the group, and although we could not find every individual at each moment, the results at each stage provide some strong indications of mobility. About 55 per cent of the 1,038 recruits had moved at least once between their birth and the 1911 Census. A similar proportion had moved sometime between 1911 and their enlistment, although this included a number of return migrations to their birthplace. Most of these changes were local or regional. Military service influenced mobility in important ways. First, the proportion moving at least once between date of enlistment and the 1921 Census rose to 73 per cent. By way of comparison, Bouchard and Huberman found that only about 12 per cent of the French-Canadian soldiers they studied had changed their address between enlistment and the 1921 Census.[65] Second, the former soldiers were much more likely to quit their home province entirely, with most heading to the United States. The proportion of men undertaking these more ambitious national and transnational migrations rose from less than 5 per cent before the war to 20 per cent after.

To better capture the mobility of this group, we looked at the 492 individuals for whom we had complete information on residence at birth, in 1911, on enlistment, and in 1921. Only 78 (16 per cent) lived in the same place throughout their lives. Meanwhile, 183 (37 per cent) were highly mobile, declaring a different residence at each point of reference. The remainder (47 per cent) had moved once or twice during their lives to that point. Clearly, during this time it was normal and indeed common for young Acadian men to move, with or without their families. Military service, which included travel for training in Canada and overseas service, intensified an existing Acadian emigration trend and widened the scope of potential destinations. Indeed, for those who moved just once, three-quarters of them did so after enlistment, which suggests that the decision was at least partly motivated by their time in uniform.

Improved Health and Weight Gain

A recent study found that "serving in the CEF was good for the general health of many Canadian males." As reasons for this, the authors cite access to medical and dental services as well as to plentiful if not always desirable food, finding that the majority of men discharged as fit had experienced a noticeable weight gain.[66] We similarly compared the weight recorded at attestation and demobilization, choosing sixty soldiers (about 10 per cent of those going overseas) who had not suffered serious injury or long-term hospitalization for illness. It was important to differentiate between the physically mature adults and those still teenagers when they enlisted. One group was composed of thirty soldiers between the ages of twenty-four and twenty-nine; the other included thirty soldiers who were not yet eighteen years old. Not surprisingly, the age of the volunteers had a significant impact on the findings.

The B surname sample of 22,214 CEF soldiers studied by Clarke, Cranfield, and Inwood included men between 21 and 50 years old at enlistment, and these scholars did not differentiate between age groups. They noted an average weight gain from attestation to demobilization of 6 lbs (2.7 kg). They also calculated the body mass index (BMI) of the recruits and found that "far from being straight-backed and muscle-bound northern supermen, the majority of CEF members had decidedly unimposing physiques."[67] Given their relative poverty, similar results might be expected for the Acadian volunteers in the 165th Battalion. Indeed, the results for the sample of sixty soldiers are virtually identical; if anything, they gained slightly more weight in the CFC camps. The BMI calculations at attestation found that only two of the soldiers were underweight, while seven would have been considered overweight by current standards. At the end of the war, this latter category increased to twelve men. The majority of the recruits were well within the normal range throughout. This suggests that the level of poverty and malnutrition before the war should not be exaggerated.

When dividing the group into older and younger cohorts, what does become clear is that teenagers bulked up considerably more during their service and that this would have been at least partly attributable to normal physical maturation no matter where they served. My own experience joining the army fits this model. Due to a high metabolism and a lanky build, I struggled to put weight on throughout adolescence.

Table 5.4
Average weight (in lbs) of CEF soldiers and 165th Battalion volunteers

	Attestation	Demobilization	Change
B surname sample	142	148	6
165th Bn sample	139	147	8
165th Bn 24–9 years old	148	150	2
165th Bn under 18	130	145	15

When I enlisted in 1997 at 19 years of age, I weighed 130 pounds; by the end of my first full summer of training I had added nearly 15 pounds to my frame. Of course, most of the Acadian volunteers in 1916 would already have been working physically demanding jobs on farms or in factories, mines, and lumber camps, so in their case the results are probably more about reaching physical maturity rather than being exposed to hard labour. In fact, the group of under-18 volunteers gained on average nearly 1.5 inches in height during their military service. Joseph Melanson of Rogersville, New Brunswick, stood out in this regard: he grew 5 inches and gained 30 pounds while in uniform. Meanwhile, those already well into their twenties at attestation did not gain much weight at all. The results suggest that at least for the Acadians, the younger soldiers had simply caught up to the BMI of the older soldiers by the end of their service.

Post-War Reintegration for Specific Groups

The database allows comparison of some specific groups within the 165th Battalion in order to determine how distinct wartime experiences may have influenced post-war reintegration. To that end, we identified three twenty-person samples of those who had suffered from venereal disease, those with disciplinary problems related to alcohol, and those who had been recognized for their good conduct while in the CFC. To avoid false correlations, we excluded those who would have fit more than one of these categories or experienced other notable issues, such as physical injuries or influenza while with the CFC. The results offer intriguing trends but no definitive conclusions; in addition, not all of these issues can be entirely attributable to military service. For example, social class, family history, and medical history may have played a role in personal choices and opportunities. When people struggle, the origins of the problem are often complex.

Table 5.5
1921 trends among selected sub-groups of 165th Battalion volunteers

	GCB	VD	Alcohol	165th Bn
Average declared age at enlistment (years)	21.0	26.1	22.9	23.1
Average salary ($)	$726	$1,002	$530	$749
Average household salary ($)	$1,134	$1,236	$857	$1,406
Relationship = Son (%)	47	44	36	38
Relationship = Head (%)	23	31	29	42
Boarding/lodging (%)	25	18	21	13
Agriculture OCC (%)	41	13	43	24
Labourer OCC (%)	41	19	29	26
Natural resource OCC (%)	5	19	14	16
Skilled OCC (%)	5	38	0	28
Out of work in 1921 (%)	24	38	43	30
Urban residence (%)	35	75	7	29
Emigration to US (%)	19	18	14	19

Several trends stand out from this comparative analysis: the relative youth of those who had received a good conduct badge; the older and more urban setting of those who had been hospitalized with VD; and the difficult economic circumstances of those who had been disciplined for drunkenness.

First, the strong performers recognized by CFC leadership for their good conduct. They were on average two years younger than their counterparts among the 165th Battalion. Not surprisingly, then, they were more likely to still be living in the parental home in 1921 and twice as likely to be boarding or lodging after the war. Most had not yet had the opportunity to get married or set themselves up as heads of household in their own right. Like the group of volunteers overall, they seemed to benefit from higher individual salaries after the war, even though most of them declared jobs as farmhands and labourers. Perhaps due to their discipline and willingness to work hard, they were also less likely to be out of work in 1921. These results reflect life course as much as military service; these younger men would need more time to establish themselves after coming home but appeared to be on the right path. Joseph Chenard was an interesting case. He was living at a group home and going to school in Caraquet, New Brunswick, in 1911. He signed up on the eve of his eighteenth birthday and declared a stepbrother living in Saskatchewan as his next of kin. However, after the war, he seems to have reunited with his birth family, for he was living on their farm in Saint-Pacôme, Quebec.

The group that had suffered from venereal disease tended to be older. Nearly all of these men were living in cities after the war and often held skilled, well-paying jobs. This group included some men already married before the war, but also others who had returned to the parental home. Martha Hanna found that married men were much less likely to have contracted venereal disease and that those who did posed a serious health risk to their wives and unborn children.[68] Judging by the difference between their individual and household salaries, most of the men in this sample were the principal family breadwinners, although almost 40 per cent of them declared that they were out of work in 1921. Life course could certainly explain why this group had a much higher proportion of men with skilled trades, but symptoms of their illness and social stigma might explain their relatively high rate of unemployment and also the fact that despite being older, more of these men had not yet married or established their own households. Did those who were already married disclose their condition when they got home? How had their relationships with their wives and children evolved? Desmond Morton alludes to the psychological effects of absence and "guilty conscience" for many married CEF soldiers.[69] From sons like Chenard returning to complex family dynamics to unfaithful partners trying to re-establish themselves as husbands and fathers, we are only scratching the surface of the "vast emotional repercussions" of the war.[70]

Those who had been disciplined for drunkenness in the CFC camps were much more likely to experience economic hardship after the war. Nearly half of them were out of work in 1921, and those who did report a salary earned one-third less than their counterparts among the former 165th Battalion volunteers. The household income for these former soldiers was also much lower than for the group as a whole. Further indicators that these men were struggling include the fact that they were much less likely to be a head of household and more likely to board or stay with part of their extended family. Nearly all of them were living in the countryside, and none of them declared a skilled occupation in 1921. The picture certainly seems to be one of poverty. Life course does not appear to have been a factor here, as the average age was virtually identical to that of the former Acadian soldiers as a whole. Many Canadian war wives had to deal with returned spouses who drank too much. Some of them left their marriage; others were abandoned by their husbands.[71]

Alcohol abuse was not a new issue in post-war Canada. Temperance groups like the Women's Christian Temperance Union (WCTU) had successfully lobbied for prohibition in many Canadian provinces by the end of the war. Their efforts to deny alcohol to soldiers overseas had failed in the face of strenuous opposition from commanders and the rank and file, and they worried that "inexperienced boys" would become "infected" by a taste for alcohol that would lead to "misery and depravity" after the war.[72] The results here suggest that they were not wrong about the potential destructive consequences of addiction to drink. However, there are also larger questions about why soldiers, veterans, and other Canadians drank; perhaps it was a symptom rather than the determining cause of marginalization, trauma, and despair. Indeed, Jonathan Vance found at least one former soldier from the township of East Flamborough who wrote about alcohol soothing the "restlessness" he felt after returning from war.[73]

CONCLUSION

This chapter has explored some of the seen and unseen consequences of military service, including challenges around demobilization and the return to civil society. While some of the Acadian foresters appear to have benefited from army life and the opportunity to gain new skills, others struggled in post-war economic conditions that were particularly difficult in Atlantic Canada. A few experienced especially negative outcomes due to injury, illness, or conflict with military authorities. Life course played an important role in the fortunes of the veterans. Many of the young, single recruits had missed out on opportunities to establish themselves as married heads of household and breadwinners. Some quickly rebounded when they returned; like many of the men of East Flamborough Township in southern Ontario, they "apparently stepped back into their lives with barely a hiccup."[74] Others struggled to reintegrate and quit the region entirely.

While job-seeking and mobility were already features of the Acadian landscape before the war, there is plenty of evidence that military service and post-war economic conditions intensified these trends and enlarged the field of prospective destinations. The higher average individual and household income gain of former Acadian soldiers in 1921, relative to other groups of veterans and the larger population, further suggests that military service could diminish socio-economic inequalities for minority groups.[75] Regular income, a consistent diet, and access to health services would certainly have been a benefit for those previously living in relative poverty. At the same time, some individuals clearly suffered as a result of their absence, or their injuries abroad. Individual choices mattered; scholars should remember that the returned soldiers had agency.[76] As more data emerge with the release of the 1931 Canadian census and with more studies using longitudinal analysis reaching fruition, it should be possible to dedicate entire research projects to complex post-war realities. This would allow us to move beyond the often polemical discourses of military officials, politicians, and veterans' advocacy groups and gain a clearer understanding of veterans' experiences in different regions of Canada.

Conclusion

In calling for the creation of an Acadian national unit for the Canadian Expeditionary Force, Pascal Poirier asserted that Acadians already serving had been "lost in the crowd" of anglophone soldiers from the Maritime provinces. The assembly of notables he was addressing was quick to agree, emphasizing that Acadians needed their own French-speaking, Catholic unit led by officers of their own in order to ensure that Acadian soldiers received proper leadership and spiritual support. Perhaps even more importantly, they hoped that the 165th Battalion, having been promptly approved by the federal government as part of a larger initiative of "special identity" units meant to boost flagging voluntary recruitment, would counteract increasingly polemical political and public discourses that accused French-Canadians across the country of "slacking," as well as contribute in the longer term to greater political rights and recognition for Acadians everywhere.

The Acadians were not alone in viewing military service as an opportunity to demonstrate their loyalty and to improve the visibility and circumstances of their minority group. Melissa Shaw discusses the case of Afro-Canadians in Ontario lobbying for full inclusion in the CEF, while Katharine McGowan explains how Indigenous recruits from James Bay moved south with their families to enlist.[1] Of course, the Acadians were white and did not face the same prejudice and institutional barriers to service, but they also mobilized notions of race and nation to emphasize their distinctiveness. These notions were closely tied, in their case, to language and religion. As Acadians serving in anglophone Maritime battalions discovered, it was not always easy to speak French or gain access to the Catholic Mass in the CEF. Thus, the campaign for the creation of an Acadian national unit was a microcosm of the larger struggle for greater representation in Canadian society.

The 165th Battalion fell short of the admittedly unrealistic expectations of its creators. There would be no great victories won single-handedly by the Acadian national unit, but none of the new CEF units formed in 1916 were preserved intact, as the war effort required reinforcements for existing units already at the front. Individual Acadians contributed to every significant battle fought by the CEF from the iconic seizing of Vimy Ridge to the miserable advance in the mud-choked fields of Passchendaele. Acadian newspapers published letters from some of the soldiers who were there. Indeed, the 165th Battalion volunteers were simply the tip of the iceberg of a considerable Acadian contribution that numbered at least 5,000 volunteers.

In many ways, the 165th Battalion did achieve its goals. It attracted more than 1,200 new volunteers, including more than 1,000 Acadians from across the Maritime provinces as well as the diaspora in Quebec and the United States. The unit ultimately sent almost 600 men overseas. Most made a different kind of contribution to the war effort in the CFC, supplying the timber, planks, spars, and frames that the CEF required for everything from duckboards to airframes. First World War historiography continues to focus on the trenches, in part because of the assumption that audiences are less interested in supply and logistics.[2] The disinterest was also apparent at the time: Acadian newspapers shared fewer letters from the Acadian foresters once the 165th Battalion had been broken up. Acadian communities certainly followed the news, and they shared in the general merriment and relief with other Canadians after the Armistice. Andrew Theobald recounts a particularly colourful celebration in Cap-Pélé, New Brunswick, where the crowd shot an effigy of Kaiser Wilhelm with a colonial-era cannon.[3]

Although curiously absent in scholarly works, the Acadian contribution to the First World War never completely disappeared from public memory. In 1965, Clément Cormier, the president (*recteur*) of the newly established Université de Moncton, wrote a letter to the Royal Commission on Bilingualism and Biculturalism (the Laurendeau–Dunton Commission). The commission was examining the inclusion of francophones in a wide variety of federal arenas, including the military, and Cormier related with pride how his father had been one of the principal advocates of the creation of the

165th Battalion, the only francophone unit authorized outside of Quebec during the First World War.[4] At least one high school textbook in 1970s New Brunswick included an Acadian soldier's letter.[5] Local newsletters and historical societies also mentioned the military service of prominent Acadians.[6] Our own work with communities from Pubnico and Chéticamp in Nova Scotia to Moncton and Bathurst in New Brunswick revealed enduring local connections to military service; dozens of copies of the 165th Battalion photo album organized by the unit CO, Louis Cyriaque Daigle, remain preserved by families along with letters, postcards, photographs, and other memorabilia. A special song composed for the 165th Battalion during the war was recorded by ethnographers in the 1970s in several different regions of New Brunswick.[7]

One reason why the history of the 165th Battalion seems largely unknown or forgotten by scholars and institutions has to do with the Acadian minority situation – something that notables like Poirier and Cormier understood very well when they lobbied for its creation. The story of the Acadian national unit does not fully resonate with the dominant English-Canadian narrative of combat and sacrifice in the trenches, nor does it with the common French-Canadian narrative of an imperial war forced on an unwilling populace. Indeed, Acadians shared with their anglophone neighbours a public support for the war and a significant voluntary enlistment rate, even while agreeing with French-Canadians in Quebec that conscription should be opposed. Acadians had their own motives for enlisting, tied to specific local identities, opportunities, and needs. The history of the 165th Battalion points to a third way and, indeed, to much more complex and diverse experiences of Canada's First World War. In this sense, these Acadians soldiers are significant not only for Acadian or Atlantic Canadian history but also as part of a broader national discussion about the First World War and its consequences. This conflict was more than a great victory and nation-building moment for the young Dominion; it was also, to use Theobald's eloquent expression, "a costly victory in a brutal war that fractured the basic fabric of the country."[8] Current research is demonstrating that overly simplified English-Canadian and French-Canadian narratives of the war do not reflect the complex motivations of historical actors. For example, recruitment posters published in French by private organizations demonstrated a "loyalist" and Catholic French-Canadian viewpoint to encourage enlistment.[9] The enthusiastic, even "frenzied" homecoming of the 22nd Battalion (Canadien-Français) highlighted the support of many Quebecers for the war.[10]

It is time to finally put to bed the notion that just 35,000 French-Canadians enlisted voluntarily in the CEF and indeed the broader idea that French-Canadians were somehow less loyal citizens.[11] The repetition of this harmful and false discourse continues to damage relationships within Canada and to colour how we commemorate the war. Instead of exclusionary themes that classify communities as more or less loyal, and veterans as more or less worthy of remembrance based on how much they suffered in the trenches, we should adopt more inclusive histories and commemorative practices. The rejected volunteers and those deemed too young or unsuitable for the trenches were no less motivated or deserving of our attention than their counterparts who "made it" to the mud in Flanders. We should be able to honour the sacrifice of those who died in combat while also remembering those who died in accidents or due to illness, suicide, and other forms of violence. As other scholars have pointed out, the war divided Canadians against one another and exposed systemic barriers to minority groups of many kinds in the new nation.

By the same token, studying difficult topics like desertion, venereal disease, and alcoholism should not be seen as insulting to veterans; rather, we should view those things as essential components of the challenges faced by soldiers, military authorities, and local communities. These problems were not specific to army life; rather, they point to wider social phenomena affecting families of all backgrounds. We can also take a closer look at those awarded good conduct badges, promotions, and technical pay not just to celebrate accomplishments but to get a sense of what was valued by peers and superiors and how social class, education, and professional experience were reflected in these choices.

The army, with its copious documentation, offers unique opportunities to study a group of Canadians who were not a perfect microcosm of the larger Dominion but were certainly representative of a specific generation of young men for whom military service fit within larger trends of wage-seeking and geographic and professional mobility, as well as within the quest for acceptance in masculine culture. This was certainly true of the Acadians, who had been migrating to factory towns in Massachusetts and Maine since the mid-nineteenth century in search of wages and a better life; this, at a time when Moncton was emerging as an industrial city and transportation hub. Military service, then, was not only a patriotic duty keenly felt by some individuals and families but also a viable option for young, unmarried men, who were expected to contribute to the household economy.

From a distinctly Acadian perspective, the experience of the 165th Battalion reveals specific regional patterns. It is no coincidence that Clément Cormier spoke with pride about the Acadian national unit. Cormier was the scion of an elite class based in southeastern New Brunswick that sought to create a new Acadie. They saw themselves as the natural leaders to support francophone communities across the region through social services, post-secondary education, and political representation. Not surprisingly, they also formed the officer class of the 165th Battalion. Not everyone appreciated the efforts of this group; we saw how the choice of Daigle as CO over other Acadians with significant military experience created resentment, particularly in northern New Brunswick. It was also no coincidence that the largest contingent of 165th Battalion recruits were residing in Moncton when they enlisted. Social pull and peer pressure played important roles – fourteen recruits from the tiny village of Adamsville followed their *curé* Jean V. Gaudet into the Acadian national unit. Our research also found that in many regions, including North Shore New Brunswick communities and Prince Edward Island, enlistment followed years of service in local militia regiments.

A great advantage of conducting a longitudinal analysis linking military attestation papers to census records and other kinds of historical sources is that it provides new insights into our understanding of what motivated voluntary military service. While it is no great surprise that younger people were more likely to sign up, the relative youth of the Acadian recruits, even when compared to their counterparts across the CEF, points to the importance of life course. An astounding one in four of the 165th Battalion volunteers were not yet eighteen years old when they enlisted; we would never have known this without linking them to census records in order to deduce their real age. While it is undoubtedly true that the number of underage recruits in the CEF greatly exceeded the 3 per cent estimated using official records,[12] more research is needed to determine the true extent of this and whether the 165th Battalion was exceptional in this regard (probably not). Our analysis reveals other insights about Acadian recruits that differentiate them from general CEF trends, such as their tendency to come from large, rural households and to already have had some experience with temporary or permanent migration.[13] While many scholars have attempted to calculate voluntary enlistment rates for specific categories of Canadians such as by primary language, provincial origin, occupational category, and urban or rural background, this analysis of the 165th Battalion recruits over time reveals that people moved, changed, and could be more than one thing at the same time. Some of our categories may provide false impressions.[14]

Morton famously distinguished between idealists and idlers as a way to interrogate the conjecture that unemployed or underemployed men were more likely to enlist. He found that most of the recruits left good jobs behind, which is in line with the findings of Caroline D'Amours in her study of Second World War recruits.[15] The problem with this approach is that it entails a value judgment about motives. Many of the 165th Battalion volunteers did leave good jobs behind, but that does not mean they did not see economic advantages in joining the army. Similarly, those who had not yet found permanent, well-paying jobs near home may well have had patriotic motives. Life course played a significant role in what the records say about these recruits, particularly those just starting out on their own. Our look at desertion and those left behind when the 165th Battalion deployed overseas also revealed considerable diversity of socio-economic circumstances. A few men clearly saw putting on a uniform as one among many options for seasonal employment and had no great desire to deploy overseas. Others struggled to fit in and decided that the military was not for them. Still others really wanted to go but were declared unfit by the doctors. A few re-enlisted on multiple occasions, refusing to take no for an answer. In the ranks of the 165th, there was a full spectrum of individuals from idealists to idlers and everything in between.

Indeed, our longitudinal analysis suggests that there are no easy answers when seeking to generalize about First World War experience. Nowhere is this more evident than in our study of the returned men. Some certainly fit the traditional description of disillusioned or injured veterans experiencing challenges reintegrating with civil society. Others did quite well, leveraging their military skills for new occupational positions and improved salaries. While our ability to reconstitute individual lives will invariably fall short, the research does demonstrate that factors like life course, family support, social class, bilingualism, and education, as well as geographic origin, all played considerable roles. Some men quickly married and set up households of their own, while others languished at home. Many chose to quit the region entirely, heading for the United States or western Canada. Comparatively more men chose to emigrate after the war when compared with pre-war trends. Perhaps their world had become bigger as a result of their time overseas. Or perhaps they were simply older and more willing to leave. The results provide a fascinating cross-section of a generation of Acadian men but defy easy characterization.

To what extent were the 165th Battalion volunteers different from other soldiers in the CEF? On the whole, they were much younger, more mobile, and more rural. Their language, faith, and culture provided common points of reference, and the Acadian national unit was broadly representative of an entire region – indeed, a diaspora – rather than a single town or county. In general, they deserted a little less and had fewer disciplinary problems compared to some of their counterparts in other battalions, but they also had similar rates of venereal disease and perhaps even more difficulty with drunkenness. Like other units, including special identity units recruiting in 1916, the 165th Battalion did not reach full strength and was ultimately disbanded.[16] Most of the recruits ended up in the CFC. When compared with other CEF veterans, the former members of the 165th seemed to have higher salaries and more geographic and professional mobility in 1921.

When Acadians in large numbers – approximately 23,000 – signed up for military service during the Second World War,[17] they were continuing an existing tradition originating not just in the First World War but also in regional militia service. A new research project by Philippe Volpé is finding that the Canadian Officer Training Corps program was very well established and enthusiastically adopted in colleges and universities across Acadie.[18] Recapturing the history of the 165th Battalion can fill some critical gaps in Acadian history, shedding new light on the Acadian renaissance and larger social, economic, and political transformations. This was the first objective of the present book.

I have also sought to offer a new and more comprehensive approach to Canada's First World War, leveraging social history methods and longitudinal analysis focused on the soldiers and their families. The findings of this study demonstrate the value in combining information from multiple sources, including military files, censuses, newspapers, correspondences, and official archives. There is still much to do and that can be done with the sources at our disposal, both for Acadians and for other regional units. Indeed, further studies using these methods with other groups of CEF soldiers from different regions and in different age groups would shed light on a variety of trends, from underage recruitment to the selection of leaders, and from family strategies of support to driving factors in post-war outcomes. This would be valuable not only in the context of First World War history but also for broader inquiries such as how to support veterans in the future. Addressing the third objective of this book – to broach difficult topics such as desertion and discipline – enhances this reconstruction of soldiers' lives and the interconnections between individual choices, family obligations, and regional trends.

The volunteers of the Acadian national unit deserve to be remembered even if most of them did not win glory on the battlefield. This history of Acadian volunteers before, during, and after the First World War features soldiers but also families,[19] heroes but also anti-heroes,[20] idealism but also pragmatism. Their experiences add to the burgeoning literature on this conflict, a literature that is leading to more inclusive history and fostering better insights into how the war affected a generation of families in the Maritime provinces and across the Dominion of Canada, and continues to shape public memory today.

Notes

INTRODUCTION

1 Vance, *Death So Noble*, 12–13.
2 Theobald, *The Bitter Harvest*, 10.
3 Nicholson and Humphries, *Canadian Expeditionary Force*, 35.
4 Shaw, "Expanding the Narrative," 399.
5 Granatstein and Hitsman, *Broken Promises*, 26–8.
6 Copp, with Maavara, *Montreal at War*, 66–9.
7 One of the best scholarly works available in English on early Acadian history is Griffiths, *From Migrant to Acadian*.
8 2021 Canadian Census, https://www12.statcan.gc.ca/census-recensement/index-eng.cfm.
9 McKay and Swift, *The Vimy Trap*, 9.
10 Cook, *Vimy*, 380–1.
11 Wood, *Militia Myths*.
12 Miller, *Painting the Map Red*, 439.
13 Cook, *Vimy*, 171–222. One of the most important works on this issue remains Granatstein and Hitsman, *Broken Promises*, esp. 22–104.
14 Landry and Lang, *Histoire de l'Acadie*, 237–9; Couturier and Leblanc, *Économie et société en Acadie*.
15 Chiasson, *Petit manuel d'histoire d'Acadie*, 14.
16 Roy, *L'Acadie des origines à nos jours*, 222.
17 Godin and Basque, *Histoire des Acadiens*; Massicotte and LeBlanc, "L'Acadie et la Seconde Guerre mondiale," 49–67.
18 Cook, *Vimy*, 144. For more on the 26th Battalion, CEF, see Wilson, *A Family of Brothers*.
19 Léger, *Le bataillon acadien*, 81.

20 Theobald, *The Bitter Harvest*, 72.
21 Ibid., 37–57.
22 "Echos d'un tag day," *L'Évangéline*, 21 April 1917.
23 "L'Acadie offre son bataillon," *L'Évangéline*, 8 December 1915.
24 Le majeur J.A. Léger à l'honorable J.B.M. Baxter, *Le Moniteur acadien*, 9 August 1917, translation of letter published on 6 December 1917. 7
25 "Marching Out State of the 165th (OS) Battalion, CEF," 24 March 1917, LAC, RG 24, vol. 4563.
26 Léger, *Le bataillon acadien*, 209.
27 Henderson and Keshen retrace the emergence of a more sophisticated field of military history in Canada and the importance of local and regional studies in "Canadian Perspectives on the First World War," 285–6.
28 One excellent recent example among many is Campbell, *It Can't Last Forever*.
29 Léger, *Le bataillon acadien*, 133, 144–7. A unit nominal role dated 13 February 1917 counted 784 soldiers, and Léger indicates that the new exams were held in March, just before the battalion left Saint John.
30 CEAAC, Louis Cyriaque Daigle, fonds 566, Registre de déserteurs, 165e bataillon.
31 Martin, *Un siècle d'oubli*, 92.
32 In the official instructions for the Canadian census, enumerators were to record the *de jure* population, that is, the people who would normally be present in the household whether they were actually there that day or not. This led to varying interpretations in practice. On the work of the enumerators, see Kennedy and Inwood, "A New Prosopography," 65–77.
33 Bouchard and Huberman, "Les anciens combattants canadiens-français," 558.
34 Cunningham, "After 'it's over over there,'" 213.
35 CEAAC, fonds Hilarion LeBlanc, boîte 308, J. Ulric LeBlanc to his parents, 25 October 1915.
36 CEAAC, "Mandement de Monseigneur Édouard LeBlanc, évêque de Saint-Jean, au Clergé, aux Ordres Religieux et aux Fidèles de son Diocèse, 1915" (Saint John, 1915).
37 Nicholson and Humphries, *Canadian Expeditionary Force, 1914–1919*, 499; for No. 2 Construction Battalion, see Ruck, *Canada's Black Battalion*.
38 Fred Frigot to Léotine Frigot, *Le Moniteur acadien*, 25 October 1917.

Notes to pages 15–22

39 LAC, RG 9 III-B-3, vol. 3818-3819, Daily Routine Orders (DRO), 5th District (Jura), CFC.
40 Devigne, *Les faiseurs de sciure*, 93–6.
41 Clearly intended to be humorous; "fricot" is a traditional Acadian chicken soup.
42 For more on these events, part of a SSHRC-funded Connection Project called *Cultural Communities, Memory and the First World War*, see https://museum.novascotia.ca/firstworldwar.
43 Morton, "Le Canada français," 43.
44 Pépin, "1914–1918," 31–7.
45 Morton, *When Your Number's Up*, 34, 55.
46 Djebabla, "Historiographie francophone," 407, 413.
47 Morton, *When Your Number's Up*, 62.
48 Brown and Loveridge, "Unrequited Faith," 17–18.
49 Sharpe, "Enlistment in the Canadian Expeditionary Force," 20–4.
50 Mainville, *Till the Boys Come Home*, 18.
51 Martin, *Un siècle d'oubli*, 18–29.
52 Ibid., 94-5.
53 Marti, "Embattled Communities," 103, 116.
54 Le majeur J.A. Léger à l'honorable J.B.M. Baxter, *Le Moniteur acadien*, 9 August 1917, translation of letter published on 6 December 1917.
55 Nicholson and Humphries, *Canadian Expeditionary Force*, 215, 546.
56 Brown and Loveridge, "Unrequited Faith," 12.
57 Marti, "Embattled Communities," 101.
58 Copp, *Montreal at War*, 87–9.
59 Léger, *Le bataillon acadien*, 72.
60 O'Connor, "The 105th," 8.
61 Léger, *Le premier régiment North Shore*.
62 "Notre bataillon acadien," *L'Évangéline*, 15 March 1916.
63 Martin, "Francophone Enlistment," 10.
64 Clarke, *Unwanted Warriors*, 12, 50–4.
65 The government reduced the height requirement from five feet three inches to five feet two inches in July 1915 in order to increase the potential recruiting pool. Morton, *When Your Number's Up*, 56.
66 Clarke, *Unwanted Warriors*, 62–3.
67 Léger, *Le bataillon acadien*, 82–4.
68 Ratch relates that this unit shared a fate much like that of the 165th Battalion. Doctors declared 150 recruits unfit – several were underage – and those who did make it overseas were turned into a

railway construction battalion because they were seen as unsuitable for the trenches. Sauer Ratch, "'Do Your Little Bit.'"
69 Clarke, Cranfield, and Inwood, "Fighting Fit?," 94.
70 Morton, *When Your Number's Up*, 279.
71 Black and Boileau, *Old Enough to Fight*; Cook, "'He was determined to go,'" 42.
72 Cook, "'He was determined to go,'" 60. Holt supplies the figure of 33,000 men or about 5 per cent of CEF enlistments who were underage or overage. *Filling the Ranks*, 79.
73 Marti, "Embattled Communities," 112.
74 Nicholson and Humphries, *Canadian Expeditionary Force*, 499–500; Marti, "Embattled Communities," 134; Sauer Ratch, "Do Your Little Bit," 6.
75 Bouvier, *Déserteurs et insoumis*, 30–1.
76 Iacobelli, "No Example Is Needed," 72; Dagenais, "'Une permission! C'est bon pour une recrue,'» 3–5.
77 Bouvier, *Déserteurs et insoumis*, 9.
78 Morton, *When Your Number's Up*, 60.
79 Morton, "The Short, Unhappy Life," 75.
80 Also see Kennedy, "Struck Off Strength and from Memory."
81 Léger, *Le bataillon acadien*, 209.
82 Morton, *When Your Number's Up*, 270; Morton and Wright, *Winning the Second Battle*.
83 Scotland, "And the Men Returned," 149.
84 Bouchard and Huberman, "Les anciens combattants canadiens-français," 547; Clarke, Cranfield, and Inwood, "Fighting Fit?," 94.
85 Plourde and Frenette, "Essor démographique," 111–14.
86 Humphries, "Between Commemoration and History," 385, 395–6.
87 Rutherdale, *Hometown Horizons*, xiii.
88 Gagnon, *Le 22e bataillon*; Wilson, *A Family of Brothers*.
89 Morton, *When Your Number's Up*, 51.
90 D'Amours, " Idéalistes, pragmatiques et les autres," 125–47.

CHAPTER ONE

1 For an overview of the Acadian renaissance and the First World War, see Doucet, "La politique et les Acadiens," 310–20; and Landry and Lang, *Histoire de l'Acadie*, 189–96.
2 Theobald, *The Bitter Harvest*, 43–4.

3 This was a reproduction of his first speech in Saint John, included in a later article about recruitment, "Le bataillon acadien," *Le Moniteur acadien*, 28 September 1916, 1.
4 Basque, *La Société Nationale de l'Acadie*, 94.
5 Andrew, "La montée des élites acadiennes au Nouveau-Brunswick."
6 Roy, *L'Acadie des origines à nos jours*, 216–21.
7 Couturier, "Perception et pratique de la justice," 75.
8 LeBlanc, "Une communauté en transition."
9 LeBlanc, "La recherche fondamentale en histoire des femmes et du genre en Acadie," in Thibeault et al., *Paroles et regards de femmes en Acadie*, 30.
10 Frenette, "L'historiographie des Franco-américains"; Plourde et Frenette, "Essor démographique," 113. Classic studies of French Canadian emigration include Lavoie, *L'émigration des Canadiens aux Etats-Unis*; and Roby, *Les Franco-Américains de la Nouvelle-Angleterre*.
11 Deschambault, Haché-Chiasson, and Kennedy, "Vers une reconstitution de la mobilité des Acadiennes."
12 Bourque and Richard, *Les conventions nationales acadiennes*, vols. 1–2.
13 Sharpe, "Enlistment in the Canadian Expeditionary Force," 38. Sharpe actually said twelve; he missed the 165th Battalion.
14 Louis-Cyriaque Daigle, "Le 165ieme Bataillon Acadien", LAC, RG 9, vol. 4702, folder 75, file 12.
15 "The Acadian Battalion," *The Daily Telegraph and Sun* (Saint John), 20 December 1915.
16 Desjardins, "La maudite guerre."
17 Duguid's work is reproduced by Vance in "Provincial Patterns of Enlistment." See also Sharpe, "Enlistment [...] A Re-evaluation," 50. Holt employed an innovative methodology, extrapolating from registration results under the Military Service Act of 1917; *Filling the Ranks*, 82.
18 CEAAC, Hilarion C. LeBlanc, fonds 308, archives privées; Saindon, "Étude des correspondances."
19 Theobald, *The Bitter Harvest*, 43-6.
20 Louis-Cyriaque Daigle, "Le 165ieme Bataillon Acadien," LAC, RG 9, vol. 4702, folder 75, file 12.
21 Sharpe, "Enlistment [...] A Re-evaluation," 34.
22 Léger, *Le bataillon acadien*, 56.
23 Today this site is occupied by the Crowne Plaza Hotel in downtown Moncton.

24 Léger, *Le bataillon acadien*, 63–6.
25 Ibid., 59.
26 Basque, *La Société Nationale de l'Acadie*, 84.
27 "L'Acadie offre son bataillon," *L'Évangéline*, 8 December 1915.
28 Daigle, *Un aperçu historique*, 4; CEAAC, fond Rufin Arsenault, Le premier ministre Robert Borden à A. Sormany et R. Arsenault, 4 December 1915.
29 Telegram OC 6th Division, 13 December 1915, LAC, RG 24, vol. 1388, file HQ 593-6-1-165, 0024.
30 Léger, *Le premier régiment North Shore*, 62–3.
31 Daigle, *Un aperçu historique*, 4.
32 "M. L. Cyriaque Daigle recommandé pour le poste de Commandant du Bataillon Acadien," *Le Moniteur acadien*, 16 December 1915.
33 "Aux Acadiens Français," *L'Évangéline*, 29 December 1915.
34 "Battalion for Acadian Race," *The Daily Gleaner* (Fredericton), 8 December 1915.
35 "The Acadian Battalion," *The Daily Telegraph and Sun* (Saint John), 20 December 1915.
36 Léger, *Le bataillon acadien*, 73–4.
37 Daigle, *Un aperçu historique*, 3.
38 "Battalions vie with one another in their efforts for an early completion," *The Daily Telegraph and Sun* (Saint John), 7 January 1916.
39 Adjutant-General to General Officer Commanding Military District No. 6 (Halifax), 1 May 1916, LAC, RG 24, vol. 1388, file HQ 593-6-1-165, 0020.
40 Léger, *Le premier régiment North Shore*, 75-6.
41 "Lieut. Col. Daigle says no difficulty will be found in raising the 165th," *Campbellton Graphic*, 5 January 1916.
42 "Le Col. Daigle et le régiment des Acadiens," *Le Moniteur acadien*, 20 January 1916.
43 Although, to the consternation of many, it also published a short series of editorials against Acadian military participation by an apparent disciple of Henri Bourassa. Léger, *Le bataillon acadien*, 103.
44 "Le Col. Daigle et le régiment des Acadiens," "Choses militaires, en avant 'arche!" *L'Évangéline*, 2 February 1916.
45 Translation: "Soon you will greet France / Soldiers, who would not envy such a fate? / It is also for their deliverance that you are going to fight hard / It is the former motherland / That opens its arms to you today / Go and fight their battles / For your honour and your life / Stand up Acadian people! Forward for honour! / For you, and for your

Notes to pages 44–9　　　　251

children's happiness." F.M. Lanteigne, prêtre, "Le Bataillon Acadien: chanson dédié aux soldats du bataillon acadien," *L'Évangéline*, 1 March 1916.
46 Jonathan F. Vance, *A Township at War* (Waterloo: Wilfrid Laurier University Press, 2018), 104–7.
47 Vance, *A Township at War*, 109–10.
48 "Grande Assemblée de Recrutement," *L'Évangéline*, 29 December 1915.
49 Daigle, *Un aperçu historique*, 3.
50 Sirois, "La participation des Brayons," 6.
51 Léger, *Le bataillon acadien*, 88.
52 "Chez nos militaires: le 165e bataillon acadien, assemblée de recrutement, Tignish," *L'Évangéline*, 14 June 1916.
53 Miller, *Torontonians and the Great War*, 100.
54 Unity creates strength.
55 "Aux officiers et membres de la fanfare du 165e Bat.," *L'Évangéline*, 17 June 1916.
56 "Alphonse Melanson of the 165th died in hospital," *Campbellton Graphic*, 30 November 1916.
57 "Adresse aux officiers du 165e bataillon acadien," *L'Évangéline*, 27 June 1916.
58 Léger provides a few details about the involvement of the band in recruiting; *Le bataillon acadien*, 101–6.
59 "La fanfare du Bataillon Acadien," *Le Moniteur acadien*, 4 May 1916.
60 CEAAC, fond 566, Louis-Cyriaque Daigle, Captain J. Malenfant au Lieutenant-Colonel Daigle, 12 March 1918.
61 "La Fanfare l'Assomption fait une démonstration en l'honneur de son directeur et de ses membres enrégimentés dans la Fanfare du 165e," *Le Moniteur acadien*, 4 May 1916.
62 "Moncton's Bands Patriotic," *Daily Times* (Moncton), 3 June 1916.
63 "Au 165ième Bataillon Acadien," 23 February 1916.
64 "Notre bataillon acadien," 15 March 1916.
65 Jacques La Tour, "Le Lt-Col. D'Aigle et les soldats acadiens," *L'Évangéline*, L6 April 1916.
66 Daigle, *Un aperçu historique*, 3.
67 BGen H.H. McLean, G.O.C. Troops, New Brunswick, to 6th District Halifax, 5 December 1916, LAC, RG 24, vol. 1662, file HQ 683-316-5.
68 Marti, "Embattled Communities," 53–4.
69 Jacques La Tour, "Le Lt-Col. D'Aigle et les soldats acadiens," *L'Évangéline*, 6 April 1916.

70 "Le Régiment Acadien," *L'Évangéline*, 26 January 1916.
71 "Le Lieutenant-Colonel Daigle," *Le Moniteur acadien*, 9 March 1916.
72 CEAAC, fonds Hilarion LeBlanc, Joseph Ulric LeBlanc to his parents, 11 July 1916.
73 "En avant le 165e," *L'Évangéline*, 31 May 1916.
74 "Capt. Arthur Legere Honored at Dalhousie," *Campbellton Graphic*, 9 March 1916.
75 MGen W. Hodgins, Adjutant General – Canadian Militia to 6th District (Halifax), 16 May 1916, LAC, RG 24, vol. 1388, file HQ-593-6-1-165.
76 "Senior Major in French Battalion," *The Daily Gleaner*, 29 May 1916; "Second in Command of 165th Batt., Long Military Career of Major Bissonnette," *Saint John Globe*, 30 May 1916.
77 Morton, "The Short, Unhappy Life."
78 Holt, *Filling the Ranks*, 25–9.
79 GOC Military District 6 (Halifax) to the Secretary of the Militia Council (Ottawa), 12 June 1916, LAC, RG 24, vol. 1388, file HQ-593-6-165 – 0013 and 0014, LAC.
80 Major J.F. Bissonnette to Commander, 1st Brigade, Valcartier Camp, 8 July 1916, LAC, RG 24, vol. 1388, file HQ-593-6-165 – 0010.
81 Major J.F. Bissonnette to Commander, 1st Brigade, Valcartier Camp, 8 July 1916, LAC, RG 24, vol. 1388, file HQ-593-6-165 – 0009.
82 Adjutant-General, Canadian Militia (Ottawa), to GOC Military District 6 (Halifax), 16 June 1916, LAC, RG 24, vol. 1388, file HQ-593-6-165 – 0012.
83 Adjutant-General, Canadian Militia (Ottawa), to GOC Valcartier Camp, 22 August 1916, LAC, RG 24, vol. 1388, file HQ-593-6-165 – 0005.
84 Adjutant-General, Canadian Militia (Ottawa), to GOC Valcartier Camp, 27 September 1916, LAC, RG 24, vol. 1388, file HQ-593-6-165 – 0004.
85 Vance, *A Township at War*, 52–3.
86 Morton, *When Your Number's Up*, 57–60.
87 Miller, *Torontonians and the Great War*, 71–72; Marti, "Embattled Communities," 117. Holt describes the difficulties in recruiting several bantam units across Canada; ultimately nearly 1,700 of them were sent overseas, but fewer than half proved eligible for front-line service; *Filling the Ranks*, 60–1.
88 Brown and Loveridge, "Recruiting the CEF," 12; Nicholson and Humphries, *Canadian Expeditionary Force*, 546.
89 Brown and Loveridge, "Unrequited Faith," 14.

90 Léger, *Le bataillon acadien*, 105.
91 Morton, *When Your Number's Up*, 51–2.
92 More detailed census schedules on agriculture and household production were not preserved by LAC.
93 Godin and Basque, *Histoire des Acadiens du Nouveau-Brunswick*, 68; Leblanc, "Une communauté en transition,": 133–6.
94 Michel Roy, *L'Acadie des origines à nos jours*, 212–18.
95 Landry and Lang review the challenging economic circumstances and opportunities brought by industrialization and urbanization in *Histoire de l'Acadie*, 212–27.
96 The total population of French origin figures taken from Roy, "Settlement and Population Growth," 167.
97 Daigle, *Un aperçu historique*, 3.
98 "Le Bataillon Acadien," *L'Évangéline*, 9 February 1916.
99 For the situation in the Madawaska, see Sirois, "La participation des Brayons," 2–13.
100 For more on this family, see Stehelin, *Electric City*.
101 For more on this family and the region, see Kennedy, "The Baie Sainte-Marie Goes to War," 123–31.
102 "Le Recrutement au 165e," *L'Évangéline*, 28 June 1916.
103 "Nouvelles locales," *Le Moniteur acadien*, 22 June 1916.
104 "Nouvelles locales," *Le Moniteur acadien*, 9 March 1916.
105 Morton, *When Your Number's Up*, 62.
106 Brown and Loveridge, "Unrequited Faith," 18.
107 Vance, "Provincial Patterns of Enlistment," 75–8.
108 Sharpe, "Enlistment [...] A Regional Analysis," 33–4.
109 Plourde et Frenette, "Essor démographique," 111–14; Landry and Lang, *Histoire de l'Acadie*, 2e éd., 252–5.
110 Craig and colleagues have provided the best historical synthesis of the Madawaska region as an integrated social and economic zone, although their treatment ends at the beginning of the First World War. See *The Land in Between*.
111 LeBlanc, "Une communauté en transition," 34.
112 Sylvester, "Rural to Urban Migration."
113 Sandwell, *Canada's Rural Majority*, 3–5, 181–3.
114 Ibid., 22–3.
115 Burke, "Transitions."
116 Miller, *Torontonians and the Great War*, 68.
117 Rutherdale, *Hometown Horizons*, 43–5.

CHAPTER TWO

1. Daigle, *Un aperçu historique*, 3.
2. "Le départ du Bataillon Acadien," *Le Moniteur acadien*, 6 July 1916.
3. *The Daily Telegraph and Sun*, 29 June 1916, 3.
4. Daigle, *Un aperçu historique*, 3; G.O.C. Valcartier Camp to G.O.C. M.D. No. 6 (Halifax), 8 July 1916, LAC, RG 24, vol. 4563.
5. CEAAC, fonds 566 Louis-Cyriaque Daigle, Alphée Langis to Clément Cormier (?), June 1916.
6. *The Daily Telegraph and Sun*, 14 July 1916, 3.
7. "140th Battalion Team is Winner," *The Daily Gleaner*, 29 July 1916, 9.
8. Keshen, *Propaganda and Censorship*, 78.
9. Adjutant-General, Canadian Militia (Ottawa) to GOC District No. 6 (Halifax), 14 November 1916, LAC, RG 24, vol. 1388, file HQ-593-6-1-165, 0003, LAC.
10. "Lettre d'un soldat," *Le Moniteur acadien*, 1 August 1916.
11. 165th Battalion Camp Valcartier, 1916, Personal Collection of Jonathan Vance.
12. "145th, Westmorland's Best, Off to Valcartier," *The Daily Telegraph and Sun*, 26 June 1916, 3.
13. "News of Valcartier," *The Daily Telegraph and Sun*, 12 July 1916, 3.
14. Morton, *When Your Number's Up*, 17.
15. 17 August 1916, "Le 165e à Valcartier," *Le Moniteur acadien*, 1.
16. "Recruiting in Province continues without Marked Improvement," *The Daily Telegraph and Sun*, 2 September 1916, 3.
17. "Machine Gun Squad of 165th Composed of Fine Soldiers," *St. John Standard*, 30 October 1916, 10.
18. "Le bataillon acadien," *Le Moniteur acadien*, 28 September 1916, 1.
19. Tim Cook notes that the Canadian Corps, after suffering 8,000 total casualties in two weeks during the Battle of Mount Sorrel, was lucky to have missed the first two months of the Somme Campaign, but the Newfoundland Regiment, serving with the 29th British Division at Beaumont Hamel 1 July 1916, was "all but annihilated." *Vimy*, 20.
20. Keshen, *Propaganda and Censorship*, 27–54.
21. "165th is 850 Strong; Getting Armory Ready," *The Daily Telegraph and Sun*, 29 September 1916, 3.
22. "Honneur au 165ème," *Le Moniteur acadien*, 9 November 1916, 2.
23. Daigle, *Un aperçu historique*, 4.

24 "Nouvelles militaires," *Le Moniteur acadien*, 12 October 1916, 4; "The 165th Battalion was Warmly Welcomed to City," *St. John Standard*, 3 October 1916, 2.
25 "Another Military Unit May Arrive Here Tonight," *St. John Standard*, 6 October 1916, 10; "French-Acadians, on Route March, Captivate St. John," 5 October 1916, *The Daily Telegraph and Sun*, 3.
26 Daigle to MacLean, 29 August 1916, LAC, RG 24, vol. 1401, HQ 593-6-2, vol. 18.
27 "Good Soldiers," *The Daily Telegraph and Sun*, 6 November 1916, 5.
28 "With the 165th," *The Daily Telegraph and Sun*, 6 October 1916, 3.
29 "Bayonet and Bomb Fighting Now Occupy French Acadians," *The Daily Telegraph and Sun*, 9 October 1916, 3.
30 "French-Acadians Splendid Marchers," *The Daily Telegraph and Sun*, 7 October 1916, 6.
31 "Trench Warfare for 165th," *The Daily Telegraph and Sun*, 25 October 1916, 4.
32 "St John is Preparing for More Troops; 'Battlefield' Required," *The Daily Telegraph and Sun*, 8 November 1916, 3.
33 "Canada to Hold Forces at Home, Preparing for the Spring Offensive," *The Daily Telegraph and Sun*, 15 December 1916, 3.
34 "Field Ambulance Wants Officers," *The Daily Telegraph and Sun*, 9 February 2017, 6.
35 "Entertainment by 165th Was Huge Success," *St. John Standard*, 8 November 1916, 2.
36 "165th Concert Brought out Fine Talent," *The Daily Telegraph and Sun*, 8 November 1916, 9; "Field Ambulance Filled: Territorial Unites to Re-Inforce, the New Plan," *The Daily Telegraph and Sun*, 22 November 1916, 3.
37 "165th Reception and Dance Most Brilliant Affair," *The Daily Telegraph and Sun*, 17 February 1917, 9.
38 "Entertaining the 165th Battalion," *St. John Globe*, 2 December 1916, 5.
39 Miller, *Torontonians and the Great War*, 113–19.
40 "165th Wins First from Ambulance Corps, 4–3," *The Daily Telegraph and Sun*, 20 January 1917, 15.
41 Reid Studio to Daigle, 25 November 1916, LAC, RG 9, vol. 4702, folder 75, file 12, 14.
42 Mortimer Company to Daigle, 12 March 1917, LAC, RG 9, vol. 4702, folder 75, file 12, 9.

43 CEAAC, fonds 566 Louis-Cyriaque Daigle, J. Malenfant to Daigle, 12 March 1918.
44 "Strong Drafts soon to be Raised for 26th," *The Daily Telegraph and Sun*, 14 December 1916, 3.
45 "Twelve Units, 7000 Men, on way to N.B.," *The Daily Telegraph and Sun*, 27 February 1917, 4.
46 *The Kings County Record*, 10 March 1916, 2.
47 "Weddings," *The Daily Telegraph and Sun*, 13 February 1917, 5.
48 "Hebert-Chase," *The Daily Telegraph and Sun*, 20 February 1917, 5.
49 "Sent to Dorchester," *The Campbellton Graphic*, 3 May 1917, 3; "Five Years for Burglary," *The North Shore Leader*, 4 May 1917, 5.
50 "Soldier Struck by Auto," *St. John Standard*, 23 March 1917, 3.
51 "Officer's Narrow Escape," *The Daily Telegraph and Sun*, 19 February 1917, 10.
52 Telesphore Richard, statement before notary public in Bathurst, 17 March 1917, from military personnel file of Antoine Nowlan, 666804, LAC.
53 J. Theophilus Doucet, statement before notary public in Bathurst, 17 March 1917, from military personnel file of Antoine Nowlan, 666804, LAC. See also "Un soldat du 165e écrasé par un char," *L'Évangéline*, 21 March 1917.
54 Léger, *Le premier régiment North Shore*, 98.
55 Daigle, *Un aperçu historique*, 4.
56 CEAAC, Fonds Clément Cormier 177.2341, D.W. Simpson to Daigle.
57 "Untitled," *Saint John Globe*, 29 January 1917, 10.
58 "Sequel of Raid by Policemen," *Saint John Globe*, 17 January 1917, 10.
59 "Y.W.P.A. favor Police Women," *Saint John Globe*, 27 January 1917, 2.
60 "Com. M'Lellan had a Change of Heart," *Saint John Globe*, 8 November 1916, 5.
61 "Acadians and Enlistment," *Saint John Globe*, 12 March 1917, 10.
62 Theobald, *The Bitter Harvest*, 56–7.
63 Col. A. Mignault, Director of French recruiting in Montreal, to LCol Daigle, 23 December 1916, and response 14 January 1917, LAC, RG 24, vol. 4574, file MD7 3-8-1 (0002-0003).
64 "The French Acadians in War," *St. John Standard*, 30 November 1916, 4.
65 Miller, *Torontonians and the Great War*, 114–15.
66 "Echos d'un 'Tag Day'" *L'Évangéline*, 21 February 1917.
67 "Le Lt-Col. Daigle remercie les dames de l'Assomption," *L'Évangéline*, 9 May (publication d'une lettre rédigée le 5 avril à bord le *S.S. Metagama*).

68 Adjutant-General, MD 6 (Halifax), to 165th O/S Battalion dated 8 March 1917, LAC, RG 24, vol. 4563.
69 Holt, *Filling the Ranks*, 192–3.
70 "Le Bataillon Acadien," *Le Moniteur acadien*, 28 December 1916, 1.
71 "Notre bataillon!," *L'Évangéline*, 3 January 1917, 1, 8.
72 "New Battalion for This Province," *The Daily Gleaner*, 19 August 1916, 4.
73 Holt, *Filling the Ranks*, 192–9.
74 Nicholson and Humphries, *Canadian Expeditionary Force*, appendix C, 546.
75 "Recruiting," *St. John Globe*, 21 November 1916, 3.
76 Mainville, *Till the Boys Come Home*, 37.
77 Daigle, *Un aperçu historique*, 4.
78 Léger, *Le premier régiment North Shore*, 99–101.
79 Anonymous letter to Robert Borden dated 21 November 1916; MGen W.E. Hodgins (Ottawa) to MGen Benson (Halifax), 27 November 1916; BGen H.H. McLean to MGen Benson, 5 December 1916, LAC, RG 24, vol. 1662, file HQ 683-316-5 (0004-0007).
80 MGen Hodgins to MGen Benson, undated (December 1916); BGen McLean to MGen Benson, 20 December 1916; Maj Legere to BGen McLean, 19 December 1916, LAC, RG 24, vol. 1662, file HQ-683-316-5 (0002-0006).
81 Clarke, *Unwanted Warriors*, 106–9.
82 MGen Benson (Halifax) to Militia Council (Ottawa), 3 March 1917, LAC, RG 24, vol. 4563, file MD 6 133-36-1 (0001).
83 "Une foule considérable salue les soldats du 165e," *L'Évangéline*, 28 March 1917.
84 Morton, "The Short, Unhappy Life," 75.
85 "Le bataillon acadien," *Le Moniteur acadien*, 28 December 1916.
86 "Daring Escape," *Saint John Globe*, 21 November 1916, 3.
87 Keshen, *Propaganda and Censorship*, 77–9.
88 Wright et al., *Security, Dissent, and the Limits of Toleration in Peace and War*, 19.
89 Marquis, "Policing the New Dominion" in *Policing Canada from 1867 to 9/11*; "Revised instructions for dealing with deserters and absentees without leave," Ottawa: King's Printer, 1917, 39–42, 48–9.
90 Léger, *Le premier régiment North Shore*, 79–80.
91 Preliminary findings about the 187 deserters identified in the unit register appeared previously in Kennedy, "Struck Off Strength and from Memory."
92 Holt, *Filling the Ranks*, 92, 193.

93 According to a statement by the Chief of the Defence Staff, the CAF lost nearly 15 per cent of its strength during the pandemic years 2020–22. With recruitment slowed and the number of requests for voluntary release increasing, the organization suffered a net loss of approximately 10,000 people. Murray Brewster, "Military personnel shortage will get worse before it gets better, top soldier says," CBC News, 6 October 2022.
94 Bouvier, *Déserteurs et insoumis*, 30–1.
95 Iacobelli, "No Example Is Needed," 72; Dagenais, "Une permission!," 3–5.
96 Bouvier, *Déserteurs et insoumis*, 124.
97 Dagenais, "Une permission!," 7.
98 Bouvier, *Déserteurs et insoumis*, 9.
99 Vance, *A Township at War*, 117.
100 "Le bataillon acadien," *L'Évangéline*, 27 September 1916.
101 Morton, *When Your Number's Up*, 235.
102 Hanna, *Anxious Days and Tearful Nights*, 95–108.
103 For more on the creation of the Special Services Companies in the Maritime provinces, see M.D. No. 6 (Halifax) to G.O.C. Troops NB (Saint John), 30 November 1916, LAC, RG 24-C-8, vol. 4574, file 3-9-23 Recruitment.
104 Clarke, *Unwanted Warriors*, 121.
105 Theobald, *The Bitter Harvest*, 97.
106 Further details on these regulations can be found in "The Manual of Military Law," London: HMSO, 1907, LAC; Bouvier, *Déserteurs et insoumis*, 38–41; in an interview with the author in 2021, Mark Minenko noted that there were many arrests and sentences for desertion in Alberta.
107 "Extend Pardon for Deserters," *The Daily Gleaner*, 13 December 1916, 5.
108 Hanna, *Anxious Days and Tearful Nights*, 52.
109 "Was Not Guilty of Desertion," *Saint John Globe*, 2 November 1917, 10.
110 Theobald, *The Bitter Harvest*, 65–7.
111 "Absent without Leave from Duty," *Saint John Globe*, 10 November 1916, 9.
112 Cook, "'He was determined to go,'" 61–2; Holt, *Filling the Ranks*, 78.
113 Morton, *Fight or Pay*, 44.
114 Hanna, *Anxious Days and Tearful Nights*, 95. Morton and Wright, in *Winning the Second Battle*, include an appendix with a table

estimating basic living costs for a family (food, fuel, rent) in each province. Even with support from the Canadian Patriotic Fund, military pay and allowances were not enough. See Morton, *Fight or Pay*, 245.
115 LeBlanc, "Une communauté en transition," 134–6.
116 Theobald, *The Bitter Harvest*, 49.
117 Elder, "Family History and the Life Course," 280.
118 Hareven, "The History of the Family," 1, 95.
119 Gagnon, *Le 22e bataillon*, 365.
120 Nicholson and Humphries, *Canadian Expeditionary Force*, 212–19.
121 Brown and Loveridge, "Unrequited Faith," 18.
122 Vance, "Provincial Patterns of Enlistment," 78.
123 Duguid's work is reproduced by Vance, "Provincial Patterns of Enlistment," 75–8.
124 Sharpe, "Enlistment [...] A Regional Analysis," 20–2; Sharpe, "Enlistment [...] A Re-evaluation," 50.
125 Chaballe, *Histoire du 22ᵉ bataillon canadien-français*, 20.
126 Nicholson and Humphries, *Canadian Expeditionary Force*, 548; Cormier, "Militaires ayant des patronymes," unpublished database, shared with the author in 2014.
127 Landry and Lang, *Histoire de l'Acadie*, 238.
128 Mainville, *Till the Boys Come Home*, 18–19, 111–13.
129 Lazarenko, "Francophone Alberta," *Active History*.

CHAPTER THREE

1 "Le Fonds Régimentaire du 165e Bataillon," *L'Évangéline*, 14 March 1917.
2 "Socks for Soldiers," *Saint John Globe*, 24 March 1917, 11; "Un beau geste des marchands de Saint-Jean," *L'Évangéline*, 28 mars 1917.
3 "More Troops Soon to Come to St. John?," *The St. John Standard*, 26 March 1917, 12.
4 "165th, 198th and Field Ambulance Given Ovation in City Streets," *The Daily Telegraph*, 26 March 1917, 3.
5 "198th Overseas Battalion," *Queen's Own Rifles Museum and Archives*, consulted 15 June 2020, https://qormuseum.org/history/timeline-1900-1924/the-first-world-war/perpetuated-battalions/198th-battalion-cef.
6 "Une foule considerable salue les soldats du 165e," *L'Évangéline*, 28 March 1917.

7   25 March 1917, François DeGrâce à ses parents, *Le Moniteur acadien*, 17 May 1917.
8   "La présentation des Couleurs au 165e," *L'Évangéline*, 21 March 1917.
9   Jaddus P. Lanteigne to Edmond Lanteigne, 8 April 1917, *Le Moniteur acadien*, 24 May 1917.
10 Adjutant-General, Canadian Militia to O.C. Districts, "Physical Standards for Recruits for Forestry Battalions," 16 June 1916, cited in "Returned Soldiers: Proceedings of the Special Committee Appointed to ... report upon the Reception, Treatment, Care, Training and Re-Education of the Wounded, Disabled and Convalescent who have served in the Canadian Expeditionary Forces" (Ottawa: Parliament, House of Commons, 1917), 249. On Stehelin being appointed to command a forestry company, see G.O.C. NB Troops to OC French Acadian Forestry Coy (Yarmouth) dated 4 Apr 17, LAC, RG 24-C-8, vol. 4574, file 3-9-23 Recruitment.
11 "New Units Not Unlikely," *The Daily Telegraph*, 24 March 1917, 3.
12 Adjutant-General, Canadian Militia to O.C. Districts, "Notes on the Examination of Recruits for Special Service," 26 July 1916, "Returned Soldiers," 250–2.
13 Holt, *Filling the Ranks*, 184.
14 Excerpt from Hansard of House of Commons, p. 1804, 25 May 1917, communicated by Militia Department to Adjutant-General, 26 May 1917, LAC, RG 24, vol. 1662, HQ 683-316-5-0002; "Complaint by Standard up in Commons," *St. John Standard*, 26 May 1917, 1.
15 "Inspection," *Saint John Globe*, 29 May 1917, 9.
16 "Proceedings of a Board of Officers assembled at West St. John, 19 June 1917 for the purpose of reporting on clothing on charge to men attached to 62nd Regiment awaiting disposition," LAC, RG 24, vol. 1662, HQ 683-316-4-0039.
17 "Proceedings of a Board of Officers assembled at St. John, 18 June 1917, for the purpose of reporting upon the clothing of men of the 165th Battalion, C.E.F., who were left in Canada medically unfit," Quartermaster-General to General Officer Commanding N.B. Troops, 27 June 1917, LAC, RG 24, vol. 1662, HQ 683-316-4-0036 to 0038.
18 "Le bataillon acadien," *Le Moniteur acadien*, 29 March 1917.
19 "Le 165ème Bataillon est arrivé en Angleterre," *Le Moniteur acadien*, 19 April 1917.
20 François DeGrâce to his parents, 28 March 1917, *Le Moniteur acadien*, 17 May 1917.

21 Iréné Gallant to his parents, 28 March 1917, *Le Moniteur acadien*, 17 May 1917.
22 Jaddus P. Lanteigne to Edmond Lanteigne, 8 April 1917, *Le Moniteur acadien*, 24 May 1917.
23 CEAAC, dossier 408. Capt. J.V. Gaudet, journal de guerre, mardi 27 March 1917.
24 François DeGrâce to his parents, "Journal à bord le *S.S. Metagama*," 25 March to 7 April 1917, *Le Moniteur acadien*, 17 May 1917.
25 Iréné Gallant to his parents, "Journal à bord le *S.S. Metagama*," 25 March to 8 April 1917, *Le Moniteur acadien*, 17 Mai 1917.
26 Jaddus P. Lanteigne to Edmond Lanteigne, 9 April 1917, *Le Moniteur acadien*, 24 May 1917.
27 CEAAC, dossier 408, Capt. J.V. Gaudet, journal de guerre, 24 March to 8 April 1917.
28 CEAAC, fond 131, carnet de Ferdinand Malenfant, Anna Malenfant.
29 CEAAC, dossier 408, Capt. J.V. Gaudet, journal de guerre, 7 April 1917.
30 Félicien Landry to his parents, 6 May 1917, *Le Moniteur acadien*, 31 May 1917.
31 For more on official censorship of soldiers' letters, see Keshen, *Propaganda and Censorship*, esp. 153–86.
32 We found reminders of this prohibition in the Daily Routine Orders of the 5th District, Canadian Forestry Corps. This is one reason why we have so few photographs of the Acadian foresters in the Jura.
33 Meyer, *Men of War*, 15.
34 Saindon, "Étude des correspondances," esp. ch. 2.
35 Litalien, *Écrire sa guerre*, 14, 21–3.
36 Ibid., 39, 130–3.
37 Andrès, *L'Humour des Poilus canadiens-français*, 5.
38 Ibid., 140–1.
39 CEAAC, Ulric LeBlanc to his parents, 5 June 1915.
40 Hebb, *In Their Own Words*, 1.
41 CEAAC, Lionel LeBlanc to his parents, 26 September 1918.
42 Martineau, " Entre les lignes."
43 Victorien Lagacé au Rév. Père Van De Moortel, 5 August 1917, *L'Évangéline*, 5 September 1917.
44 Pierre Vautour to Elmina Babineau, 3 June 1917, *Le Moniteur acadien*, 23 August 1917.
45 Edmond Barrieau to his parents, 15 August 1917, *Le Moniteur acadien*, 27 September 1917.

46 Rutherdale, *Hometown Horizons*, 59.
47 Morin-Pelletier, "The Anxious Waiting Ones at Home," 357–8.
48 Flavelle, 'Not Enough Food and Too Many Military Police," 94.
49 Ibid., 98.
50 CEAAC, dossier 408, Capt. J.V. Gaudet, journal de guerre, 17 April 1917.
51 Jérôme Arsenault to his parents, 12 April 1917, *L'Évangéline*, 2 May 1917.
52 Abel Belliveau to his parents, 5 June 1917, *Le Moniteur acadien*, 5 July 1917.
53 Jean-Baptiste Nowlan to Corinne Nowlan, 19 May 1917, *L'Évangéline*, 27 June 1917.
54 Eddie Mazerolle to his parents, undated (mid-April 1917), *L'Évangéline*, 9 May 1917.
55 For a detailed discussion of how reinforcements were processed in England and France, see Holt, *Filling the Ranks*, 209–50.
56 Vance, *A Township at War*, 138.
57 Eddie Mazerolle to his parents, undated (mid-April 1917), *L'Évangéline*, 9 May 1917.
58 CEAAC, dossier 408, Capt. J.V. Gaudet, journal de guerre, 13 April 1917.
59 CEAAC, fond 131 Anna Malenfant, carnet de Ferdinand Malenfant, 13 April 1917.
60 Léger, *Le bataillon acadien*, 149.
61 For example, more than 250 men from the 132nd Battalion ended up fighting with the 26th Battalion. See MacGowan et al., *A History of the 26th New Brunswick Battalion, C.E.F., 1914–1919*, 331–2.
62 "Canadian Forestry Corps – Guide to Sources Relating to Units of the Canadian Expeditionary Force," LAC, 60-1.
63 Capt. J.V. Gaudet, 5 May 1917, *L'Évangéline*, 30 May 1917.
64 "The Accident to Lt.-Col. D'Aigle," *Saint John Globe*, 2 June 1917, 12; "Unité forestière," *Le Moniteur acadien*, 14 June 1917, 4.
65 Léger, *Le bataillon acadien*, 154.
66 Theobald, *The Bitter Harvest*, 65–98; Dutil and Mackenzie, *Embattled Nation*, esp. 163–85 for events in French Canada.
67 Dutil and Mackenzie, *Embattled Nation*, 331–2.
68 Clarke, *Unwanted Warriors*, 103–6.
69 Clarke, Cranfield, and Inwood, "Fighting Fit?," 83.
70 Clarke, *Unwanted Warriors*, 12; Miller, *Torontonians and the Great War*, 104.

71 Morton, *When Your Number's Up*, 277–9.
72 Morton, *Fight or Pay*, 23-6.
73 Holt, *Filling the Ranks*, 13–33; Windsor et al., *Loyal Gunners*, 28–52. Brent Wilson is working on a study of New Brunswick home defence as part of the SSHRC-funded partnership development project *Military Service, Citizenship, and Political Culture in Atlantic Canada*.
74 Curtis Mainville is also working on this study as part of the above-mentioned project.
75 Léger, *Le premier régiment North Shore*, esp. ch. 1.
76 Frenette, Rivard, and St-Hilaire, *La francophonie nord-américaine*, 281.
77 Kennedy, Haché-Chiasson, and Montour, "Transition démographique."
78 Morton, *When Your Number's Up*, 9–10.
79 Sharpe, "Enlistment [...] A Regional Analysis," 22.
80 Martin, *Un siècle d'oubli*, 22.
81 Vance, "Provincial Patterns of Enlistment," 77–8.
82 Campbell, *It Can't Last Forever*, 8.
83 Sharpe, "Enlistment "Enlistment [...] A Re-evaluation," 34.
84 Morton, *Fight or Pay*, 30.
85 Ibid., 38–42; Hanna, *Anxious Days and Tearful Nights*, 88.
86 Hanna, *Anxious Days and Tearful Nights*, 95–123.
87 McGowan, "A Question of Caste and Colour," 103–23.
88 Morton, *Fight or Pay*, 202.
89 Ibid., 90–1.
90 Morton, "Le Canada français et la milice canadienne."
91 Campbell, *It Can't Last Forever*, 8.
92 Rutherdale, *Hometown Horizons*, 13.
93 Morton, *When Your Number's Up*, 277–9.
94 Vance, "Provincial Patterns of Enlistment," 78.
95 Theobald, *The Bitter Harvest*, 28–9.
96 LeBlanc, "Que nous apprennent les synthèses historiques," 30–1.
97 Deschambault, Haché-Chiasson, and Kennedy, "Vers une reconstitution de la mobilité.»
98 Hanna, *Anxious Days and Tearful Nights*, 107–8.
99 Morin-Pelletier, "'The Anxious Waiting Ones at Home,'" 368.
100 Kennedy et al., "La mobilité des conjointes des soldats acadiens pendant la Première Guerre mondiale" (in production).
101 Terry Copp relates that military pay and allowances proved insufficient to motivate most Canadian-born residents of Montreal to enlist; *Montreal at War*, 66.

102 Smith, "Comrades and Citizens," 244.
103 Morton and Wright, *Winning the Second Battle*, 112–13.

CHAPTER FOUR

1 Vance, *A Township at War*, 135.
2 CEAAC, fonds 556, archives privées, Louis-Cyriaque Daigle to Director Timber Operations, London, CFC, 16 May 1917; Marti, "Embattled Communities," 112.
3 "Guide to Sources Relating to Units of the Canadian Expeditionary Force: Canadian Forestry Corps," LAC, https://www.bac-lac.gc.ca/eng/discover/military-heritage/first-world-war/Documents/canadian%20forestry%20corps.pdf.
4 Fedorowich, "The 'Sawdust Fusiliers,'" 532.
5 Bartlett, "Yeoman of the Woods," 7, 90–9.
6 Nicholson and Humphries, *Canadian Expeditionary Force*, 499–500.
7 DROS, 5th District (Jura) CFC, 9 December 1918, LAC.
8 Morton, *Fight or Pay*, 202.
9 Leger, *Le bataillon acadien*, 149.
10 "165th Broken Up and Some Going to France," *The Daily Telegraph*, 31 May 1917, 3a.
11 "Unité forestière," *Le Moniteur acadien*, 14 June 1917, 4a.
12 "Le 165e Bataillon," *L'Évangéline*, 13 June 1917.
13 Fred Frigot to Léotine Frigot, *Le Moniteur acadien*, 25 October 1917.
14 Victorien Lagacé au Révérend Père Van de Moortel, 5 August 1917, *L'Évangéline*, 5 September 1917.
15 Louis C. Daigle to his parents, August 1917, *Le Moniteur acadien*, 6 September 1917.
16 Devigne, *Les faiseurs de sciure*, 93–6.
17 Grosmaire, *Acadissima*, 206.
18 Ibid., 217.
19 Paratte, "Jura-Acadie."
20 Bartlett, "Yeoman of the Woods," 54.
21 Fedorowich, "The 'Sawdust Fusiliers,'" 532. For Indigenous volunteers, see Winegard, *For King and Kanata*; for Afro-Canadian volunteers, see Shaw, "Most Anxious to Serve," 534–80.
22 The circumstances of this transfer are sensitive. Two men of No. 2 Construction Battalion were accused of sexual assault against a French civilian, court-martialled, and sentenced to death. Their punishment was then commuted to hard labour. The incident

provoked outrage from the local population. The woman concerned wrote a petition directly to the King of England. See HQ Claims Commission (British Armies in France) to HQ Forestry Directorate (Paris), 11 December 1917, RG 9-III-C-8, vol. 4515, file 8, Claims from French Civilians, No. 5 District, CFC, 1917–18, LAC.
23 DROS, 5th District (Jura) CFC, 29 December 1917, 15 January 1918, 17 May 1918, LAC.
24 Freeman, "Charlie's War," 463.
25 Journal de guerre, J.V. Gaudet, 17 July 1917 et le 1 July 1917. Gaudet claimed that a Black soldier had assaulted a French woman in the crowd on Dominion Day, but he provided no further detail.
26 Grosmaire, Acadissima, 216.
27 Aimé Leger au Révérend J.-A. Labelle, vicaire à Rogersville, 7 November 1917, L'Évangéline, 31 July 1917.
28 Freeman, "Charlie's War," 461.
29 Devigne, Les faiseurs de sciure, 13.
30 Bartlett, "Yeoman of the Woods," 73.
31 24 March 1917, "New Units not Unlikely," *The Daily Telegraph*, 3c.
32 Bartlett, "Yeomen of the Woods," 84.
33 Fedorowich, "The 'Sawdust Fusiliers,'" 535.
34 Joseph Edmond Barrieau to his parents, 2 March 1917, *L'Évangéline*, 11 March 1917.
35 Eddie Mazerolle to his parents, 2 March 1917, *L'Évangéline*, April 1917.
36 Louis C. Daigle to his parents, 20 April 1917, *Le Moniteur acadien*, 24 May 1917.
37 Jean Malenfant to his wife, Marie, 20 August 1918.
38 CEAAC, fonds 131, Anna Malenfant, Carnet de Ferdinand Malenfant, June–July 1917.
39 Félicien Landry to his parents, 16 June 1917, *Le Moniteur acadien*, 19 July 1917.
40 Nicholson and Humphries, *Canadian Expeditionary Force*, 499.
41 Fedorowich, "The 'Sawdust Fusiliers,'" 533–4.
42 Cook, *Vimy*, 54.
43 Windsor, et al., *Loyal Gunners*, 107–14.
44 Fedorowich, "The 'Sawdust Fusiliers,'" 529.
45 Including a great shot of the entire 48th Company. Devigne, *Les faiseurs de sciure*, 61-2.
46 Johnston to DTO on arrival of 118th Auxiliary M.T. Petrol Coy, dated 15 August 1918, LAC, RG 9-III-C-8, vol. 4515, file 6, Canadian Army Service Corps and 5th District.

47 Bartlett, "Yeoman of the Woods," 82–4.
48 CEAAC, fond 131 Anna Malenfant, carnet de Ferdinand Malenfant, July 1917.
49 Louis C. Daigle to his parents, August 1917, *Le Moniteur acadien*, 6 September 1917.
50 CEAAC, fonds 408, Capt. J.V. Gaudet, journal de guerre, 30 December 1917,
51 Fred Frigot to Madame R. Chiasson, 25 October 1917, *Le Moniteur acadien*, 6 December 1917.
52 DROS, 5th District (Jura) CFC, 26 June 1918, 17 September 1918, 8 October 1918, 16 October 1918, 28 October 1918, LAC; Rewegan et al., "The First Wave," 638–45.
53 DROS, 5th District (Jura) CFC, 4 December 1917, LAC; DTO to CFC districts, dated 27 March 1918, RG 9-III-C-8, vol. 4515, file 3, Agriculture, LAC.
54 DROS, 5th District (Jura) CFC, 10 October 1918, LAC.
55 The French were largely happy with the work done by 5th District according to a report after the war. See Conservateur Bazaille des Eaux et Forets to Director Timber Operations, 28 December 1918, LAC, RG 9-III-C-8, vol. 4515, file 9, Clearances.
56 Fedorowich, "The 'Sawdust Fusiliers,'" 544.
57 Bartlett, "Yeoman of the Woods," 112.
58 Fedorowich, "The 'Sawdust Fusiliers,'" 528.
59 CEAAC, fonds 408, Capt. J.V. Gaudet, journal de guerre, 1 July 1917; CEAAC, fond 131, Anna Malenfant, carnet de Ferdinand Malenfant, July 1917.
60 DROS, 5th District (Jura) CFC, 14 June, 2 July, 3 July 1918, LAC.
61 DROS, 5th District (Jura) CFC, 21 February 1918, LAC.
62 DROS, 5th District (Jura) CFC, 2 January 1918, LAC.
63 DROS, 5th District (Jura) CFC, 9–10 December 1917, 7 January 30 March, 23 May, 3 June, 17 July, 17 August 1918, LAC.
64 DROS, 5th District (Jura) CFC, 7 December 1917, 15 February, 20 February, 13 March, 14 June, 17 July, 28 August 1918, LAC.
65 DROS, 5th District (Jura) CFC, 6 September 1918, LAC.
66 For example, Pte Deveau of 22nd Company was instructed to pay a bill of fifty-nine francs to a café owner in Chapois. Captain Wallace, Adjt No. 5 District, to Johnson (OC Jura Group), 8 July 1918, LAC, RG 9-III-C-8, vol. 4515, file 8, Claims from French Civilians, No. 5 District, CFC, 1917–18.

67 DROS, December 1917–January 1918, 10 August 1918, LAC.
68 DROS, 15 August 1918, LAC.
69 DROS, 6 December, 19 December 1917, 26 August 1918, LAC.
70 War Establishment for Canadian Forestry Corps, 22 February 1917, LAC.
71 Fedorowich, "The 'Sawdust Fusiliers,'" 536–7.
72 CEAAC, fond 131, Anna Malenfant, carnet de Ferdinand Malenfant, July 1917, December 1917. Malenfant underlined the words *for ever* in his notebook.
73 CEAAC, fond 131, Anna Malenfant, carnet de Ferdinand Malenfant, 11 December 1917, 27 October 1917.
74 War Establishment of the Canadian Forestry Corps, 1917, LAC.
75 DROS 5th District, CFC, 12 December 1917, 25 February 1018, LAC.
76 Cook, "Anti-Heroes of the Canadian Expeditionary Force," 182–3.
77 McKay and Swift, *The Vimy Trap*, 255.
78 Morton, *When Your Number's Up*, 250–1.
79 Godefroy, *For Freedom and Honour?*; "Canadian Soldiers executed in WWI to get pardon," CBC News, 15 August 2006, https://www.cbc.ca/news/world/canadian-soldiers-executed-in-ww1-to-get-pardon-1.596886.
80 Bouvier, *Déserteurs et insoumis*, 49, 88–105.
81 Iacobelli, "No Example Is Needed," 72.
82 Pugsley, "Learning from the Canadian Corps," 7–8.
83 Bouvier, *Deserteurs et insoumis*, 124.
84 Dagenais, "Une permission!," 5–9.
85 Ibid., 10–11.
86 With Bill C-77 in 2019, the CAF moved to a new internal disciplinary process called "summary hearings" rather than summary trials. The goal remains the quick resolution of minor infractions, but with administrative hearings and reduced powers of punishment. Legislative Summary, Library of Parliament (Ottawa), https://lop.parl.ca/sites/PublicWebsite/default/en_CA/ResearchPublications/LegislativeSummaries/421C77E.
87 Hemond, "Military Law," 56.
88 Ibid., 53.
89 Dagenais, "Une permission!," 5.
90 Cook, "More as a medicine," 7–22.
91 Cook, "Wet Canteens and Worrying Mothers," 320.
92 Iacobelli, "No Example Is Needed," 82.
93 Wilson, "Booze, Temperance, and Soldiers."

94 Correspondence concerning a bill from Villiers-sous-Chalamont, RG 9-III-C-8, vol. 4515, file 8, Claims from French Civilians, No. 5 District, CFC, 1917–1918, LAC.
95 Canteen Accounts for 22nd, 39th, and 40th Companies, CFC, 31 October 1918, RG 9-III-C-8, vol. 4515, file 4, Canteen Statements, LAC.
96 Abel Belliveau to his parents, 8 October 1917, *Le Moniteur acadien*, 15 November 1917.
97 Fedorowich, "The 'Sawdust Fusiliers,'" 537.
98 Félicien Landry to his parents, 16 June 1917, *Le Moniteur acadien*, 19 July 1917.
99 Bartlett, "Yeoman of the Woods," 107.
100 Léger, *Le bataillon acadien*, 192.
101 CEAAC, fond Anna Malenfant, carnet de Ferdinand Malenfant, 27 June, 1 July, 15 December.
102 Fred Frigot to his sister Léonide, July 1917, *Le Moniteur acadien*, 25 October 1917; Fred Frigot to his mother and his parents, 25 October 1917, *Le Moniteur acadien*, 6 December 1917.
103 CEAAC, William P. Forest au révérend père J.D. LeBlanc, 26 November 1917.
104 Carnet de Ferdinand Malenfant, 25–6 October 1917.
105 DROS, 26 August 1918, 27 December 1918.
106 DROS, 24 August 1918, 14 November 18.
107 CEAAC, dossier 408. Capt. J.V. Gaudet, journal de guerre, 20 June 1918.
108 Personnel record, L/Cpl Jean-Baptiste Daigle – Report by Members of the Court in absence of President into circumstances surrounding the death of No. 666043 L/Cpl J.B. D'aigle, Proceedings of Court of Inquiry assembled 10 June 1918 by order of LCol Strong, Officer Commanding No. 5 District, CFC, LAC.
109 Gunner describes these jobs in detail: "Canadian Lumber Camp Earthan and Slindon: 1917 till 1919." http://www2.westsussex.gov.uk/learning-resources/LR/canadian_lumber_camp_eartham_and_slindon10a2.pdf?docid=888517b6-083c-445e-a4b9-b98727fae3e2&version=-1.
110 Brown relates that for the Second World War, it became standard practice to assign NCOs to acting rank for three months before confirming them in their new positions; *Building the Army's Backbone*, 28.
111 Brown, *Building the Army's Backbone*, 3.

112 Windsor, "Replacing Leaders," 219.
113 Malcolm Gladwell, in *Blink*, points out that preconceived notions relating physical stature to able leadership continue to the present day as one of many forms of unconscious bias.
114 Abel Belliveau to his parents, 8 October 1917, *Le Moniteur acadien*, 15 November 1917.
115 Devigne, *Les faiseurs de sciure*, 94.
116 For a recent treatment of the situation in the CEF, see Rewegan et al., "The First Wave," 638–45.
117 Brenyo, "Whatsoever a Man Soweth," 8–10.
118 The best reference on venereal disease in Canada remains Jay Cassel, *The Secret Plague*. Cassel noted the military leadership's reluctance to set up supervised brothels to protect the soldiers, for this would have promoted immorality (124).
119 CEAAC, fonds 408, apt J.V. Gaudet to l'abbé D.J. LeBlanc, 14 May 1917.
120 Rosenthal, "New Battlegrounds," 59; Bogaert, "Patient Experience," 7.
121 DROS, 19 November 1917, 26 August 1918.
122 Bogaert, "Patient Experience," 6.
123 Shah et al., "Recent Change"; Wright and Judson, "Relative and Seasonal Incidences."
124 Cassel estimates that about 16 per cent of the CEF contracted VD at some point during their overseas military service, six times the rate for other members of the British Expeditionary Force. See *The Secret Plague*, 123.
125 Crouthamel, "Male Sexuality and Psychological Trauma," 60–84; Harvey, "Homosexuality and the British Army," 313–19.
126 Djebabla, "Historiographie francophone," 413.
127 Keelan, "The Forgotten Few."
128 Nicholson and Humphries, *Canadian Expeditionary Force*, 548.
129 CEAAC, J. Ulric LeBlanc to his parents, 25 October 1915; J. Ulric LeBlanc to a friend, *Le Moniteur acadien*, September 1916.
130 CEAAC, J. Ulric LeBlanc to his parents, 4 January and 21 January 1918.
131 CEAAC, Joseph Edward Devarennes to his sister, 22 March and 30 August 1917.
132 J. Ulric LeBlanc to a friend, undated *Le Moniteur acadien*, 5 September 1917.
133 CEAAC, Joseph Edward Devarennes to his sister, 8 October 1917.
134 CEAAC, J. Ulric LeBlanc to his parents, 30 January 1919.

135 CEAAC, J. Ulric LeBlanc to his parents, 8 September 1917.
136 J. Ulric LeBlanc to a friend, undated, *Le Moniteur acadien*, 5 September 1917.
137 CEAAC, Albert Devarennes to his sister, 7 October 1917.
138 CEAAC, Joseph Edward Devarennes to his sister, 22 March 1917.
139 J. Ulric LeBlanc to a friend, undated, *Le Moniteur acadien*, 5 September 1917.
140 CEAAC, J. Ulric LeBlanc to his parents, 28 April 1918.
141 CEAAC, J. Ulric LeBlanc to his parents, 21 February 1916, 4 November 1916.
142 CEAAC, Albert Devarennes to his father, 8 November 1917.
143 CEAAC, Albert Devarennes to his sister, 7 October 1917.
144 André Arsenault to his parents, 3 September 1918, *L'Évangéline*, 9 October 1918.
145 Humphries, *A Weary Road*, 134.
146 Edmond Barriault to his parents, 20 June 1918, *L'Évangéline*, 14 August 1918.
147 Édouard LeBlanc to his parents, 13 November 1917, *Le Moniteur acadien*, 20 December 1917.
148 Adolphe T. Robichaud to his mother, 13 May 1918, *Le Moniteur acadien*, 20 June 1918.
149 CEAAC, J. Ulric LeBlanc to his parents, 4 January 1918.
150 CEAAC, Joseph Edward Devarennes to his sister, 22 March 1917, 1 November 1917.
151 Major J.A. Léger à J.B.M. Baxter, 9 August 1917, *Le Moniteur acadien*, 6 December 1917.
152 Saindon, "Étude des correspondances," Chapter 2.
153 CEAAC, Joseph Edward Devarennes to his sister, 22 March 1917.
154 CEAAC, Joseph Edward Devarennes to his sister, 1 November 1917.
155 CEAAC, J. Ulric LeBlanc to his parents, 25 January 1919.
156 Shaw, "Expanding the Narrative," 403.

CHAPTER FIVE

1 Bowker, "The Long 1919," 12.
2 MacLean and Elder, "Military Service in the Life Course," 188.
3 There are several documents in this file, including a statement of production from commencement until 28 December 1918, a detailed listing of the infrastructure and vehicles used or built by the CFC, and the final report from the French official from the Department of Waters and Forests, RG 9-III-C-8, vol. 4515, file 9, Clearances, LAC.

4 DROS, 5th District, CFC – 18 November 1918, 12 December 1918; 12th District – 14 November 1918, 22 November 1918, 27 November 1918, LAC.
5 Oliver, "Coming Home."
6 Morton and Wright, *Winning the Second Battle*, 109.
7 Nicholson and Humphries, *Canadian Expeditionary Force*, 531–2.
8 Smith, "Comrades and Citizens," 232; Morton, "Kicking and Complaining."
9 Campbell, *It Can't Last Forever*, 510–17.
10 Prost, "The Military Cemeteries of the Great War."
11 Isitt, "Mutiny from Victoria to Vladivostok."
12 Windsor discusses the contribution of New Brunswick gunners to the CSEF in *Loyal Gunners*, 167–70.
13 Smith, "Comrades and Citizens," 219.
14 "Men from the Celtic Reach City," *The Daily Telegraph and Sun*, 20 March 1919, 6.
15 "Home on the Aquitania," *The Daily Telegraph and Sun*, 23 June 1919, 9.
16 "Soldiers from Olympic were on Derailed Train," *The Daily Telegraph and Sun*, 10 July 1919, 4.
17 "Soldats acadiens enrolés," *L'Évangéline*, 24 March 1919.
18 Leger, *Le bataillon acadien*, 209.
19 "Retour du soldat Victorin Lagacé," *L'Évangéline*, 21 April 1919.
20 "Moncton Boys Home," *Moncton Daily Times*, 11 February 1919, 7.
21 Grosmaire, *Acadissima*, 335–41.
22 "Sergt. Major Abel Belliveau Welcomed," *Moncton Daily Times*, 21 February 1919, 7.
23 DROS, 5th District – 15 October 1918, 28 October 1918; 12th District – 16 October 1918, 7 November 1918, LAC.
24 Morton and Wright, *Winning the Second Battle*, 231.
25 Ibid., 10–90.
26 Morton, *Fight or Pay*, 147; Morton, *When Your Number's Up*, 264.
27 Morton and Wright, *Winning the Second Battle*, 25.
28 Humphries, "War's Long Shadow," 530.
29 Smith, "Comrades and Citizens," 245. Landry and Lang affirm that some Acadians did join the Great War Veterans' Association in New Brunswick; *Histoire de l'Acadie*, 239.
30 Morton, *Fight or Pay*, 151, 163.
31 Humphries, "War's Long Shadow," 518.
32 Ibid., 521.
33 "Soldat de retour," *L'Évangéline*, 6 November 1918.

34 Brenyo, "Whatsoever a Man Soweth," 28.
35 Rosenthal, "New Battlegrounds," 57.
36 Humphries, "Wilfully and With Intent," 373.
37 Smith, "Comrades and Citizens," 51; Shaw, "Expanding the Narrative," 403.
38 Thanks to Rémi Frenette for forwarding this reference. "Un soldat commet le suicide à Tracadie," *L'Évangéline*, 23 February 1922.
39 "Le rétablissement des soldats dans la vie civile," *L'Évangéline*, 21 June 1923.
40 Morton and Wright, *Winning the Second Battle*, 25, 231.
41 CEAAC, J. Ulric LeBlanc to his parents, 5 November 1915, 10 November 1917.
42 LeBlanc frequently wrote to Marcelline during the war, and we find them living in Shédiac with an infant daughter in 1921.
43 Bouchard and Huberman, "Les anciens combattants canadiens-français," 547.
44 Scotland, "And the Men Returned," 160–3.
45 Morton and Wright, *Winning the Second Battle*, 118, 214.
46 Morton, *When Your Number's Up*, 270.
47 Morton and Wright, *Winning the Second Battle*, 102, 155–6.
48 Nicholson and Humphries, *Canadian Expeditionary Force*, 534.
49 Keshen, *Propaganda and Censorship*, 59–60.
50 Smith, "Comrades and Citizens," 243.
51 21 June 1923. "Le rétablissement des soldats dans la vie civile," *L'Évangéline*, 21 June 1923.
52 Humphries, "War's Long Shadow," 530.
53 Morton, *Fight or Pay*, 151, 137–8.
54 Cook, *Vimy*, 173.
55 Morton and Wright, *The Second Battle*, 117.
56 LeBlanc, "Une communauté en transition," 134–6.
57 Statistics Canada, "Percentage distribution of rural and urban population, by provinces and territories, 1891, 1901, 1911, and 1921," *Canada Year Book*, 1927–28.
58 CEAAC, Ulric LeBlanc to his parents, 7 December 1917.
59 Bouchard and Huberman, "Les anciens combattants canadiens-français," 560.
60 Ibid., 551.
61 Campbell, "'We who have wallowed in the mud of Flanders,'" 125.
62 Windsor, *Loyal Gunners*, 177–80.

63 Campbell, "'We who have wallowed in the mud of Flanders,'" 148–9.
64 Cousley, Siminki, and Ville, "The Effects of World War II Military Service," 838–65.
65 Bouchard and Huberman, "Les anciens combattants canadiens-français," 560.
66 Clarke, Cranfield, and Inwood, "Fighting Fit?," 80, 89.
67 Ibid., 80.
68 Hanna, *Anxious Days and Tearful Nights*, 151–6.
69 Morton, *When Your Number's Up*, 236.
70 Shaw, "Expanding the Narrative," 403.
71 Hanna, *Anxious Days and Tearful Nights*, 151, 179.
72 Cook, "Wet Canteens and Worrying Mothers," 328.
73 Vance, *A Township at War*, 250.
74 Ibid., 249.
75 MacLean and Elder found this for African-American veterans of the Second World War and the Vietnam War. This is an intriguing finding that merits further inquiry; "Military Service in the Life Course," 189.
76 Cunningham, "After 'It's Over Over There,'" 225.

CONCLUSION

1 Shaw, "Most Anxious to Serve," 534–80; Katharine McGowan, "A Question of Caste and Colour," 103–23.
2 Fedorowich, "The 'Sawdust Fusiliers'," 7–9.
3 Theobald, *The Bitter Harvest*, 105.
4 Robichaud and Basque, *Audacieux et téméraire*, 71–3.
5 Degrâce, *Histoire d'Acadie par les textes*, fascule C, 1867–1930.
6 To cite just one example, Léger, "Isidore Bourque de Shédiac: un précurseur de la renaissance acadienne," 17–19. Other local resources include *Les Cahiers de la Société historique acadienne* and *La Société Nicolas-Denys*.
7 CEAAC, "Le bataillon acadien," recordings from 1977 and 1978, Chansons C100.
8 Theobald, *The Bitter Harvest*, 10.
9 Cotton-Dumouchel, "French Canada and Enlistment," 54.
10 Durflinger, "L'honneur de notre race," 72.
11 Jean Martin, *Un siècle d'oubli*, 94.
12 Tim Cook offers the figure of up to 20,000 underage CEF soldiers in "He Was Determined to Go," 41–74.

13 Sharpe, "Enlistment [...] A Regional Analysis," 20–1.
14 Here, I am inspired by some of Jonathan Vance's work; see "Provincial Patterns of Enlistment," 78.
15 D'Amours, "Idéalistes, pragmatiques et les autres," 125–47.
16 For example, Jonathan Vance relates the disbanding of several units from southern Ontario once they arrived in England in 1916; *A Township at War*, 138.
17 Massicotte and LeBlanc, "L'Acadie et la Seconde Guerre mondiale," 49–67.
18 Philippe Volpé, "Jeunesse étudiante acadienne et Corps-école des officiers canadiens, 1941–1964," Billet de blogue, *Acadiensis* (2020), https://acadiensis.wordpress.com/2020/07/27/jeunesse-etudiante-acadienne-et-corps-ecole-des-officiers-canadiens-1941-1964-1-2.
19 Shaw, "Expanding the Narrative," 393.
20 Cook, "Anti-heroes of the Canadian Expeditionary Force," 191.

Bibliography

ARCHIVES

Library and Archives Canada

4th District (Bordeaux)
  Daily Routine Orders, RG 150, vol. 190
5th District (Jura)
  Claims, Accounts, Clearances, RG 9-III-C-8, vol. 4515
  Daily Routine Orders, RG 9-III-B-3, vols. 3818–19
  Establishment, RG 9-III-B-1, vol. 1608
165th Battalion, Canadian Expeditionary Force
  Louis-Cyriaque Daigle, RG 9, vol. 4702, folder 17
  Official Correspondence, RG 24, vols. 1388, 1401, 1662, 4563–79
Adjutant-General, Canadian Militia to O.C. Districts. "Physical Standards for Recruits for Forestry Battalions," 16 June 1916, cited in "Returned Soldiers: Proceedings of the Special Committee Appointed to ... Report upon the Reception, Treatment, Care, Training and Re-Education of the Wounded, Disabled and Convalescent who have served in the Canadian Expeditionary Forces." Ottawa: Parliament, House of Commons, 1917.
Canadian Forestry Corps, Canadian Expeditionary Force
  Guide to Sources Relating to Units of the Canadian Expeditionary Force. Ottawa: LAC, n.d. 162. https://www.collectionscanada.gc.ca/obj/005/f2/005-1142.29.010-e.pdf
Department of Militia and Defence. "Revised instructions for dealing with deserters and absentees without leave." Ottawa: Dept. of Militia and Defence, 1918.

Great Britain. War Office. "The Manual of Military Law." London: HMSO, 1907.
Personnel records of the First World War
Ministry of the Overseas Military Forces of Canada, RG 150, https://www.bac-lac.gc.ca/eng/discover/military-heritage/first-world-war/personnel-records/Pages/personnel-records.aspx
Statistics Canada. "Percentage distribution of rural and urban population, by provinces and territories, 1891, 1901, 1911 and 1921." *Canada Year Book*, 1927–28.
– "Total number of wage earners and average yearly earnings, census years 1911 and 1921, in cities of 30,000 population and over." *Canada Year Book*, 1927–28.

CEAAC *(Centre d'études acadiennes Anselme Chiasson)*

ARCHIVES PRIVÉES

Rufin A. Arsenault, fonds 506 (documents sur le 165e bataillon)
Clément Cormier, fonds 177 (dossier 165e bataillon)
Louis-Cyriaque Daigle, fonds 566 (correspondance, documents officiels, histoire)
Jean V. Gaudet, fonds 408 (journal de guerre, correspondance, photos)
Napoléon Landry, fonds 18 (correspondance d'Eddy J. Devarennes)
Hilarion LeBlanc, fonds 308 (correspondance de Joseph Ulric LeBlanc)
Anna Malenfant, fonds 131 (correspondance, carnet de Ferdinand Malenfant)

NEWSPAPERS

L'Évangéline
Le Moniteur acadien
Moncton Times and Transcript

PROVINCIAL ARCHIVES OF NEW BRUNSWICK*

Campbellton Graphic
The Daily Gleaner (Fredericton)
The Daily Telegraph (Saint John)
The Daily Telegraph and Sun (Saint John)
The Daily Times (Moncton)
The Kings County Record

The North Shore Leader
Saint John Globe
St. John Standard
* Many of the articles concerning the 165th Battalion were generously shared by Curtis Mainville.

PUBLISHED AND OTHER SOURCES

Andrès, Bernard. *L'Humour des Poilus canadiens-français de la Grande Guerre*. Québec: Presses universitaires de Laval, 2018.

Andrew, Sheila. "La montée des élites acadiennes au Nouveau-Brunswick, 1861–1881." In *Économie et société en Acadie, 1850–1950: Nouvelles études d'histoire acadienne*, edited by Jacques Paul Couturier and Phyllis LeBlanc, 36–41. Moncton: Éditions d'Acadie, 1996.

Bartlett, Cameron. *La Société Nationale de l'Acadie: Au cœur de la réussite d'un peuple*. Moncton: Les Éditions de la francophonie, 2006.

– "Yeoman of the Woods: The Operations of the Canadian Forestry Corps during the Great War 1916–1919." MA Thesis, University of Calgary, 2019.

Black, Dan, and John Boileau. *Old Enough to Fight: Canada's Boy Soldiers in the First World War*. Toronto: James Lorimer and Company, 2013.

Bogaert, Kandace. "Patient Experience and the Treatment of Venereal Disease in Toronto's Military Base Hospital during the First World War." *Canadian Military History* 26, no. 2 (2017).

Bouchard, Carl, and Michael Huberman. "Les anciens combattants canadiens-français de la Première Guerre mondiale et leur réintégration professionnelle." *Histoire sociale/Social History* 53, no. 109 (November 2020): 545–68.

Bourque, Denis, and Chantal Richard. *Les conventions nationales acadiennes*, vols. 1–2. Moncton: Institut d'études acadiennes, 2013, 2018.

Bouvier, Patrick. *Déserteurs et insoumis: Les Canadiens français et la justice militaire (1914–1918)*. Québec: Athéna éditions, 2003.

Bowker, Alan. "The Long 1919: Hope, Fear, and Normalcy." In *Canada 1919: A Nation Shaped by War*, edited by Tim Cook and J.L. Granatstein, 12–26. Vancouver: UBC Press, 2020.

Brenyo, Brent. "'Whatsoever a Man Soweth': Sex Education about Venereal Disease, Racial Health, and Social Hygiene duringthe First World War." *Canadian Military History* 27, no. 2 (2018): 1–35.

Brown, Andrew L. *Building the Army's Backbone: Canadian Non-Commissioned Officers in the Second World War*. Vancouver: UBC Press, 2022.

Brown, Robert, and Donald Loveridge. "Unrequited Faith: Recruiting the CEF 1914–1918." *Canadian Military History* 24, no. 1, (2015).

Burke, Stacie D.A. "Transitions in Household and Family Structure: Canada in 1901 and 1991." In *Household Counts: Canadian Households and Families in 1901*, edited by Eric W. Sager and Peter Baskerville, 34–7. Toronto: University of Toronto Press, 2007.

Campbell, David. *It Can't Last Forever: The 19th Battalion and the Canadian Corps in the First World War*. Waterloo: Wilfrid Laurier University Press, 2017.

Campbell, Lara. "'We who have wallowed in the mud of Flanders': First World War Veterans, Unemployment, and the Development of Social Welfare in Canada, 1929–1939." *Journal of the Canadian Historical Association* 11, no. 1 (2000): 125–49.

Cassel, Jay. *The Secret Plague: Venereal Disease in Canada 1839–1939*. Toronto: University of Toronto Press, 1987.

Chaballe, Joseph. *Histoire du 22e bataillon canadien-français, 1914–1919*. Québec: Les éditions Chantecler, 1952.

Chiasson, Anselme. *Petit manuel d'histoire d'Acadie: les Acadiens de 1867 à 1976*. Moncton: Université de Moncton, 1976.

Clarke, Nic. *Unwanted Warriors: The Rejected Volunteers of the Canadian Expeditionary Force*. Vancouver: UBC Press, 2015.

Clarke, Nic, John Cranfield, and Kris Inwood. "Fighting Fit? Diet, Disease, and Disability in the Canadian Expeditionary Force, 1914–1918." *War and Society* 33, no. 2 (2014): 80–97.

Cook, Tim. "Anti-Heroes of the Canadian Expeditionary Force." *Journal of the Canadian Historical Association* 19, no. 1 (2008): 171–93.

– "'He was determined to go': Underage Soldiers in the Canadian Expeditionary Force." *Histoire sociale/Social History* 41, no. 81 (2008): 41–74.

– "'More as a medicine than a beverage': 'Demon Rum' and the Canadian Trench Soldier in the First World War." *Canadian Military History* 9, no. 1 (Winter 2000): 7–22.

– *Vimy: The Battle and the Legend*. Toronto: Penguin Random House, 2017.

– "Wet Canteens and Worrying Mothers: Soldiers and Temperance Groups in the Great War." *Histoire sociale/Social History* 35, no. 70 (June 2003): 311–30.

Copp, Terry, with Alexander Maavara. *Montreal at War, 1914–1918*. Toronto: University of Toronto Press, 2021.

Cormier, Ronald. "Militaires ayant des patronymes d'origine acadienne ou française des Provinces Maritimes morts au cours de la Première Guerre mondiale." Unpublished database, generously shared with the author in 2014.

Cotton-Dumouchel, Emmanuelle. "French Canada and Enlistment in the First World War: A Study of Recruitment Posters." *Canadian Military Journal* 22, no. 2 (Spring 2022): 54–61.

Cousley, Alex, Peter Siminki, and Simon Ville. "The Effects of World War II Military Service: Evidence from Australia." *Journal of Economic History* 77, no. 3 (September 2017): 838–65.

Couturier, Jacques Paul. "Perception et pratique de la justice dans la société acadienne, 1870–1900." In *Économie et société en Acadie, 1850–1950: Nouvelles études d'histoire acadienne*, edited by Jacques Paul Couturier and Phyllis LeBlanc, 43–75. Moncton: Éditions d'Acadie, 1996.

Couturier, Jacques Paul, and Phyllis E. Leblanc. *Économie et société en Acadie, 1850–1950*. Moncton: Éditions-d'Acadie, 1996.

Craig, Beatrice, Maxime Dagenais, et al. *The Land in Between: The Upper Saint John Valley, Prehistory to World War I*. Thomaston: Tilbury House, 2009.

Crouthamel, Jason. "Male Sexuality and Psychological Trauma: Soldiers and Sexual Disorder in World War I and Weimar Germany," *Journal of the History of Sexuality*, 17, no. 1 (January 2008): 60–84.

Cunningham, Angela R. "After 'it's over over there': Using Record Linkage to Enable the Reconstruction of World War I Veterans' Demography from Soldiers' Experiences to Civilian Populations." *Historical Methods: A Journal of Quantitative and Interdisciplinary History* 51, no. 2 (2018): 203–29.

Dagenais, Maxime. "'Une permission! C'est bon pour une recrue': Discipline and Illegal Absences in the 22nd (French-Canadian) Battalion, 1915–1919." *Canadian Military History* 18, no. 4 (2015): 3–5.

D'Amours, Caroline. "Idéalistes, pragmatiques et les autres: Profil des volontaires du Régiment de la Chaudière, 1939–1945." *Histoire sociale/Social History* 51, no. 103 (May 2018): 125–47.

Deschambault, Lauraly, Noémie Haché-Chiasson, and Gregory Kennedy. "Vers une reconstitution de la mobilité des Acadiennes à l'époque de l'industrialisation: l'émigration familiale et l'exode rurale vues à travers l'analyse longitudinale." In *Port Acadie* (forthcoming, 2023).

Desjardins, Mélanie. "La maudite guerre: l'expérience de guerre du soldat volontaire acadien, 1911–1921." MA thesis, Université de Moncton, 2018.

Devigne, David D. *Les faiseurs de sciure: le Corps forestier canadien du groupe de Bordeaux ou le plus important déploiement en France, 1917–1919*. Mérignac: l'Imprimerie Laplante, 2020.

Djebabla, Mourad. "Historiographie francophone de la Première Guerre mondiale: écrire la Grande Guerre de 1914–1918 en français au Canada et au Québec." *Canadian Historical Review* 95, no. 2 (September 2014): 407–16.

Doucet, Philippe. "La politique et les Acadiens," in *L'Acadie des Maritimes: études thématiques*, edited by Jean Daigle, 299–340. Moncton: Chaire des études acadiennes, 1993.

Durflinger, Serge Marc. "'L'honneur de notre race': The 22nd Battalion returns to Quebec City, 1919." In *Canada 1919: A Nation Shaped by War*, edited by Tim Cook and J.L. Granatstein, 72–85. Vancouver: UBC Press, 2020.

Dutil, Patrice, and David Mackenzie. *Embattled Nation: Canada's Wartime Election of 1917*. Toronto: Dundurn, 2017.

Elder, Glen H., Jr. "Family History and the Life Course." *Journal of Family History* 2, no. 4 (1977): 279–304.

Fedorowich, Kent. "The 'Sawdust Fusiliers': The Canadian Forestry Corps in Devon, 1916–1919." *Histoire sociale/Social History* 53, no. 109 (November 2020): 519–44.

Flavelle, Ryan. "'Not Enough Food and Too Many Military Police': Discipline, Food, and the 23rd Reserve Battalion, July–September 1917." *War and Society* 35, no. 2 (2016): 92–113.

Freeman, Kirrily. "Charlie's War: The Life and Death of a Black South African in the Canadian Expeditionary Force." *Journal of Imperial and Commonwealth History* 48, no. 3 (2020): 456–90.

Frenette, Yves. "L'historiographie des Franco-américains de la Nouvelle-Angleterre, 1872–2015." *Bulletin d'histoire politique* 24, no. 2 (Winter 2016): 75–103.

Frenette, Yves, Étienne Rivard, and Marc St-Hilaire. *La francophonie nord-américaine*, Quebec City: Les Presses de l'Université Laval, 2013.

Gaffield, Chad. "Language, Ancestry, and the Competing Constructions of Identity in Turn-of-the-Century Canada." In *Household Counts: Canadian Households and Families in 1901*, edited by Eric W. Sager and Peter A. Baskerville, 423–40. Toronto: University of Toronto Press, 2007.

Gagnon, Jean-Pierre. *Le 22e bataillon (canadien-français) 1914–1919: étude socio-militaire*. Québec: Les Presses de l'Université Laval, 1986.

Gladwell, Malcolm. *Blink: The Power of Thinking without Thinking*. New York: Little, Brown, 2007.

Godefroy, Andrew. *For Freedom and Honour? The Story of 25 Canadians Executed during the Great War*. Toronto: CEF Books, 1998.

Godin, Sylvain, and Maurice Basque. *Histoire des Acadiens et des Acadiennes du Nouveau-Brunswick*. Tracadie-Sheila: Éditions de la Grande Marée, 2007.

Granatstein, J.L., and J.M. Hitsman. *Broken Promises: A History of Conscription in Canada*. Toronto: Oxford University Press, 1977.

Griffiths, N.E.S. *From Migrant to Acadian: A North American Border People, 1604–1755*. Montreal and Kingston: McGill-Queen's University Press, 2004.

Grosmaire, Jean-Louis. *Acadissima*. Ottawa: les presses universitaires d'Ottawa, 2021.

Hanna, Martha. *Anxious Days and Tearful Nights: Canadian War Wives during the Great War*. Montreal and Kingston: McGill-Queen's University Press, 2020.

Hareven, Tamara. "The History of the Family and the Complexity of Social Change." *American Historical Review* 96, no. 1 (1991): 95–124.

Harvey, A.D. "Homosexuality and the British Army during the First World War." *Journal of the Society for Army Historical Research* 79 (2001): 313–19.

Hebb, Ross, ed. *In Their Own Words: Three Maritimers Experience the Great War*. Halifax: Nimbus, 2021.

Hemond, Marc-André. "Military Law, Courts Martial, and the Canadian Expeditionary Force, 1914–1918." MA thesis, University of Manitoba, 2008.

Henderson, Jarrett, and Jeffrey Keshen. "Introduction: Canadian Perspectives on the First World War." *Canadian Historical Review* 47, no. 94 (2014): 283–90.

Holt, Richard. *Filling the Ranks: Manpower in the Canadian Expeditionary Force, 1914–1918*. Montreal and Kingston: McGill-Queen's University Press, 2017.

Humphries, Mark. "Between Commemoration and History: The Historiography of the Canadian Corps and Military Overseas." *Canadian Historical Review* 95, no. 2 (September 2014): 395–6.

- "War's Long Shadow: Masculinity, Medicine, and the Gendered Politics of Trauma, 1914–1939." *Canadian Historical Review* 91, no. 3 (2010): 503–31.
- *A Weary Road: Shellshock in the Canadian Expeditionary Force, 1914–1918.* Toronto: University of Toronto Press, 2013.
- "Wilfully and With Intent: Self-Inflicted Wounds and the Negotiation of Power in the Trenches." *Histoire sociale/Social History* 47, no. 94 (June 2014): 369–97.

Iacobelli, Teresa. "No Example Is Needed: Discipline and Authority in the Canadian Expeditionary Force during the First World War." PhD diss., University of Western Ontario, 2009.

Isitt, Benjamin. "Mutiny from Victoria to Vladivostok, December 1918." *Canadian Historical Review* 87, no. 2 (June 2006): 223–64.

Keelan, Geoff. "The Forgotten Few: Quebec and the Memory of the First World War." In *The Great War: From Memory to History*, edited by Jonathan F. Vance et al., 235–60. Waterloo: Wilfrid Laurier University Press, 2015.

Kennedy, Gregory. "The Baie Sainte-Marie Goes to War: Experiences of Nova Scotia Acadians, 1916–1921." In *Speaking Up: New Voices on War and Peace in Nova Scotia*, edited by Maya Eichler, Reina Green, and Tracy Moniz. Halifax: Nimbus, 2022.
- "Struck Off Strength and from Memory: A Profile of the Deserters of the 165th (Acadian) Battalion, 1916." *Canadian Military History* 27, no. 2 (2018).

Kennedy, Gregory, Noémie Haché-Chiasson, and Amélie Montour. "Transition démographique et mobilité géographique dans la région de Kent: Le cas de Cocagne, 1871–1921." In *Histoire et origines des communautés de Kent*, edited by Mathieu Wade et al., 256–65. Quebec City and Moncton: Septentrion/Institut d'études acadiennes, 2023.

Kennedy, Gregory, and Kris Inwood. "A New Prosopography: The Enumerators of the 1891 Census in Ontario." *Historical Methods* 45, no. 2 (2012): 65–77.

Keshen, Jeffrey. *Propaganda and Censorship during Canada's Great War.* Edmonton: University of Alberta Press, 1996.

Landry, Nicolas, and Nicole Lang. *Histoire de l'Acadie.* 2nd edition. Quebec City: Septentrion, 2014.

Lavoie, Yolande. *L'émigration des Canadiens aux États-Unis avant 1930: mesure du phénomène.* Montreal: Presses de l'Université de Montréal, 1972.

Lazarenko, Rebecca. "Francophone Alberta: Deeply Engaged in the First World War." *Active History*, 27 August 2019. http://activehistory.ca/2019/08/francophone-alberta-deeply-engaged-in-the-first-world-war.

LeBlanc, Phyllis E. "Une communauté en transition: Moncton, 1870–1940." In *Économie et société en Acadie, 1850–1950: Nouvelles études d'histoire acadienne*, edited by Jacques Paul Couturier and Phyllis LeBlanc, 131–6. Moncton: Éditions d'Acadie, 1996.

– "Que nous apprennent les synthèses historiques et les contributions récentes à la recherche fondamentale en histoire des femmes et du genre en Acadie." In Thibeault et al., *Paroles et regards de femmes en Acadie*, 21–44.

Léger, Claude E. *Le bataillon acadien de la Première Guerre mondiale*. Moncton, 2001.

– *Le premier régiment North Shore: les Acadiens dans la Première Guerre mondiale*. Caraquet: Les Éditions de la Francophonie, 2019.

Litalien, Michel. *Écrire sa guerre: témoignages de soldats canadiens-français, 1914–1919*. Outremont: Athéna éditions, 2011.

MacGowan, S. Douglas, Mac Heckbert, and Byron E. O'Leary. *New Brunswick's "Fighting 26th": A History of the 26th New Brunswick Battalion, C.E.F., 1914–1919*. Sackville: Tribune Press, 1994.

MacLean, A., and Glen H. Elder, "Military Service in the Life Course." *Annual Review of Sociology* 33, no. 1 (2007): 175–96.

Mainville, Curtis. *Till the Boys Come Home: Life on the Home Front, Queen's County, NB, 1914–1918*. Fredericton: Goose Lane Editions, 2015.

Marti, Steve. "Embattled Communities: Voluntary Action and Identity in Australia, Canada, and New Zealand, 1914–1918." PhD diss., University of Western Ontario, 2015.

– *For Home and Empire: Voluntary Mobilization in Australia, Canada, and New Zealand during the First World War*. Vancouver: UBC Press, 2019.

Martin, Jean. "Francophone Enlistment in the Canadian Expeditionary Force, 1914–1918: The Evidence." *Canadian Military History* 25, no. 1 (2015).

– *Un siècle d'oubli: Les Canadiens et la Première Guerre mondiale (1914–2014)*. Outremont: Athéna Éditions, 2014.

Martineau, France. "Entre les lignes: écrits de soldats peu-lettrés de la Grande Guerre." In Tyne et al., *La variation en question*, 211–36.

Massicotte, Julien, and Mélanie LeBlanc. "L'Acadie et la Seconde Guerre mondiale." *Acadiensis* 45, no. 2 (Summer-Fall 2016): 49–67.

McGowan, Katharine. "'A Question of Caste and Colour': The Displacement of James Bay Native Soldiers' Wives during the First World War, Soldiers' Family Support, and the Maintenance of Pre-War Canadian Society." *Native Studies Review* 21, no. 1 (2012): 103–23.

McKay, Ian, and Jamie Swift. *The Vimy Trap. Or, How We Learned to Stop Worrying and Love the Great War*. Toronto: Between the Lines, 2016.

Meyer, Jessica. *Men of War: Masculinity and the First World War in Britain*. London: Palgrave Macmillan, 2009.

Miller, Carman. *Painting the Map Red: Canada and the South African War, 1899–1902*. Montreal and Kingston: McGill-Queen's University Press, 1993.

Miller, Ian. *Our Glory and our Grief: Torontonians and the Great War*. Toronto: University of Toronto Press, 2002.

Morin-Pelletier, Mélanie. "'The Anxious Waiting Ones at Home': Deux familles canadiennes plongées dans le tourment de la Grande Guerre." *Histoire sociale/Social History* 47, no. 94 (2014): 357–8.

Morton, Desmond. "Le Canada français et la milice canadienne, 1868–1914." In *Le Québec et la Guerre*, edited by Jean-Yves Gravel, 24–43. Montreal: Les Éditions du Boréal Express, 1974.

– *Fight or Pay*. Vancouver: UBC Press, 2004.

– "'Kicking and Complaining': Demobilization Riots in the Canadian Expeditionary Force, 1918–1919." *Canadian Historical Review* 61, no. 3 (1980): 334–60.

– "The Short, Unhappy Life of the 41st Battalion, CEF." *Queen's Quarterly* 81, no. 1 (1974): 70–80.

– *When Your Number's Up: The Canadian Soldier in the First World War*. Toronto: Random House, 1993.

Morton, Desmond, and Glenn Wright. *Winning the Second Battle: Canadian Veterans and the Return to Civilian Life, 1915–1930* [1987]. Toronto: University of Toronto Press, 2018.

Nicholson, G.W.L., and Mark Osborne Humphries. *Canadian Expeditionary Force, 1914–1919: Official History of the Canadian Army in the First World War*. Montreal and Kingston: McGill-Queen's University Press, 2015.

O'Connor, Ryan. "The 105th: The Rise and Fall of the Island's Battalion." *Island Magazine* 60 (Fall/Winter 2006): 2–9.

Oliver, Dean F. "Coming Home: How the Soldiers of Canada and Newfoundland Came Back." In *Canada 1919: A Nation Shaped by War*, edited by Tim Cook and J.L. Granatstein, 27–41. Vancouver: UBC Press, 2020.

Paratte, Henri-Dominique. *Jura-Acadie: deux communautés francophones et leur évolution*. Delémont: Rassemblement jurassien et le Comité permanent des communautés ethniques de langue française, 1980.

Pépin, Carl. "1914–1918: la guerre des Canadiens-Français." *Revue historique des armées* 266 (2012): 31–7.

Plourde, Stéphane, and Yves Frenette. "Essor démographique et migrations dans l'Acadie des Maritimes, 1871–1921." In *La francophonie nord-américaine*, edited by Yves Frenette, Étienne Rivard, and Marc St-Hilaire, 111–14. Quebec City: Les Presses de l'Université Laval, 2013.

Prost, Antoine. "The Military Cemeteries of the Great War, 1914–1940." *Le movement social* 237, no. 4 (2011): 135–51.

Pugsley, Christopher. "Learning from the Canadian Corps on the Western Front." *Canadian Military History* 15, no. 1 (Winter 2006): 7–8.

Rewegan, Alex, Kandace Bogaert, Melissa Yan, Alain Gagno, and D. Ann Herring. "The First Wave of the 1918 Influenza Pandemic among Soldiers of the Canadian Expeditionary Force." *American Journal of Human Biology* 27 (2015): 638–45.

Robichaud, Marc, and Maurice Basque. *Audacieux et téméraire: le père Clément Cormier, c.s.c. (1910–1987), recteur-fondateur de l'Université de Moncton*. Moncton: Institut d'études acadiennes, 2018.

Roby, Yves. *Les Franco-Américains de la Nouvelle-Angleterre: 1776–1930*. Quebec City: Septentrion, 1990.

Rosenthal, Lyndsey. "New Battlegrounds: Treating VD in Belgium and Germany, 1918–1919." In *Canada 1919: A Nation Shaped by War*, edited by Tim Cook and J.L. Granatstein, 57–71. Vancouver: UBC Press, 2020.

Roy, Michel. *L'Acadie des origines à nos jours: Essai de synthèse historique*. Montréal: Amérique, 1981.

Roy, Muriel K. "Settlement and Population Growth." In *The Acadians of the Maritimes*, edited by Jean Daigle, 166–70. Moncton: Centre d'études acadiennes, 1982.

Ruck, Calvin. *Canada's Black Battalion: No. 2 Construction, 1916–1920*. Halifax: Society for the Protection and Preservation of Black Culture in Nova Scotia, 1986.

Rutherdale, Robert. *Hometown Horizons: Local Responses to Canada's Great War*. Vancouver: UBC Press, 2005.

Saindon, Samuelle. "Étude des correspondances de Joseph Ulric LeBlanc, soldat acadien de la Première Guerre mondiale." MA thesis, Université de Moncton, 2023.

Sandwell, R.W. *Canada's Rural Majority: Households, Environments, and Economies, 1870–1940.* Toronto: University of Toronto Press, 2016.

Sauer Ratch, Sandra. "'Do Your Little Bit': The 143rd Battalion Canadian Expeditionary Force, 'BC Bantams.'" *British Columbia Studies* 182 (2014): 151–76.

Scotland, Jonathan. "And the Men Returned: Canadian Veterans and the Aftermath of the Great War." PhD diss., University of Western Ontario, 2016.

Shah, Ami P., et al. "Recent Change in the Annual Pattern of Sexually Transmitted Diseases in the United States." *Chronobiology International* 24, no. 5 (2007): 947–60.

Sharpe, Chris. A. "Enlistment in the Canadian Expeditionary Force, 1914–1918: A Re-evaluation." *Canadian Military History* 24, no. 1 (2015).

– "Enlistment in the Canadian Expeditionary Force, 1914–1918: A Regional Analysis." *Journal of Canadian Studies* 18, no. 4 (Winter 1983): 20–4.

Shaw, Amy. "Expanding the Narrative: A First World War with Women, Children, and Grief." *Canadian Historical Review* 95, no. 2 (September 2014): 398–406.

Shaw, Melissa. "Most Anxious to Serve Their King and Country: Black Canadians Fight to Enlist in WWI and Emerging Race Consciousness in Ontario 1914–1919." *Histoire sociale/Social History* 49, no. 100 (2016): 534–80.

Sirois, Georges. "La participation des Brayons à la Grande Guerre: 1914–1918." *Revue de la Société historique du Madawaska* 16, nos. 3–4 (1988): 3–53.

Smith, Nathan. "Comrades and Citizens: Great War Veterans in Toronto, 1915–1919." PhD diss., University of Toronto, 2016.

Stehelin, Paul H. *Electric City: The Stehelins of New France.* Halifax: Nimbus, 1999.

Sylvester, Kenneth. "Rural to Urban Migration: Finding Household Complexity in a New World Environment." In *Household Counts: Canadian Households and Families in 1901*, edited by Eric W. Sager and Peter Baskerville, 147–79. Toronto: University of Toronto Press, 2007.

Theobald, Andrew. *The Bitter Harvest of War: New Brunswick and the Conscription Crisis of 1917*. Fredericton: Goose Lane Editions, 2008.
Thibeault, Jimmy, Michael Poplyansky, Stéphanie Saint-Pierre, and Chantal White, eds. *Paroles et regards de femmes en Acadie*, Quebec City: Les Presses de l'Université Laval, 2020.
Tyne, Henry, et al., eds. *La variation en question: hommages à Françoise Gadet*. Brussels: Peter Lang, 2017.
Vance, Jonathan. *Death So Noble: Meaning, Memory, and the First World War*. Vancouver: UBC Press, 1997.
– "Provincial Patterns of Enlistment in the Canadian Expeditionary Force." *Canadian Military History* 17 (2008): 75–8.
– *A Township at War*. Waterloo: Wilfrid Laurier University Press, 2018.
Wadsworth Longfellow, Henry. *Evangeline: A Tale of Acadia*, 1847.
Wilson, Brent. *A Family of Brothers: Soldiers of the 26th New Brunswick Battalion in the Great War*. Fredericton: Goose Lane Editions, 2018.
Wilson, Faye. "Booze, Temperance, and Soldiers on the Home Front: The Unraveling of the Image of the Idealized Soldier in Canada." *Canadian Military History* 25, no. 1 (2016): 6–8.
Windsor, Lee. "Replacing Leaders: Lieutenant Roy Duplissie and the Hundred Days Campaign." In *Portraits of Battle: Courage, Grief, and Strength in Canada's Great War*, edited by Peter Farrugia and Evan J. Habkirk, 199–223. Vancouver: UBC Press, 2021.
Windsor, Lee, et al. *Loyal Gunners: 3rd Field Artillery Regiment (The Loyal Company) and the History of New Brunswick's Artillery, 1893–2012*. Waterloo: Wilfrid Laurier University Press, 2016.
Winegard, Timothy C. *For King and Kanata: Canadian Indians and the First World War*. Winnipeg: University of Manitoba Press, 2012.
Wood, James. *Militia Myths: Ideas of the Canadian Citizen Soldier, 1896–1921*. Vancouver: UBC Press, 2010.
Wright, R.A., and F.N. Judson. "Relative and Seasonal Incidences of the Sexually Transmitted Diseases: A Two-Year Statistical Review." *British Journal of Venereal Diseases* 54, no. 6 (1978): 433–40.

Index

5th District (Canadian Forestry Corps), 15, 129, 145, 151, 153–60, 169–70, 174, 183–91, 209. *See also* France: Jura
12th District (Canadian Forestry Corps), 129, 145, 209. *See also* France: Bordeaux
22nd Battalion (Canadien-Français), 16–19, 34, 102, 121, 128–46, 239; chaplains, 108, 197; discipline, 25, 88, 165–6, 170–1; at front, 65, 193, 210–11
25th Battalion (Nova Scotia), 34, 166, 192, 208
26th Battalion (New Brunswick), 19, 38–9, 127–39, 170–1, 207; Acadians serving in, 6–7, 34–5, 50, 106, 146, 150, 192; at the front, 61, 71, 142, 194–5, 198
105th Battalion (Prince Edward Island), 20, 41, 56, 66, 106, 129, 131
132nd Battalion (North Shore), 20, 69, 77, 106, 131–3; recruitment, 40–2, 87, 103, 108; overseas, 83, 129

145th Battalion (Moncton), 41, 66, 68–9, 82, 84, 195; men transferred to 165th Battalion, 48, 91, 108, 186

Acadian renaissance, 6, 31–46, 65; *Ave Maria Stella*, 115–16, 124; national conventions, 31–3; public assemblies, 14, 36, 44–7; Société de l'Assomption, 32–7, 45–7, 111, 135; Société nationale de l'Acadie, 6, 32, 111
Adamsville (NB), 42, 55, 60–1, 186, 217–18, 240
agriculture, 32, 54–5, 63, 99–100, 134, 187, 218, 225–7, 232
alcohol, 26, 78, 160, 170, 174, 180, 202, 221, 231–4, 239; temperance, 170, 174, 234
Antigonish (NS), 41, 52, 57, 67, 210
Atlantic, crossing, 115–18, 204–5

bands, 47, 112
Borden, Robert, 3, 19, 38, 68, 84, 109, 190

Canadian Expeditionary Force
  (CEF), 3, 87–9, 106–7, 109–10,
  120–1, 143, 183, 200–2, 210,
  215–16; Acadian participation,
  6–11, 35, 44, 185, 192–6;
  composition, 24, 28, 51–5, 85,
  130–9, 230–1, 236–7; discipline,
  170–1, 174, 189–92; French-
  Canadian enlistment, 16–21, 165,
  239–40; recruitment, 60, 79–82,
  102, 146–50; veterans, 26–7,
  205, 208, 213, 221–2, 242–3
Canadian National Railway (CNR),
  32–3, 37, 214, 222, 224–5, 228
Canadian Patriotic Fund (CPF),
  137, 147
Cape Breton Island (NS), 44–5,
  57, 59, 61, 182, 184, 197, 208,
  214, 217
Caraquet (NB), 24, 54, 65, 67,
  112, 147, 175, 225, 232; train,
  67, 77; training depot, 41–2, 52;
  support for recruitment, 47,
  57–9, 83, 103, 138
Catholic Church, 14, 32–3, 44;
  bishop, 8, 14, 31, 42, 111, 130;
  confession, 116–17, 124, 151,
  196–7; Mass, 115–18, 124, 149,
  196–7, 202, 209, 236; priests,
  23, 39, 44, 46–7, 75, 81, 196;
  role in enlistment, 44, 64, 79,
  102, 106, 208–9
censorship, 10, 68, 120, 195
Collège Saint-Joseph, 32, 36
conscription, 3–7, 10, 19, 25, 52,
  79, 93–4, 107, 130, 200, 238;
  in Quebec, 4–5, 7, 19, 79,
  107, 238
Cormier, Clément, 37, 237, 240
correspondence. *See* soldiers' letters

Daigle, Louis Cyriaque, 11, 34–5,
  38–50, 57–61, 67–9, 72–84,
  111, 127–30, 238–40
demobilization, 10, 140, 143, 196,
  202–35; return to Canada, 26–7,
  130, 147, 173, 185, 195, 198
desertion, 12, 25–8, 81 85–93, 98,
  103–4, 168–9, 180, 239–41;
  in other units, 51, 109, 165–7,
  172, 207
Devarennes, Eddie, 195, 197–8
discipline, 25–6, 55; 87–8, 95, 126,
  164–9, 202, 204–5, 207, 243;
  charges, 164, 167–8, 170–3,
  176, 183, 191; courts martial,
  25, 88, 165–7, 180; ensuring,
  71, 78, 109, 161; execution,
  165; field punishment, 26, 167;
  hard labour, 168, 170, 173, 176,
  231–2; loss of position, 163–4,
  167, 172, 185; in other units, 51,
  126; summary trials, 88
Dominion Police, 86–7, 91, 94

education, 32–4, 36, 56, 184,
  186–7, 190, 205, 239–40; anti-
  French policies, 16; bilingualism,
  31, 226, 237, 241

family, archives, 15–16, 25, 76,
  93–5, 124–5, 196; children, 40,
  137, 141–3, 212, 228, 233;
  household economy, 53–6, 58–9,
  90–1, 98–103, 182, 224–6, 233;
  mothers, 40, 49, 97, 112, 140–2,
  199–200, 215, 219, 222;
  networks, 33, 61, 63–6, 105,
  134–6, 140–3, 199, 218–20;
  reconstitution methods, 9–12,
  20, 28, 106–7, 217, 243;

Index

recruitment, 35, 46, 49, 118, 198; siblings, 64, 120, 143, 184, 218, 220, 224; support to soldiers, 112, 120, 137–8, 209, 215. *See also* marriage

farming, 32, 42, 64–5, 134–5, 196, 218, 221; as occupation, 53–5, 98, 184, 224–6. *See also* agriculture

fishing, 32, 46, 54–6, 62, 90, 99–102, 187, 210, 225–6

forestry, sawmills, 90, 153, 157, 159, 206, 226; lumber camps, 9, 15, 24, 26, 59, 94, 99, 146, 152, 162–3, 181–2, 231; seasonal work, 55, 90, 99–100, 226–7

France, 4, 41–5, 49, 72–76, 121, 145–6, 154–5, 199, 205, 209; Andelot, 151–2, 176; Bordeaux, 8, 15, 129, 145, 147, 152–3, 189, 206, 209; Champagnole, 152, 175–6, 192; Dijon, 151; Jura, 8, 15, 20, 129, 145, 147–57, 169, 174, 176, 188–9, 209, 217; Paris, 151, 161, 170, 192, 202; Passchendaele, 65, 142, 146, 196, 198, 237; Rouen, 151, 168, 170, 173, 175, 188, 213–14; Saint Pierre and Miquelon, 4, 61, 133, 135; service at front, 119, 126, 129, 195–6; soldiers from, 58–61, 97, 135; Vimy Ridge, 5–6, 133, 152, 197, 199–200, 237

Gaudet, Jean V., 42, 45, 60–1, 115–19, 126, 129, 145, 149, 153, 180, 190–2, 197, 240

good conduct badge (GCB), 181, 183, 202, 226, 232, 239

Great Britain, 19, 31, 34, 59, 121; British Expeditionary Force (BEF), 3, 17, 24, 165, 190, 192; London, 129, 146, 151, 190–2, 202, 206; Shoreham-by-Sea, 119, 126–9, 183; Sunningdale, 150–1, 182

Halifax, 4, 36, 39, 84, 109; port of embarkation, 11, 29, 91, 112, 115–17, 208; recruiting, 42, 44–6, 57; return port, 205–6, 210, 212, 214

health, 42, 77, 89, 114, 160, 172, 189, 209–17, 230–5; mental health, 95, 212–13; weight, 17, 22, 27, 154, 158, 230–1

hospital admissions, 15, 189, 190–2, 216; influenza, 15, 24, 60–1, 149, 155, 189, 190, 203, 206, 209, 210–11, 216, 231; wounds, 91, 133, 142, 190, 193–4, 198, 210–12

Hughes, Samuel, 35–6, 38, 41, 52, 82, 114, 132, 136, 174

Landry, Pierre-Amand, 31, 37

leave (military), in Canada, 76–7, 92–3, 109, 198; in CFC, 155, 160–5, 181, 192, 201–5, 209; in England, 119. *See also* desertion

LeBlanc, Édouard A., 14, 31, 142, 199

LeBlanc, Joseph Ulric, 14, 35, 49, 64, 120–4, 195, 204, 216, 218–19, 222, 224

Léger, Léo (Fricot), 15, 75, 162–3

Legere, J. Arthur, 7, 15, 50, 74, 128

Madawaska (NB), 22, 33, 44, 50, 55, 57–9, 62, 75, 83, 92–4, 98, 103–4, 182, 184–5, 226
Magdalen Islands (QC), 62, 171
Malenfant, Ferdinand, 118, 127–8, 151–2, 157, 162–3, 175
marriage, 27, 100, 136, 190, 201, 217; prior to enlistment, 134, 205; war brides, 15, 201; widowers, 54; widows, 40, 142, 215; wives, 40, 51, 54, 79, 90–1, 97, 118, 136–7, 140–2, 151, 162, 176–9, 206, 226, 233
McLean, H.H., 74, 84–6
Meteghan (NS), 41, 50, 52, 55, 57, 59, 67, 92, 98, 104, 138
migration, 33, 65–6, 101, 134–5, 199, 229, 241; international, 33, 61–5, 199, 211; mobility, 53–6, 103, 140, 187, 229, 242
militia, 48–52, 84–5, 92, 114; in Canada, 5, 16, 138–9; in Maritime provinces, 79, 118, 131–3, 228, 240, 242; other military experience, 9, 50, 130, 132, 146, 184–6, 240
mining, 32, 54, 56–7, 187, 225
Moncton (NB), 6–7, 79–80, 237–8; assemblies, 36–8, 85, 111–12, 117–18, 208–9; economic hub, 29–33, 98, 103, 134, 143, 224–7, 240; recruitment, 41–4, 47, 52, 56–68, 92–3, 138, 187, 195; residence of soldiers, 95, 97, 101, 133, 141, 176, 184–5, 214, 217–18
Montreal (QC), 4, 20, 62, 95, 138, 150, 165, 169, 199, 227

mortality (deaths), 116–18, 141, 176–80, 201, 215; in combat, 29, 106–7, 193–5; disease, 60, 155, 184–5, 189–92; fear of, 81, 121, 199–200

non-commissioned officers (NCOs), 55, 65, 71–3, 116, 126, 139, 152, 182–9

officers (military), 7, 15, 36–9, 76–7, 81–2, 86, 114–18, 120, 143; in CFC, 150–2, 156, 160, 166, 179–80, 185–7, 199; profile, 52, 55, 64, 128–30, 132; recruitment, 7, 14, 20–2, 41, 44–6, 67, 79, 108, 139; training, 7, 48–52, 71–5, 109, 111, 116
Ottawa, 39, 42, 57, 60, 73, 75, 82, 84–5, 114, 150

pensions, 40, 211–13, 215, 221–2
Poirier, Pascal, 6, 37, 80, 236
professions: public service, 36, 221, 226; sales, 54, 99–100, 186–7, 218, 225; teaching, 55, 73, 184–5
promotion, 61, 116, 118, 143, 145, 164, 181, 183–7, 191, 202, 239; to company sergeant-major, 74; to sergeant, 60, 61, 116, 118, 133, 183; junior NCOs, 183, 187. See also non-commissioned officers (NCOs).
propaganda, 23, 59. See also censorship

Quebec City (QC), 5, 21, 34, 45, 73, 79, 135, 138, 168, 206, 223–4

railway, 24, 32–3, 56, 62, 78, 135, 146, 152, 154, 199, 207, 214, 221, 225–7. *See* Canadian National Railroad (CNR)
recruitment, 9, 30, 34, 38, 42, 50, 52, 56, 60, 65, 80, 82–3, 85, 105, 236, 238, 243; age requirement, 23, 94, 113, 205; medical exams, 11–12, 21–2, 40, 86, 91, 108, 112, 126, 164, 169, 205, 212; physical standards, 22, 113, 212, 230; wives' permission, 136
rejected volunteers, 9, 21–4, 113, 131, 150, 205, 215, 239; overage, 24, 61, 150; underage, 52–3, 60, 62, 93–4, 96, 104, 219, 240; unfit, 48, 84–7, 91, 104, 113–14, 131, 212

Saint John (NB); 11–12, 14, 29, 33, 54, 72–114, 131–3, 169, 200, 217–18, 223–4
salary, 40, 55–6, 98, 101, 105, 138, 141, 143, 220, 223, 226–7, 232; post-war, 222–7, 233
Shediac (NB), 28, 37, 47, 60, 62, 94, 105, 142, 175, 200, 206, 222
soldiers' letters, 14–16, 39, 68, 112, 115–30, 140, 145–9, 162, 164, 195–201, 237–8

Spanish flu, 24, 155, 208, 213. *See* hospital admissions
special identity battalions, 9, 19, 47, 52, 57, 109, 121, 236, 242
Stehelin, Émile, 57, 77, 95, 104, 113, 150

trades, 54–5, 60, 65, 98–102, 136, 165, 181, 186–7, 225–7, 233

unemployment, 10, 27–8, 53, 102, 221, 227, 233
United States, 25, 27, 32–3, 56, 60–4, 77, 134–5, 140–1, 199–200, 203, 211, 217–18, 237, 242; Maine, 94, 97–8, 103, 135, 183, 206, 211, 239; Massachusetts, 64, 95, 97, 103, 105, 206–7, 214, 239; US Army, 61–2, 133, 141, 193. *See also* migration

Valcartier (QC), 35, 47–9, 51, 53, 59, 66–72, 75, 83–4, 89–93, 95, 101–2, 109–10, 113, 133, 168
venereal disease, 78, 126, 161, 189–91, 213, 216, 231–3, 239, 242; gonorrhea, 29, 191, 213, 216–17; orchitis, 164; syphilis, 191, 216–17; treatment, 161, 190–1